SCREENS OF POWER

SCREENS OF POWER

Ideology, Domination, and Resistance in Informational Society

Timothy W. Luke

University of Illinois Press
Urbana and Chicago

This book is printed on acid-free paper.

Library of Congress Cataloging-in-Publication Data

Luke, Timothy W.
    Screens of power : ideology, domination, and resistance in
informational society / Timothy W. Luke.
        p. cm.
    Includes index.
    ISBN 0-252-01629-7 (alk. paper)
    1. Power (Social sciences) 2. Ideology. 3. Communication in
politics. 4. Information technology—Political aspects. I. Title.
JC330.L38 1989
303.3'3—dc19   88-37528
                                               CIP

To Kay

Contents

Acknowledgments   ix

Part I
Scanning the Screens of Power

Introduction   3

Part II
Creating a Post-Marxist Critique of Postindustrialism

1. Finding New Puzzles of Power
   in the Riddle of the Commodity   19

Part III
Power and Ideology in Informational Society

2. The Contradictory Capital of Culture:
   The Neoconservative Critique of the
   Cultural Contradictions of Capitalism   61

3. From Fundamentalism to Televangelism   86

4. Regulating the Haven in a Heartless World:
   The State, Firm, and Family under
   Advanced Capitalism   98

5. Discourses of Charisma and Televisual
   Electoral Politics   129

6. History as an Ideopolitical Commodity:
   The 1984 D-Day Spectacle   159

Contents

7. "Packaging" Chernobyl: The Manufacture of
   Meaning from a Transnational Ecological
   Disaster   181

Part IV
Oppositional Politics in Informational Society

8. Power and Resistance in Informationalizing
   Postindustrial Societies   207

9. The New Left, Critical Intellectuals, and Social
   Revolution: The Role of the
   New Media in the Politics of Image   240

   Index   259

Acknowledgments

This book in many ways is an extended essay composed of many smaller essays. Written at different times and under varying circumstances, each chapter expresses an aspect of my critical thinking during the last eight years. Together they provide a tentative theoretical appraisal of how the workings of power and ideology are shifting decisively in the present era into new, less traditional forms of both domination and resistance. Sections of Chapter 1 initially appeared in a different form as "Jean Baudrillard's Political Economy of the Sign," in *Art Papers* 12, no. 2 (1986): 22–25, and in *New Political Science* 15 (Summer 1986): 103–7. Chapter 3 appeared in a slightly different version in *Telos* 58 (Winter 1983–84): 204–10, reprinted with permission. A shorter, modified version of Chapter 4 was published in *New Political Science* 7 (Winter 1981): 51–74, reprinted with permission. Small sections of it also appeared in "Critical Theory, The International Revolution, and an Ecological Path to Modernity," (coauthored with Stephen K. White), in *Critical Theory and Public Life,* ed. John Forester (Cambridge, Mass.: MIT Press, 1985), 22–33. Chapter 5 is an expanded version of "Televisual Democracy and the Politics of Charisma," published in *Telos* 70 (Winter 1986–87): 59–79, reprinted with permission. Chapter 6 is an extended version of "History as an Ideo-Political Commodity: The 1984 D-Day Spectacle," published in *New Political Science* 13 (Winter 1984), 49–67, reprinted with permission. A longer version of Chapter 7 appeared as "Chernobyl: The Packaging of Transnational Ecological Disaster," in *Critical Studies in Mass Communication* 4, no. 4 (1987): 351–75, reprinted by permission of the Speech Communication Association. Parts of Chapter 8 are included in "The New Social Movements: Conflict, Social Cleavages, and Class Contradictions in Emergent Informational Societies," *New Political Science* 16 (forthcoming). Parts of Chapter 9 initially appeared in "The Modern Service State: Public Power in America from the New Deal to the New Beginning," in *Race, Politics, and Culture: Critical Essays on the Radicalism of the 1960s,* ed. Adolph Reed, Jr., Contributions in Afro-American and African Studies, No. 95, (Westport, Conn.: Greenwood Press, 1986), copyright 1986 by Adolph Reed, Jr., reprinted with permission of editor and publisher, and in *Telos* 50 (Winter 1981–82): 125–29, reprinted with permission.

Over the past few years, many people have given me very informed and helpful criticism on parts of or all of the manuscript, including Carl Boggs, Gavan Duffy, Ellsworth R. Fuhrman, David Gross, Robert D. Holsworth, Patrick Murray, Adolph Reed, Jr., Glenn Harper, and Fred Siegel. However, I particularly wish to thank my colleague, Stephen K. White, for his friendly interest in, and insightful comments on, this manuscript as it has gradually evolved into its current form. I also want to acknowledge my sincere appreciation for the advice, editorial directions, and criticisms provided by Paul Piccone and Florindo Volpacchio. Without their suggestions, this book could not have developed as it did.

Lawrence J. Malley and Beth Bower of the University of Illinois Press managed the review and editing of my manuscript with careful attention and tremendous enthusiasm for which I am very grateful. The actual production of the text itself would have been impossible without the word processing abilities of Kim Hedge, Terry Kingrea, Maxine Riley, and Luci Zipper in the Department of Political Science at Virginia Polytechnic Institute and State University. I truly appreciate their skillful work and patience in dealing with my constant changes and revisions. I also would like to acknowledge the helpful observations and research assistance provided by some of my graduate assistants, including Paul Taggart, Guillermo Alberto Monkman, Reinhard Heinisch, Henning Arp, and Ian Walden.

My wife, Kay Heidbreder, has been very supportive over the years as I have worked on this project—never hesitating in her caring, encouragement, and tolerant understanding. I happily dedicate this book to her.

PART I

Scanning the Screens of Power

Introduction

This book is only a beginning. It is imperfect and incomplete. Given the ground that it covers, it cannot be otherwise. This ground is the still essentially contested terrain of "postindustrial," "information-based," or "informational" society as it has been forming with the globalization of advanced corporate capitalism since 1945. The distinctive features of "postindustrialism"—rising numbers of white-collar workers, decreasing numbers of blue-collar workers, a greater emphasis on services or information goods rather than industrial manufacturing, the mobilization of science as a factor in production and management, and a consumer-oriented economy of affluence—have been talked about since the mid-1950s. Yet intense debates over what these changes mean, and how far they go toward actually amounting to a new stage of development, continue today.[1] Therefore, the following chapters will examine two societies. One is not yet fully born, but it still remains entangled with another that is not yet completely dead.

Over two decades ago, Marcuse made some of the first sightings of this ground when he suggested in *One-Dimensional Man* that "when technics becomes the universal form of material production, it circumscribes an entire culture; it projects a historical totality—a 'world.'"[2] To explore the new world (circumscribed by cybernetic/electronic technics and the social modes of production it embodies) that has developed more fully since Marcuse made this observation, I outline a set of initial reference points broadly based, in large part, upon my own readings of semiotic and critical theory. My theoretical markers are simply a first step toward charting the new cultures, politics, and societies in these still largely unexplored spaces. While they are both local and transnational in their dimensions, their topographies are emerging out of electronically generated regions of awareness formed from the "airwaves," "television land," "PC worlds," "video country," "computer networks," or the "reach of radio."

Ultimately, I investigate the politics behind how cultural, economic, and social meanings are created to produce new forms of power for those who control the material and symbolic means of producing and consuming these meanings. I would be the first to admit that the following studies are tentative and fragmentary, subject to revision, and not fully developed. My eclectic readings of several theoretical traditions also do not always conform to the shifting canons of interpretation prevailing in many of the different subcultures of academic discourse, because my discussion is not a systematic review of particular critical theorists. Still, these studies begin to articulate some insights that clearly merit further exploration into how cultural meanings, political institutions, and social relations are affected by the power flowing through the new systems of symbols used in data processing, telecommunications, and the electronic mass media.

These developments have not led to the carefree utopia of cybernetic postindustrialism that fascinated early space-age America in the 1950s and 1960s. Instead, new technical and economic forces are creating a more culturally impoverished and ecologically destructive world system, which now is based upon attaining the complete commodification of all aspects of human life. With the emergence of informationalization, one can see concomitant declines in several different but interrelated spheres—environmental quality, urban life, material living standards, cultural vitality, popular political effectiveness, and ordinary everyday community. The substance and form of television and radio broadcasting, audio- and videocassettes, computer hardware and software—as key commodities in this growing web of global exchange—should be reevaluated in this sort of ideology critique to explore some of the new forms of power and ideology binding together these new transnational human communities. Within such consumption communities, the flow of goods, services, and signs is creating new, densely encoded "mediascapes," or new regions and sites of shared cultural consciousness, that continuously but cryptically display the workings of power and ideology. But whose power and whose ideology?

As Harold A. Innis and Marshall McLuhan argue, there is usually a systematic bias in society, tied to the "distorting power of the dominant imagery and technology of any culture," that can be used to guide the course of critical social research.[3] The forms of organized power in a world increasingly dominated by the networks of transnational corporate capital (based mainly in Japan, North America, and Western Europe) and weak transnational zone-regimes (tied to either the Soviet or the American superpower) reveal their biases most directly in the electronic imagery and technology underpinning contemporary mass consumption and production. What are these powers, how might they distort human activity, why is their bias destructive, and when might they be resisted? During the strategic deadlock of Soviet and American superpower throughout the past four decades, the everyday commerce of transnational corporate capitalism has significantly transformed the established cultures, politics, and society of many nation-states by developing electronically mediated consumption communities within and alongside their traditional ways of life.[4] The bases of power, ideology, and resistance are changing within these regions, but in ways that still are unclear, contradictory, and incomplete.

SEMIOTIC APPROACHES AND CRITICAL THEORY AS METHOD

What conceptual assumptions and methodological practices are implied here by adopting a semiotic-based mode of analysis? I understand semiotics basically as a conceptual means for examining the exchange of messages, the systems of signing or coding that anchor them, and the nature of the social relations that frame the production, exchange, and interpretation of their meaning. The study of messages and their constituent signs often "deals with those general principles which underlie the structure of all signs whatever and with the character of their utilization within messages, as well as with the specifics of the various sign systems and the diverse messages using those different kinds of signs."[5] Nonetheless, defining the nature of signs and their meaning is complex. And, at this stage of its development, no explication of semiotics or signification can be identified as definitive.[6] However, Eco's definition of the sign as *"everything,* that, on the grounds of a previously established social convention, can be taken as *something standing for something else"* will be used as a guidepost here.[7] It echoes Morris's assertion that "something is a sign only because it is interpreted as a sign of something by some interpreter. . . . Semiotics, then, is not concerned with the study of a particular kind of objects, but with ordinary objects insofar (and only insofar) as they participate in semiosis."[8]

Eco also argues that semiotics spans a broad range of analysis, extending from the study of mass communication to rhetoric to proxemics to text theory to paralinguistics.[9] While I see some problems with Eco's formalistic construction of semiotics, my critical interpretation of informationalism mainly borrows from three subfields of interpretive semiosis that he identifies; namely, investigating *systems of objects,* which, like industrial artifacts, are studied as communicative devices; *cultural codes,* such as behavioral and value structures, which are seen as complex sign systems; and *modes of visual communication,* like architecture, design styles, fashions, films, or maps, implied by intricate iconographic systems.[10] In examining some of the workings of informationalizing society, several twists and turns in the logic of commodification can be traced here through systems of images and objects, which constitute systematic modes of visual or symbolic communication while expressing complex cultural codes.

To develop a useful analysis of the meaning-formation underlying commodification, some basic models of communication perhaps should be outlined. They are far from perfect, but for my purposes here they are useful. Standard information theorists typically have employed the elements of sender, message, addressee, and code.[11] Messages in these theories are quanta of information sent to addressees sharing a common code with the sender. Yet these approaches do not capture the nuances of many communicative interactions. Jakobson goes beyond information theory and delineates a new model of communication that assumes six elements: addresser, context, message, contact, code, and addressee. In his model, a communicative act involves the addresser's sending a message to an addressee.[12] To be effective, a message requires a context or referential setting in which at least partially shared codes of expression and interpretation can be situated. Their contact is some physical channel interactively connecting addressee and addresser in communication. Although Jakobson did not conceptualize these relations simply as a mechanical unimodal or bimodal transfer of message cargoes between two points, critics have complained about an implicit "pipeline" theory of informational transfer in this model.[13] To partially correct these misconceptions, Eco outlines a more complex (albeit still imperfect) schema that builds in filters, back loops, noise, and distortion.[14]

Eco's model, which in many ways is also too "clean," highlights the complex textual qualities of the message, stressing what Barthes identifies as "the plurality of the text: a plurality of semantic levels (codes), whose 'braiding' forms the text."[15] Critical interpretation here can trace out the several networks of distinct subcodes interoperating on many different levels of signified meaning. In examining objects, for example, Eco points out at least five separate levels of possible meaning: as physical objects, as functional entities (or use values), as commodities (or exchange values), as social entities (or status, rank, and position markers), and as semantic elements with culturally discursive applications. Eco, then, replaces the mechanistic pipeline theory of communication borrowed from information theory with an interactive model based on the social production and consumption of sign expressions and interpretations. The sender, using codes and subcodes that may or may not be shared with the receiver, produces a coded text or message in the channels of communicative contact. The provisional "text of expression" is situated in a larger context of social circumstances. The receiver must receive this text and transform its codes and subcodes. In this interaction, the addressee produces a working "text of interpretation" from the expressed text to construct some sense of the content of the coded text or message sent by the addresser. Communication, then, occurs with the production of imperfect equivalences of partial understanding from the constantly reconstructed expressions and interpretations of diverse signs grounded within evolving codes.

It is from this interlocution of the addressee and addresser that content or meaning is constructed. Because of variations in decoding, the significations "produced" by the sender usually are "consumed" on only one or a few of their levels of content. Therefore, meaning "surpluses" and "deficits" are intrinsic to the interaction. The message expression, as a source of meaningful content, is constrained by the sender's private bias, ideological precepts, ambiguous presentation, and tacit subcoding. By the same logic, the message content, as an interpreted source of expressive meaning, is reduced by the receiver's private codes, ideological filters, interpretative failures, and implicit subcoding.[16] Within a given context of ongoing communication, then, the addresser and addressee continuously encode and decode a sign flow to try to express and apprehend the meaning of sign vehicles; countercoding, miscoding, and noncoding all are inherent in the interactivity of communication.

Granting this brief overview of communication, how can the workings of informationalism be examined? This analysis approaches political behaviors, social forces, institutional structures, and cultural activities as densely encoded but largely decodable *texts.* Texts are volatile and fragile tissues of codes, knitting together diverse signification fragments charged with mythologies, plural meanings, and many different values. The text is never fully controlled by its author; instead, it is itself finally "finished" or "produced" in its reading by others, inevitably leaving meaning surpluses behind and fulfilling meaning deficits when they arise. The production of meaning, as Eagleton argues, then, "cannot be easily nailed down, it is never fully present in any one sign alone, but rather is a constant flickering of presence and absence." The production and consumption of signs encourages one "to carve them up, transpose them into different discourse, produce his or her semi-arbitrary play of meaning athwart the work itself" such that one always must remember how "the reader or critic shifts from the role of consumer to that of producer."[17]

I also see the analysis in the following chapters as a form of critical theory that is partly inspired but not entirely guided by my own interpretations of Marx, Adorno, Horkheimer, and Marcuse, as well as Barthes, Debord, and Baudrillard. As with semiotics, there are perhaps as many understandings of critical theory as there are critical theorists.[18] Despite such variations, I would argue that critical theory is characterized by at least three fundamental qualities.

First, such theories are essentially reflective, reflexive, and ironic rather than positive, objective, and methodologically formalistic. In seeking a reflective, reflexive, or ironic knowledge of social relations, critical theorizing repudiates a positivistic mode of knowing tied uncritically to natural science models of investigation. Consequently, this analysis will not follow the set-piece research strategies of formalistic methodologies intent upon grinding some preprocessed empirical data through an allegedly objective but still theory-laden mathematical model. The results of such productions almost always fail to resonate with reality. Critical theory instead is a way of seeing and a form of knowing that employs historical knowledge, reflexive reasoning, and ironic awareness to give people some tools to realize new potentials for the emancipation and enlightenment of ordinary individuals today.

By adopting here some perspectives from semiotic and critical theory, I also do not see semiotics as an all-powerful science of signs that provides a special, correct consciousness of contemporary society. This danger resides in nearly every corner of modern semiotics. The rise of informational societies arguably places a high premium upon the professional study of codes and communication. Rather than developing semiotics as the open-ended, critical study of how meaning is produced and communicated, experts working in the discipline often seem to reduce it to nothing but a formalized science of signs or methodologies for systematizing signification. To the extent that informationalization travels upon formalized signification systems in the corporate and state rationalization of the economy and society, semiotics as a "science" does perhaps increasingly serve as its "appropriate technology" of both self-disclosure and self-mystification. Its partial deployment in the areas of artificial intelligence, public relations, cryptography, advertising, software engineering, product design, and cognitive science all illustrate some of these trends. Culture, meaning, and values, however, are much more than merely modes of "communication" or genres of "information." And a critical semiotics can be engaged politically and culturally in disclosing the sources of mystification, power, and domination in the social production and consumption of meaning. When directed to these purposes, it also might broaden the analytical perspective of critical theory on the social context of generating and interpreting knowledge.

Second, critical theory adopts the goal of guiding human actions to realize greater emancipation and enlightenment in the lives of people today. By refining people's thinking abilities and moral sensibilities, critical theorists hope to equip individuals with a new consciousness of what must be done and how to do it. This consciousness might help them determine what their best interests should be besides gauging how far they must move away from currently held beliefs that embody elements of domination and exploitation. By helping people come to such realizations, critical theory advances human emancipation from the victimization that people impose on themselves from within or that is forced upon them from without. Such domination is seen as preventing people from attaining their best interests through fully conscious, reasoned activity by blocking the conditions that would allow them to realize liberation.

At the same time, however, critical theory must acknowledge the cultural and psychological groundings of the people it addresses. There are few general categories or universal classes that can be addressed with complete certainty. While transnational forces clearly are at work on a global scale, their impact on any particular individual, group, locality, or region always has unique peculiarities. Such variations cannot be entirely explained away or ignored by abstract critical systems. On the contrary, these particularities in the diverse variations of everyday life must be faced locally in the agenda for change of each individual, group, or region.

And third, critical theory also advances a systematic radical critique of society. It demystifies how power, position, and privilege relate to class, group, and personal inequalities. By elaborating this ideally open-ended and changing critique with an interest in human enlightenment and emancipation, critical theorists can provide some guideposts for the actual resistance groups always forming at the margins of society. Radical critique aims at identifying in a particular society how ideologies and forms of domination might be overcome in this context and time to obtain greater liberation for more people. Yet its ironic outlook also must alert these resistance efforts to the always unexpected and unintended results of any human action as individuals and groups oppose the prevailing systems of power, position, and privilege.

More specifically, critical theory must guard against millenarian fantasies of total redemption through political action. All human beings are entangled and enmeshed in a recalcitrant reality made of enduring cultural traditions, the demands of everyday existence, and often-unyielding personal identities that no critical theorist can ever wholly unravel. Any critical theory that ignores these realities runs the risk of presuming too much as it allegedly traces out the ruses of reason into some Jacobin or Stalinist excuse for an infallible road map to the irresistible future. This sense of irony always should remind us that the future is almost always resistible, and there are few reliable road maps to anywhere.

In developing a critical theory for an informationalizing society, however, it is also essential to begin developing a post-Marxist critique of commodity production and exchange. By retooling insights from many diverse discourses, I stake out some preliminary benchmarks for at least one kind of a post-Marxist critique in these studies. This eclectic grounding can provide some of the frameworks for a needed post-Marxist critique of postindustrialism because these discourses all have recognized the limits of classical Marxian reasoning. They all come after Marx and clearly depart from Marx, but much of their analyses draw creatively from Marx's critique of power, ideology, and domination. They recognize how completely commodification has come to dominate every aspect of culture, while realizing that the "base" and "superstructure" of such capitalist societies are totally interpenetrated. Most important, they junk much of the economistic apparatus of orthodox historical materialism that has led many recent Marxist critiques down nineteenth-century theoretical paths in dealing with the crises of a twenty-first-century world.[19]

AN OVERVIEW OF THE ANALYSIS

The following chapters assemble a more textured, but still incomplete, picture of how these contradictory symbolic and material forces come into play within the social system that I examine in terms of an ideal type, namely, informational society. Ideal types, as Weber suggests,

> will help to develop our skill in imputation in research: it is no "hypothesis" but it offers guidance to the construction of hypotheses. It is not a description of reality but it aims to give unambiguous means of expression to such a description. . . . An ideal type is formed by the one-sided accentuation of one or more points of view and by the synthesis of a great many diffuse, discrete, more or less present and occasionally absent concrete individual phenomena, which are arranged according to those one-sidedly emphasized viewpoints into a unified analytical construct *(Gedankenbild)*. In its conceptual purity, this mental construct *(Gedankenbild)* cannot be found empirically anywhere in reality. It is a utopia.[20]

To begin this conceptual synthesis, I see an informational society as a complex new order whose social and political structures are dominated increasingly by the development, elaboration, and expression of formalized discourses and scientific disciplines. These structures' changing codes of substantive values and knowledge have come to define meaning, generate power, and frame the choices of everyday life. Informationalism's new strategic economic resources are the means and methods behind the computerized processing of numbers, words, documents, and pictures. Data-intensive management techniques, robotized materials processing, numerically controlled tools, aesthetically intensified marketing tactics, and the telecommunication of images all are used now to add value in the production process. In turn, most cultural codes of behavior and values are increasingly defined, mediated, and enforced through these informational modes of economic production and cultural reproduction. While this is a largely structural conception, it captures the essential basis of informationalization as the creation of new social formations tied to the exchange-driven production, distribution, consumption, interpretation, and reproduction of information as contextually or instrumentally rationalized codes in the form of words, numbers, symbols, images, or audio.[21]

An ideal type, as Weber recommends, "is neither historical reality nor even the 'true' reality."[22] Reality instead is always much more mixed and indistinct. Televisions coexist with primitive peasant agriculture, computers work side by side with manual laborers, and creative consumer ads tumble around with traditional religious dictates. There are no purely industrial or exclusively informational societies existing as such anywhere in the world. Still, the ideal type of informationalization "has the significance of a purely ideal *limiting* concept with which the real situation or action is *compared* and surveyed for the explication of certain of its significant components. Such concepts are constructs in terms of which we formulate relationships by the application of the category of objective possibility. By means of the category, the adequacy of our imagination, oriented and disciplined by reality, is judged."[23]

The ideal type, then, essentially allows one to ask and answer certain questions in a provisional, open-ended investigation. Once some "facts" are recognized or accepted, "whether the empirical-historical course of development was actually identical with the constructed one, can be investigated only by using this construct as a heuristic device for the comparison of the ideal type and the 'facts.'"[24] Although it is extremely difficult to keep the two separate and distinct, Weber concludes that "this procedure gives rise to no methodological doubts so long as we clearly keep in mind that ideal-typical developmental *constructs* and *history* are to be sharply distinguished from each other, and that the construct here is no more than the means for explicitly and validly imputing an historical event to its real causes while eliminating those which on the basis of our present knowledge seem possible."[25]

In his "Politics as a Vocation," Weber asks: "If the state is to exist, the dominated must obey the authority claimed by the powers that be. When and why do men obey? Upon what inner justifications and upon what external means does this domination rest?" [26] These studies develop answers to Weber's question in the specific situations of an informationalizing society. This domination seems to work on many levels inasmuch as "it is a whole body of practices and expectations, over the whole of living: our sense and assignments of energy, our shaping perceptions of ourselves and our world. . . . It thus constitutes a sense of reality for most people in society." [27] In other words, our everyday experience in the various mediascapes made accessible to us by informationalization "naturalizes the odd and the appalling, offers them as common sense, in Gramsci's way of putting it. Domination filters through a thousand capillaries of transmission, a million habitual meanings. Most of the time it doesn't feel like domination, but like getting on with business." [28] The technologies of the mass media and computerization are not presented here as simply ends in themselves or as autonomous forces causing domination by themselves. Rather they will be examined in the context of the political interests that control them, using them to reinforce their power or to defuse resistance while they enlarge their domination over nature and the mass population.

With the rise of industrial society, a "market economy" gains hegemony over most social relations. Yet, with the emergence of informational society, the logic of the market increasingly pervades the total reproduction of society, establishing the technical basis for creating a highly developed "market culture." As cultural systems, the means of communicating information become critical tools for producing power and privilege for those who own, control, or manage them, who are at the same time using these cultural circuits to extend their domination over others. In Part II, Chapter 1 outlines some general frameworks for the following studies with a brief analysis of how the puzzles of power are entangled in the riddle of commodity structure, arguing that Barthes's mythologies, Debord's society of the spectacle, and Baudrillard's political economy of the sign provide some very useful initial categories for gauging how social change occurs in informational society.

Working with these insights, Part III tentatively addresses the influence of informational developments on political ideology, social class, religion, the family, history, and national security. Chapters 2 and 3 explore how the politics of image divide ideologically on informational mediascapes in contemporary America. This section examines why traditional ideology and political conflicts seem to have changed under informational conditions. Chapter 2 examines the dominant ideologies of contemporary America, reviewing the emergence of neoconservatism in the 1970s and 1980s as a reaction against the cultural crises of the 1960s. And Chapter 3 then reevaluates the ideopolitical agendas of televangelism in light of the ideological conflicts of contemporary American society. Ultimately this section illustrates how ideology can be continually recoded to produce political power for its encoders over its decoders.

Part III also reviews how the workings of power and ideology in informational society reconstruct the practical premises of key social institutions. These chapters suggest why the modes of information can function as crucial productive forces in the transnational corporate economy. Chapter 4 reconsiders change in the American family during the transition from the more traditional forms of industrial culture to the present-day informational society. It reveals how socialization in the current family regime promotes forms of personal identity and social solidarity based upon the planned consumption of sign values. Chapter 5 analyzes the effects of television-based electioneering on the conduct of party politics in democratic states. In particular, it concentrates upon the rational coproduction of image by campaign organizations in special discourses of charisma, which now embodies the core of mass democratic politics at the national level in the United States. Chapter 6 also argues that ideologies are fabricated continuously in the mythologies of the mass media. To make this case more concretely, it disassembles the various dimensions of the transnational 1984 D-Day spectacle as an ideopolitical commodity that typifies how power is coproduced in image-based consumer cultures. These themes are continued in Chapter 7 by reconsidering how the Chernobyl nuclear disaster was actively repackaged ideologically to bolster the fragile consensus on nuclear power.

After the discussion of how power relations seem to be evolving along several different lines in informational societies, the concluding speculations of Part III, Chapter 8, will examine how informational society promotes the emergence of new social movements. Unlike old laborite social movements, these seem to express new forms of popular resistance against the domination embedded in informational technics and the culture it generates. Chapter 9 asks what role critical intellectuals might play in present-day resistance movements and any future forms of oppositional politics that might challenge the domination of market culture, service states, or informational capital. It reviews the politics of image behind the rise and fall of the New Left in the mainstream media, and following up on Chapter 8, it seeks to understand how oppositional groups operate successfully or unsuccessfully on mediascapes as political forces. Although critical intellectuals are often co-opted, they have, nevertheless, unique opportunities to critique, deconstruct, and subvert informational codes of domination from within the codes themselves. This chapter suggests that the alternative media might be put to many new uses in resistance to help organize new oppositional coalitions. By redefining the progressive potentialities of informational technics, critical intellectuals might use them in new political movements to help others create more liberating and enlightened forms of human relations within the ever-changing consumption communities of informationalizing society.

NOTES

1. For a sample of these discussions, see Richard J. Barnet and Ronald E. Mueller, *Global Reach* (New York: Simon and Schuster, 1974); Daniel Bell, *The Coming of Post-Industrial Society: A Venture in Social Forecasting* (New York: Basic Books, 1973); Bell, *The Cultural Contradictions of Capitalism* (New York: Basic Books, 1976); James R. Beninger, *The Control Revolution: Technological and Economic Origins of the Information Society* (Cambridge, Mass.: Harvard University Press, 1986); Barry Bluestone and Bennett Harrison, *The Deindustrialization of America* (New York: Basic Books, 1982); Zbigniew Brzezinski, *Between Two Ages: America's Role in the Technetronic Era* (New York: Viking, 1970); Ralf Dahrendorf, *Class and Class Conflict in Industrial Society* (Stanford: Stanford University Press, 1959); Peter F. Drucker, *The New Society: The Anatomy of Industrial Order* (New York: Harper & Brothers, 1950); Christopher Evans, *The Micro Millenium* (New York: Viking Press, 1979); John Kenneth Galbraith, *The Affluent Society,* 3d ed. rev. (Boston: Houghton Mifflin, 1976); Galbraith, *The New Industrial State,* 3d ed. rev. (New York: New American Library, 1978); Alan Gartner and Frank Riessman, *The Service Society and the Consumer Vanguard* (New York: Harper and Row, 1974); Michael Hudson, *Global Fracture: The New International Economic Order* (New York: Harper and Row, 1977); Donald M. Lamberton, ed., *The Information Revolution,* vol. 412 of *Annals of the American Academy of Political and Social Science* (Philadelphia: American Academy of Political and Social Science, 1974); Fritz Machlup, *The Production and Distribution of Knowledge in the United States* (Princeton: Princeton University Press, 1962); Ernest Mandel, *Late Capitalism* (London: Verso, 1978); Yoneji Masuda, *The Information Society as Post-Industrial Society* (Bethesda, Md.: World Future Society, 1981); John Naisbitt, *Megatrends* (New York: Warner Books, 1982); Simon Nora and Alain Minc, *The Computerization of Society: A Report to the President of France* (Cambridge, Mass.: MIT Press, 1980); Marc Uri Porat, *The Information Economy: Definition and Measurement* (Washington, D. C.: Office of Telecommunications, U.S. Department of Commerce, 1977); Robert Reich, *The Next American Frontier* (New York: Times Books, 1985); Alvin Toffler, *The Third Wave* (New York: William Morrow, 1980); Alain Touraine, *The Post-Industrial Society* (New York: Random House, 1971); and Frederick Williams, *The Communications Revolution* (Beverly Hills, Calif.: Sage, 1982).

2. Herbert Marcuse, *One-Dimensional Man: Studies in the Ideology of Advanced Industrial Society* (Boston: Beacon Press, 1966), 154.

3. Marshall McLuhan, Introduction to Harold A. Innis, *The Bias of Communication* (Toronto: University of Toronto Press, 1951), xi.

4. For a detailed discussion of advanced corporate capitalism in its transnational forms of exchange, which is beyond the central focus of this analysis, see Samir Amin, *Accumulation on a World Scale: A Critique of the Theory of Underdevelopment* (New York: Monthly Review Press, 1974); Richard J. Barnet and Ronald E. Mueller, *Global Reach: The Power of Multinational Corporations* (New York: Simon and Schuster, 1974); Andre Gunder Frank, *Crisis: In the World Economy* (New York: Holmes and Meier, 1980); James O'Connor, *Accumulation Crisis* (New York: Blackwell, 1984); and Immanuel Wallerstein, *The Capitalist World Economy* (Cambridge: Cambridge University Press, 1979).

5. Roman Jakobson, "Language in Relation to Other Communication Systems," *Selected Writings,* vol. 2, *Word and Language* (The Hague: Mouton, 1971), 698.

6. For a range of different approaches to semiotics, see Ferdinand de Saussure, *Course in General Linguisics* (New York: Fontana/Collins, 1974); Charles Peirce, *Collected Papers,* vols. 1–6 (Cambridge, Mass.: Harvard University Press, 1931–60); Charles Morris, *Foundations of the Theory of Signs* (Chicago: University of Chicago Press, 1938); Louis Hjelmslev, *Prolegomena to a Theory of Language* (Madison: University of Wisconsin Press, 1961); Roland Barthes, *Elements of Semiology* (New York: Hill and Wang, 1967); and Umberto Eco, *A Theory of Semiotics* (Bloomington: Indiana University Press/Midland, 1979).

7. Eco, *A Theory of Semiotics,* 16.

8. Morris, *Foundations,* 20. Since a sign is anything that is interpreted as "standing for something else," or a sign vehicle expressing some meaning (the *signifier* and *signified* in Saussurean terms), semiotics usually examines the interpretation of signs and their coded meanings in a conventional ongoing process of semiosis. Eco's and Morris's construction of the sign is somewhat narrow inasmuch as they both assume a nominalist basis for the sign, stated in terms of some human convention of interpretation. Peirce's version of the sign is more open-ended and interpretative, resting on an ongoing chain of inferences from perceptions of reality in time. As Peirce asserts, it is "the sign and the explanation together which make up another sign, and since the explanation will be a sign, it will probably require an additional explanation, which taken together with the already enlarged sign will make up a still larger sign; and proceeding in the same way, we shall, or should, ultimately reach a sign of itself, containing its own explanation and those of all its significant parts; and according to this explanation each such part has some other part as its object" (Peirce, *Collected Papers,* vol. 2, 230).

9. Eco, *A Theory of Semiotics,* 7–14.

10. Ibid., 11–13.

11. See, for example, Claude E. Shannon, "The Mathematical Theory of Communication," *Bell System Technical Journal* 27, no. 3 (1948): 379–423, and no. 4 (1948): 623–56; and Shannon and Warren Weaver, *The Mathematical Theory of Communication* (Urbana: University of Illinois Press, 1949).

12. Roman Jakobson, "Closing Statement: Linguistics and Poetics," in *Style in Language,* ed. Thomas A. Sebeok (Cambridge, Mass.: Harvard University Press, 1960), 353.

13. See Walter J. Ong, *Orality and Literacy: The Technologizing of the Word*

(New York: Methuen, 1982), and Terry Eagleton, *The Function of Criticism: From the Spectator to Post-Modernism* (London: Verso, 1983).

14. Umberto Eco, *The Role of the Reader: Explorations in the Semiotics of Texts* (Bloomington: Indiana University Press/Midland, 1984), 3–43.

15. Roland Barthes, "Style and Its Image," in *The Rustle of Language* (New York: Hill and Wang, 1986), 99.

16. Eco, *The Role of the Reader*, 5–7.

17. Eagleton, *The Function of Criticism*, 128, 137.

18. See Fred R. Dallmayr, *Beyond Dogma and Despair: Toward a Critical Phenomenology of Politics* (Notre Dame, Ind.: University of Notre Dame Press, 1981); Dallmayr, *Polis and Praxis: Exercises in Contemporary Political Theory* (Cambridge, Mass.: MIT Press, 1984); Kathy Ferguson, *The Feminist Case against Bureaucracy* (Philadelphia: Temple University Press, 1984); David Held, *Introduction to Critical Theory* (Berkeley: University of California Press, 1980); Martin Jay, *The Dialectical Imagination: A History of the Frankfurt School and the Institute of Social Research, 1923–1950* (Boston: Little, Brown, 1973); John O'Neill, *On Critical Theory* (New York: Seabury, 1976); and Stephen K. White, *The Recent Work of Jürgen Habermas: Reason, Justice, and Modernity* (Cambridge: Cambridge University Press, 1987).

19. See Herbert Marcuse, *Soviet Marxism* (New York: Columbia University Press, 1958); Jean Baudrillard, *The Mirror of Production* (St. Louis: Telos Press, 1975); and Guy Debord, *The Society of the Spectacle* (Detroit: Red & Black, 1983).

20. Max Weber, *The Methodology of the Social Sciences* (New York: Free Press, 1949), 90.

21. See Timothy W. Luke, "Informationalism and Ecology," *Telos* 56 (Summer 1983): 59–73, and "Technique in Marx's Political Economy," *The Social Science Journal* 18, no. 2 (1981): 55–70.

22. Weber, *The Methodology of the Social Sciences*, 93.

23. Ibid.

24. Ibid., 101–2.

25. Ibid., 102.

26. Max Weber, "Politics as a Vocation," in *From Max Weber: Essays in Sociology*, ed. H. H. Gerth and C. Wright Mills (New York: Oxford University Press, 1958), 78.

27. Raymond Williams, *Marxism and Literature* (Oxford: Oxford University Press, 1977), 11.

28. Richard Ohmann, *Politics of Letters* (Middletown, Conn.: Wesleyan University Press, 1987), xii.

PART II

Creating a Post-Marxist Critique of Postindustrialism

1

Finding New Puzzles of Power
in the Riddle of the Commodity

In the years immediately following World War I, Georg Lukács partially reconstructed Marx's radical deconstruction of the commodity in his essay "Reification and the Consciousness of the Proletariat." Seeking to puzzle out how and why the proletariat had been crippled, like the bourgeoisie, under capitalism by the "reification of every aspect of its life," Lukács claimed that "commodity fetishism is a *specific* problem of our age, the age of modern capitalism."[1] Commodity fetishism also was the most *general* malady of modern life, "for at this stage of history, there is no problem that does not ultimately lead back to that question and there is no solution that could not be found in the riddle of commodity-*structure*."[2] In Lukács's reconstruction of Marx's reasoning, commodification meant pure destruction, because it potentially entailed the reification of every aspect of human activity. The essential basis of the commodity structure "is that a relation between people takes on the character of a thing and thus acquires a 'phantom objectivity,' an autonomy that seems so strictly rational and all-embracing as to conceal every trace of its fundamental nature: the relation between people."[3]

Lukács then identified a critical question that remains as alive today as it was in 1922: "How far is commodity exchange together with its structural consequences able to influence the *total* outer and inner life of society?"[4] He asserted that the essence of commodification was revealed only when it became the universal basis of all social relations under advanced capitalism: "Only then does the commodity become crucial for the subjugation of men's consciousness to the forms in which this reification finds expression and for their attempts to comprehend the process or to rebel against its disastrous effects and liberate themselves from servitude to the 'second nature' so created."[5]

The answer that Lukács gave to his own questions was limited. It still was grounded in the political conflicts and social contradictions of the

1920s. While he saw the commodity form becoming a universal basis for many social relations, it did not totally dominate the outer and inner life of even the most advanced capitalist societies of Great Britain, Germany, or the United States. Forerunners of the transition to more fully developed forms of planned corporate capitalism were emerging in each of these nations, but the "organic, irrational and qualitatively determined" practices of precapitalist relations thrived outside of most modern factories.[6] The "second nature" of reified exchange relations was not indisputably hegemonic over nature itself or many noncommodified forms of human activity.

Over six decades later, however, almost everything has changed. Since the economic crises of the 1930s, and World War II in the 1940s, commodity exchange has come to dominate the outer and inner life of global society almost completely. From the uniform computer bar coding being placed on the smallest, most mundane household products, to the rise of monetized social relations in the last reaches of the Amazon and Africa, to the interlocked twenty-four-hour machinations of global financial exchanges, to the purchase of test-tube babies and renting of surrogate mothers' wombs, to the limited adoption of market reforms in centrally planned communist economies, the logic of commodification is slowly seeping into every nook and cranny of ordinary life. State intervention into the international, national, regional, and household economies in order to sustain the ongoing accumulation and circulation of capital now virtually guarantees the hegemony of exchange-driven "second nature" over nature itself and many organic human relations. The commodity is acquiring this power as corporate capital, with state support, not only rationalizes economic production but also industrializes cultural reproduction. To control the outer and inner life of society, corporate management, as Horkheimer and Adorno suggest, has mobilized the new technologies of "the culture industry," whose marketing strategies aim at "no more than the achievement of standardization and mass production, sacrificing whatever involved a distinction between the logic of the work and that of the social system. This is the result not of a law of movement in technology as such but of its function in today's economy. The need which might resist central control has already been suppressed by the control of the individual consciousness."[7]

Of course, everything that exists is not necessarily a functional subassembly of transnational capitalism. Corporate groups cannot and do not purposefully design or manage every aspect of life everywhere. The nation-state frustrates their operations as often as it facilitates them. As the global economic instabilities of the past two decades indicate, transnational capital is internally divided and contradictory, too, as different national segments, industrial sectors, technological groups, and financial conglomerates struggle against each other for markets, growth, and technical dominance in the world economy. Still, there are strong tendencies working toward the attainment of the complete commodification of cultural reproduction in the strategic business planning of many corporate groups, which seeks to erase the distinctions between the logic of work and social institutions. In contrast to the entrepreneurial capital discussed by Marx and Weber, contemporary corporate capitalism is much more organized, efficient, and managerially grounded as a scientifically planned enterprise. Similarly, the service-oriented economies of the most developed societies now predicate their future growth upon the further commodification of culture, personality, and social relations. The impact of global trade, automated industrial production, transnational mass consumption, extensive computerization, electronic communications, jet transportation, and nuclear weaponry on the traditional structures of human behavior is therefore eroding our understanding of existing industrial (or industrializing agricultural) societies. The form and substance of such systems, which were well defined by Marx and Weber, gradually are disappearing. In their place, new modes of postindustrial behavior and belief are emerging from the complex codes of global media markets, which in turn frame the outlines of a new informational culture and society. The phantom objectivity of this newly shaped "second nature," however, has yet to be fully explored, mapped, or settled by social theory.

SOME DIVERGENT BUT PARALLEL APPROACHES

Lukács's basic insights into the cycles of commodification are still sound. In this new world, however, the electronic media—as the most expressive articulation of commodification under these economic, political, and social conditions—are basic geocosmic forces that form both the molten core of today's second nature and the hard crust of its image-driven phantom objectivity. Their broadcast transmissions bubble up in an electronic primordial soup that continuously swirls around the processes of everyday life. The features of this new creation mostly are invisible until one studies the flow of images on one of the many screens of power.[8] The basic topography of its signscapes or mediascapes can be screened up from many points: from television sets, computer terminals, video recorders, audiocassette or CD players, product displays, portable computers, architectural spaces, store windows, city sidestreets, on a jet descending across urban sprawl, or inside a car traveling along a city freeway. At these and other sites, one confronts new puzzles of power, formed within the all-embracing but concealing codes of transnational capitalism's phantom objectivity.

The modernist project of the nineteenth and early twentieth centuries moved along a diachronic, linear logic of perspectival space in continual discourses about how "the new," the avant-garde, or the "latest developments" were overcoming the backwardness of traditional society. Vast regions of the "backward," "ancient," "traditional," or "historic" once served as indicators of "the new" making progress against their domain. Today, however, precapitalist tradition has been largely overcome, or at least displaced, by exchange-driven modernity as the organizing basis of most societies: Modernity "won." The capitalist world-system has penetrated almost every "backward" area, integrating each of them at least partially into the global marketplace. In turn, the linear progress of "the new" against the old increasingly is overshadowed by newer, postmodern fascinations with synchronic simultaneities of "the *now*" in a nearly universal modernity. Fresh configurations of "now" on the screens of power shift from the now-here to the now-there to the now-before to the now-coming-to-be with very little sense of real cultural progress or true social revolution.

Some of the most fruitful insights into these signscapes turn up in the thinking of Roland Barthes, Guy Debord, and Jean Baudrillard, and also among the first generation of the Frankfurt School, including Theodor W. Adorno, Max Horkheimer, and Herbert Marcuse. Drawing on my reading of their ideas, I will outline some critical approaches for understanding the puzzling flow of power through the varied terrain of market cultures under transnational capitalism. By rereading familiar images and reinterpreting their apparently obvious meanings, I hope to decipher many more less obvious meanings in response to Lukács's basic question, which is: Under informational modes of production, how far is commodity exchange together with its structural consequences able to influence the *total* outer and inner life of society today? To answer this question, several additional ones must be asked: How is power exercised on the mediascape? What kind of ideology emerges in informational society? Who dominates whom through the meanings produced on and consumed at the screens of power in these new sociopolitical spaces? How is culture commodified, produced, and reproduced under transnational televisual modes of acculturation? Where do traditional institutions, like the family, social classes, the intelligentsia, democratic politics, and national identities, fit into the mediascape as image systems? How are competitive nation-states and military conflicts framed and contained in the electronic world system of transnational capital? What types of resistance might work as new oppositional strategies?

Over the past four decades, culture, politics, and society, like all of the manufactured objects and packaged services of transnational commerce, have become screenable, image-encoded commodities, particularly in North America. These processes of informationalization now are sweeping over Asia, Europe, Latin America, and parts of Africa. As the following studies suggest, however, they are most fully elaborated within the United States and its NATO/OECD allies within the Western transnational zone-regime along the Pacific Rim or in Western Europe. There are no hard-and-fast rules for responding to these questions, but a promising start can be found in the parallel but divergent works of Barthes, Debord, and Baudrillard.

ROLAND BARTHES AND DECODING MYTHOLOGIES

The innovative theoretical contributions of Roland Barthes in the areas of semiotics, literary criticism, and linguistic analysis are quite diverse.[9] A careful survey of his works soon reveals that they essentially defy categorization and deny synthetic summations. Much of his work, however, centers upon a changing effort to contextualize the practice and place of writing in culture, discourse, and human understanding. His analyses of literary production as a mode of social practice crisscross a large range of subjects, including French history, theater, modern novels, Japanese culture, the mass media, and the fashion industry.[10] Of these important studies, it is Barthes's treatment of "mythologies" in mass media messages that perhaps is most useful for this particular analysis of power and ideology in informationalizing advanced capitalist societies.

Written in the mid–1950s for a number of journals, each of Barthes's "mythologies" is a brief consideration of some aspect of popular culture—films, wrestling, automobiles, the Tour de France, strippers, and Billy Graham religious crusades. Barthes's discussion in each piece works at demystifying the processes of producing and consuming political meanings within different kinds of textual presentations circulating in popular culture. In particular, he concentrates upon the protective illusions in these texts that obscure class stratification and exploitation in mass media images. From Adorno and Horkheimer's vantage, such mythologies are the stock-in-trade of the culture industry. Myths are vital new political alloys, fusing culture, advertising, and publicity into new technologies of power. Thus "advertising becomes art and nothing else, just as Goebbels—with foresight—combines them: *l'art pour l'art*, advertising for its own sake, a pure representation of social power. In the most influential American magazines, *Life* and *Fortune*, a quick glance can now scarcely distinguish advertising from editorial picture and text."[11]

For Barthes, myths form a way of speaking about or of making sense of the world, and are the direct obverse of politically active language, inasmuch as they project a conflict-free, noncontradictory construction of reality. They are forms of almost completely commodified communication. At the same time, these illusory visions of reality are plainly political in their thorough inversion of social realities. Such naturalized modes of commodified communication work well in a society that has learned "to satisfy all its needs in terms of commodity exchange. The separation of the producer from his means of production, the dissolution and destruction of all 'natural' production units, etc., and all the social and economic conditions necessary for the emergence of modern capitalism tend to replace 'natural' relations which exhibit human relations more plainly by rationally reified relations."[12]

Understood in this manner, Barthes argues, "*Myth is depoliticized speech.* One must naturally understand *political* in its deeper meaning, as describing the whole of human relations in their real, social structure, in their power of making the world; one must above all give an active role to the prefix *de-:* here it represents an operational movement, it permanently embodies a defaulting."[13] Each myth, as it circulates in the daily understanding of popular culture, is charged with political messages within the power-mediating systems of communication in that time and place. As a result, Barthes asserts, "we are no longer dealing here with a theoretical mode of representation: we are dealing with *this* particular image, which is given for *this* particular signification."[14] Adorno and Horkheimer also notice that these specific techniques are embedded directly in the culture industry:

> The assembly-line character of the culture industry, the synthetic, planned method of turning out its products (factory-like not only in the studio but, more or less, in the compilation of cheap biographies, pseudodocumentary novels, and hit songs) is very suited to advertising: the important individual points, by becoming detachable, interchangeable, and even technically alienated from any connected meaning, lend themselves to ends external to the work. The effect, the trick, the isolated repeatable device, have always been used to exhibit goods for advertising purposes, and today every monster close-up of a star is an advertisement for her name, and every hit song a plug for its tune. Advertising and the culture industry merge technically as well as economically. In both cases the same thing can be seen in innumerable places, and the mechanical repetition of the same culture product has come to be the same as that of the propaganda slogan. In both cases the

insistent demand for effectiveness makes technology into psychotechnology, into a procedure for manipulating men.[15]

The construction of myths in the culture industry, then, invests images with attractive attributes to allure "the buying public." Its members can mix and match the detachable, interchangeable, alienated features of these mass-produced myths to satisfy their own individual tastes within diversely coded ranges of acceptance delimited by industrialized myth-making.

This concrete grounding for Barthes's mythology analysis can be observed clearly in his famous decoding of a *Paris Match* cover, depicting a young black African in French military uniform saluting the tricolor. The photograph's denotation does not fully disclose, for Barthes, another level of politicized connotations. While it is braced within the image as denotation, the connotative level freezes the signifier and suggests a number of mythic signified qualities—France, French power, the Empire, military pride, French patriotism, the "civilizing mission" of France, Africa's domination—in the image of the photojournalistic cover. Therefore, a particular image emerges, freezes, and circulates in a very particular signification. Ultimately, Barthes maintains,

> the essential point in all this is that the form does not suppress the meaning, it only impoverishes it, puts it at a distance, holds it at one's disposal. One believes that the meaning is going to die, but it is a death with reprieve; the meaning loses its value, but keeps its life, from which the form of the myth will draw its nourishment. The meaning will be for the form like an instantaneous reserve of history, a tamed richness, which it is possible to call and dismiss in a sort of rapid alternation: the form must constantly be able to be rooted again in the meaning and to get there what nature it needs for its nutriment; above all, it must be able to hide there. It is this constant game of hide-and-seek between the meaning and the form which defines myth. The form of myth is not a symbol: the Negro who salutes is not the symbol of the French Empire: he has too much presence, he appears as a rich, fully experienced, spontaneous, innocent, indisputable image. But at the same time this present is tamed, put at a distance, made almost transparent: it recedes a little, it becomes the accomplice of a concept which comes to it fully armed, French imperiality: once made use of, it becomes artificial.[16]

The key problem here is myth's naturalization of conflictual and contradictory political circumstances in false but easily circulated images. The production and consumption of such mythologies is merely "the reflex in consciousness of the fact that the 'natural laws' of capitalist production have been extended to cover every manifestation of life in society."[17]

Whole catalogs of stereotypes—in image, sound, textual form—are continuously remanufactured to create a minimum cultural consensus for consumer capitalism. Such consensus is strong enough to generate legitimacy and to provide some rationality in the reproduction of society, but it also remains weak enough to tolerate resistance and to encourage revalorizing cultural innovations. Myths are appropriated by corporate groups and state agencies to promote their organizational interests in advertising or publicity as the personal needs of their customers and clients. In advanced capitalist societies, mythic speech and texts are charged completely with these operational intentions to reinforce the phantom objectivity of their commercialized second nature as a natural flow of universally acceptable values and needs. To have any real political impact, Barthes realizes, much more than his satirical countercodings of myths would be necessary. Still, his awareness of the political need to act does not move him past his largely anti-political position of an ironic demystifier. For the critic of such mythologies, he concludes, "the havoc which he wreaks in the language of the community is absolute for him, it fills his assignment to the brim: He must live this assignment without any hope of giving back or any assumption of payment." [18]

GUY DEBORD AND THE SOCIETY OF THE SPECTACLE

In 1957, a handful of small avant-garde groups formed the Situationist International. For the next fifteen years until the Situationist International was disbanded in 1972, its members developed a new critique of modern consumer societies. [19] As a leading figure within the Situationist International, Guy Debord drew ideas from surrealism, dadaism, and Marxism into an incisive critique of post–World War II industrialism that focused on how standardized images help to create a consumerist form of culture and social organization. A critic of film and modern urbanism, Debord provides in his *The Society of the Spectacle* an important analysis of why corporate capitalism leads to forms of life based upon images and of how images can produce and reproduce social relations. Most important, Debord considers how the meanings of power and ideology change as economies based upon mass consumption develop from within an economy of mass production. In turn, he asks what sort of resistance is appropriate to oppose the new forms of personal alienation and group exploitation in market cultures.

Debord claims that the existing world can be changed because "what is termed culture reflects, but also prefigures, the possibilities of organization of life in a given society. Our era is fundamentally characterized by the lagging of revolutionary political action behind the development of modern possibilities of production which call for a superior organization of the world." [20] Following dadaism's rejection of bourgeois values, and in keeping with surrealism's affirmation of sovereign desire to liberate new possibilities in modern life, Debord calls for an experimental, ephemeral strategy of finding new "passageways" and "situations" to transform society. In the situationist outlook, "the life of a person is a succession of fortuitous situations, and even if none of them is exactly the same as another the immense majority of them are so undifferentiated and so dull that they give a perfect impression of similitude. The corollary of this state of things is that the rare intensely engaging situations found in life strictly confine and limit this life." [21]

These confining limits follow from being entrapped within societies tied to consumption-based "spectacles." Debord, then, would agree with Adorno and Horkheimer that "culture is a paradoxical commodity. So completely is it subject to the law of exchange that it is no longer exchanged; it is so blindly consumed that it can no longer be used. Therefore, it amalgamates with advertising. The more meaningless the latter seems to be under a monopoly, the more omnipotent it becomes." [22] To oppose this amalgamation of culture with advertising, Debord's strategy of resistance calls for tactics of "contestation." By subverting the everyday exchange of image-based commodities through the challenges of art, new group organizations, or ephemeral ad hoc conventions of action, Debord hopes to discover new emancipatory possibilities beyond commodification in autonomous cultural activity.

Like Baudrillard's analysis of the code, Debord's critique tends to reify and overspecify the nature of the spectacle as a force in social relations. Nonetheless, Debord's vision of societies based upon spectacle effectively begins to describe a cultural system totally penetrated by the logic of abstract exchange. "In societies where modern conditions of production prevail, all of life presents itself as an intense accumulation of *spectacles.* Everything that was directly lived has moved away into a representation." [23] As individuals accept this unrelenting colonization of their private and public lives by commodification, many of life's most intimate situations are increasingly experienced passively and contemplatively through these endlessly circulating and evolving representations. For example, "love" is actually practiced by many as reenacted advertisements for diamonds, greeting cards, laundry soaps, life insurance, or prepaid funeral plans. Many individuals' sense of culturally appropriate action and personal identity begins, in large part, on advertising story boards and survives as a psychic urge to buy more consumer goods. These corporate-designed scripts for personal emotional expression are voluntarily self-imposed on intimate human relations not only to express emotions but also to give closure in cultural practice to corporate marketing plans.

In market cultures, "freedom" can be reduced to replaying in practice behind the wheel of a sports car (in a privately staged spectacle) a continuously remembered car ad, which defines true freedom (in the publicly projected spectacle) as roaming the roads in this kind of sports car. All of life's real excitements, joys, or passions, then, are increasingly represented as, and lived out through, commodities. This description very closely parallels Lukács's analysis of reification. The spectacle fuses the objective forms of commodified activity and the subjective content of individual consciousness into a reified and collective culture. Within societies based upon spectacle, then,

> *objectively* a world of objects and relations between things spring into being (the world of commodities and their movement on the market). The laws governing these objects are indeed gradually discovered by man, but even so they confront him as invisible forces that generate their own power. The individual can use his knowledge of these laws to his own advantage, but he is not able to modify the process by his own activity. *Subjectively*— where the market economy has been fully developed—a man's activity becomes estranged from himself, it turns into a commodity which, subject to the non-human objectivity of the natural laws of society, must go its own way independently of man just like any consumer article.[24]

The spectacle, as the site or space of meaning generation and communication, is now the product and producer, object and subject of consumer-driven economies. Therefore, "the spectacle which inverts the real is in fact produced. Lived reality is materially invaded by the contemplation of the spectacle while simultaneously absorbing the spectacle order, giving it positive cohesiveness."[25] Individuals and groups increasingly are swept into these rapidly moving currents of illusion by the pressures of living within the growing world market.

"We adapt ourselves," according to Debord, "with few variations, into a network of possible courses. We get used to it, it seems."[26] The more individuals passively contemplate the spectacle, each drawing his or her needs from its illusory currents, the less individuals understand their actual existence and own desires. Again, Debord's vision of the spectacle reinforces Lukács's critique of commodification. As reified labor, the spectacle demands a response of passive integration from each individual: "Pre-existing and self-sufficient, it functions independently of him and he has to conform to its laws whether he likes it or not. As labor is progressively rationalized and mechanized his lack of will is reinforced by the way in which his activity becomes less and less active and more and more *contemplative*."[27] The atomization, fragmentation, and isolation imposed by such "rationally refined relations" are the natural expression of spectacular modes of consciousness.[28]

To overcome this "immobile monotony" in contemporary consumerism, Debord rejects orthodox Marxist solutions. Socialist societies are also completely entwined in the global order of the evolving capitalist spectacle, as Gorbachev's "restructuring" and Deng's "guided responsibility" economic reforms in the 1980s plainly reemphasize. The ideologies of Leninism merely mystify this ugly fact: "Here the illusion of some variant of state and bureaucratic socialism is consciously manipulated by local ruling classes as simply *the ideology of economic development.*" [29] Instead, Debord's notion of resistance centers upon constructing unprecedented forms of action, or "situations" keyed to the spirit of individual moments, from within the workings of spectacular societies. Most important, he recognizes that cultural hegemony, which many Marxists see as irresistible or totalistic, is in fact always contingent, discontinuous, and elective in many of its effects. "We must try to construct situations, that is to say, collective ambiances, ensembles of impressions determining the quality of a moment. If we take the simple example of a gathering of a group of individuals for a given time, it would be desirable, while taking into account the knowledge and material means we have at our disposal, to study what organization of the place, what selection of participants and what provocation of events produce the desired ambiance.... The construction of situations begins on the ruins of the modern spectacle." [30] Each situation will be a mostly autonomous project of its particular creators, played out in immediate practice to overcome the alienation of contemplative spectatorship and its automatic reproduction of exchange values. Ideally, all individuals and groups would revolutionize their own lives by "living out" the real possibilities implicit in today's material affluence. The principle of the spectacle—passive nonintervention—would be exploded from within by active contestation of, and noncollaboration with, the system. Debord admits that "we have neither guaranteed recipes nor definitive results.... our working hypotheses will be reexamined at each future upheaval, whenever it comes." [31] Although he still casts situationism as a project for "the united action of a revolutionary *avant-garde* in culture," it is proposed as an experiment to be led into many yet to be defined directions to discover those "rare intensely engaging situations" of "collective ambiances."

Until these countercultural experiments take hold, analyzing the logic of spectacle or mapping the extent of its reach is vitally important. Such studies reveal how the phantom objectivity of naturalized domination is produced, and also how it might be resisted. In demystifying the spectacle, it becomes clear that "the worker does not produce himself; he produces an independent power. The *success* of this production, its abundance, returns to the producer, as an *abundance of dispossession.* All the time and space of his world become *foreign* to him with the accumulation of his alienated products. The spectacle is the map of this new world, a map which exactly covers its territory. The very powers which escaped us *show themselves* to us in all their force." [32]

JEAN BAUDRILLARD AND THE POLITICAL ECONOMY OF THE SIGN

Today, in the wake of the new philosophers and neoconservatives, it is not a novel claim to assert that Marxism is, at best, an inadequate framework for the critical appraisal of advanced industrial societies. Yet one of the most radical efforts to move beyond Marx has come not from the right, but from within Marxian discourse itself through the the work of Jean Baudrillard. Unlike most other thinkers on the left, as Mark Poster observes, Baudrillard systematically has "attempted a radical deconstruction of Marxism along with an alternative standpoint for today's radicalism." [33] Baudrillard's political economy of the sign also closely parallels Lukács's consideration of "the riddle of commodity-*structure*" developed in "Reification and the Consciousness of the Proletariat." Like Marx, Lukács begins from the premise that "the problem of commodities must not be considered in isolation or even regarded as the central problem in economics, but as the central, structural problem of capitalist society in all its aspects." [34] Sensing the power of this intuition, one can view Baudrillard's explorations into the new structure of contemporary commodity relations as an analysis that might "yield a model of the objective forms of bourgeois society together with all the subjective forms corresponding to them." [35] At times Baudrillard's lines of thought clearly stray off into an essentially self-referential game of allusions and allegations that have little grounding in actual economic, political, or social forces. If these excesses, however, are taken under critical consideration to control for their distortions, then his approach can contribute many useful insights.

In his first three books, written during the late 1960s and early 1970s, Baudrillard carefully develops his Marxian critique of commodification in the context of the postwar era of affluence. *Le Système des objets* (1968) and *La Société de consommation* (1970) maintain that the everyday reproduction of advanced industrial societies has transformed individual consumption into a new form of labor. [36] Trapped in a neverending flow of apparently new products, images, and experiences, Baudrillard argues, the individual must struggle to organize a limited, privativistic existence from the packaged material bits and symbolic pieces carried on these commodified tides. His *Pour une critique de l'économie politique du signe* (1972) distills most of the themes elaborated in the two previous works while at the same time beginning to move toward a break with Marxist political economy. With *Le Miroir de la production* (1973), he explicitly splits away from the purely Marxian perspective employed in the earlier studies, focusing on the play of simulacra in advanced capitalist society.

Moving beyond Marx: Baudrillard's Critique

By reexamining advanced capitalism, Baudrillard wants to reveal that dynamic where the "Marxist logic can be rescued from the limited context of political economy in which it arose, so as to account for our contradictions."[37] Returning to Marx's *The Poverty of Philosophy*, he retraces Marx's genealogy of exchange value from its first stage of surplus exchange in archaic/feudal economies, through the exchange of industrial products to the modern stage of commodifying even morals, knowledge, and consciousness. While Marx partially anticipated this transformation in capitalism, its real impact has been felt only after his death. Only a fresh appraisal of contemporary political economy can fully grasp the forms of the "universal venality" that Marx foresaw.

In retracing these steps, Baudrillard acknowledges Marx's theoretical innovations. Yet he also questions the basic foundations of the Marxian critique, doubting the historical transcendence of Marx's critical perspective: "Marx shattered the fiction of *homo economicus,* the naturalization of the system of exchange value, the market, and surplus value and its forms. But he did so in the name of labor power's emergence in action, of labor *(pro-ducere).* Isn't this a similar fiction, a similar naturalization—another wholly arbitrary convention, a simulation model bound to *code* all human material and every contingency of desire and exchange in terms of value, finality, and production?"[38] Baudrillard asserts that Marx, like most intellectuals, unwittingly accepts the *imaginary* (or the symbolic mirror of production, value, labor, and objective reality), as if it were "real" in his critical project. As a result, he substitutes one productivist fiction, tied to the processes of capitalist exchange, for another imaginary, based upon the viewpoint of revolutionary labor. Hence, Marxism constitutes a critical code only from the historically limited viewpoint of modern capitalist modes of production.

As a system of analysis, Marxism fails inasmuch as it effaces differences between the industrial capitalist modes of production and previous primitive modes of production, as well as future radical alternatives: "The blindness about primitive societies is necessarily linked to a weakness in the radical critique of political economy. This explains why, having failed to subvert the foundations of political economy, historical materialism results only in reactivating its model at a world-wide level. . . . through its most 'scientific' inclinations toward earlier societies, it "naturalizes" them under the sign of the mode of production. Here again their anthropological relegation to a museum, a process originated in bourgeois society, continues under the sign of its critique."[39] Marxism predisposes its practitioners to repeat unwittingly the productivist assumptions of bourgeois capitalism in state socialist forms of society. Given these ideological undercurrents in Marxism, Baudrillard essentially rejects the political focus of Marx's critique. "It is no longer worthwhile to make a radical critique of the order of representation in the name of production and its revolutionary formula. These two orders are inseparable and, paradoxical though it may seem, Marx did not subject *the form production to a radical analysis any more than he did the form representation.* These are the two great unanalyzed forms of the imaginary of political economy that imposed their limits on him."[40] To surpass Marx, Baudrillard works at fusing the critiques of representation and production into a single theoretical project.

Today, Baudrillard asserts, capitalism thrives in a powerful structure of control much more subtle and persuasive than classical wage-labor exploitation because it has supplanted the market-based commodity form with the code-based sign form. With the commodification of consciousness, he insists, a new *political economy of signs,* which expresses a generalized code of domination, must become the means for revitalizing Marxist criticism. The driving force behind this transformation is the rise of monopoly or corporate capital, which necessarily restructures exchange in accord with a different logic of mathematically modeled organizational planning. On this account, for example, Lukács observes that "the mathematical analysis of work-processes denotes a break with the organic irrational and qualitatively determined unity of the product. . . . The finished article ceases to be the object of the work process. The latter turns into the objective synthesis of rationalized special systems whose unit is determined by pure calculation and which therefore seem to be arbitrarily connected with each other."[41] Ultimately, Baudrillard concludes that "Marx was not in a historical position to speak scientifically, to speak the truth."[42] Therefore, Marxism becomes a theory of a now-surpassed, obsolete stage of individual commodity production or an ideology of industrial productivism. For Baudrillard, "something in the capitalist sphere has changed radically, something Marxist analysis can no longer respond to. Hence, in order to survive it must be revolutionized, something which certainly has not been done since Marx."[43]

Commodity fetishism in this new stage of capitalism focuses not exclusively on the *product,* but rather also on the *sign values* invested in the product as an object. Sign value is, in part, the synthetic outcome of those rationalized special systems that Lukács saw as being based on calculation. It centers upon products, which have been reworked with abstract or symbolic codes, producing valorized differences through symbolic intensification and imaging. Lukács, then, partially anticipates this revolutionary break in commodity valorization. He claims that "rationally reified relations" increasingly prevail when "the unity of a product as a commodity no longer coincides with its unity as a use-value: As society becomes more radically capitalistic the increasing technical autonomy of the special operations involved in production is expressed also, as an economic autonomy, as the growing relativization of the commodity character of a product at the various stages of production. It is thus possible to separate forcibly the production of a use-value in time and space. This goes hand in hand with the union in time and space operations that are related to as a set of heterogeneous use-values."[44] These "special operations," which must be constantly expressed and reconstituted in shifting sets of "heterogeneous use-values," are, to a significant extent, embodied within the coding and recoding of sign-value production and consumption. They are technically autonomous and separate from the material fabrication of products as use values, but they also are essential aspects of their exchange value under current conditions of production.

The fetishism of commodities under this regime grounds itself on the sign object that now is different and more valued because of its value-adding symbolic coding. The difference, for example, between plain old dungarees and image-intensified designer jeans sums up this mode of "post–use value" sign–form coding. Thus, "it is the sign exchange value *(valeur d'échange signe)* which is fundamental—use value is often no more than a practical guarantee (or even a rationalization pure and simple)."[45] Corporate managerialism shifts the operations of capitalism "from the form-commodity to the form-sign, from the abstraction of the exchange of material products under the law of general equivalence to the operationalization of all exchanges under the law of the code."[46] Beginning with *The Mirror of Production,* then, Baudrillard has moved progressively beyond Marx to analyze the origins and operations of these coding processes. Given the importance of sign exchange value in the code, one must now understand how this new political economy generates "a form of a general code of rational abstraction," which in turn underpins "the circulation of values and their plan of exchange in the regulated equivalence of values."[47]

Baudrillard's Political Economy of Signs

In elaborating the logic of the code, Baudrillard stresses how it reflects the general operations of monopoly capital as corporate planning effaces many of the historical contradictions between capital and labor, production and consumption, supply and demand. Traditionally, "capital only had to produce goods; consumption ran by itself. Today it is necessary to produce consumers, to produce demand, and this production is infinitely more costly than that of goods."[48] As part of the production of demand, Baudrillard argues, the forms of individual subjectivity and social consciousness are themselves manufactured to sustain consumption. Hence the social modes of existence today are essentially complex simulations of reality that are designed specifically to sustain these fragile cycles of political and economic reproduction. Since individual desires are abstractly reorganized as prepackaged needs that collectively constitute the base of society's productive forces, the structure of social existence essentially devolves into shifting aggregates of atomized individuals, who struggle to realize their personal desires in packaged meanings circulating in the corporate marketplace.

The traditional forms of both individuality and society collapse under these conditions. Like Foucault, Baudrillard discounts the autonomy of individual subjects as free reasoning moral agents. Real human needs exist, but their forms of articulation, experience, and satisfaction are actualized within a market culture that constrains individuals to realize their needs in mass-produced material packages and professionally approved behavioral scripts. Capital produces consumers, simultaneously constructing a total culture of market-dominated subjectivity for them. He argues that individuals "are only episodic conductors of meaning, for in the main, and profoundly, we *form a mass,* living most of the time in panic or haphazardly, above and beyond any meaning."[49] The masses' demand for getting and spending "disposable income" creates supplies of corporate-provided goods and services for mass "income disposal." Likewise, the attainment of ever-greater material standards of living by individual consumers increasingly requires that they live by ever-higher material standards set in the corporate marketplace. After centuries of explosive growth, then, Baudrillard holds, advanced capitalist society is now experiencing an implosive reversal as power, expressed in the form of packaging and making choices, circulates between the masses and their institutional coordinators. The mass media are at the core of this social implosion of advanced capitalism. Politics, like the media, reflect the desired choices of the audiences in the places of power; yet the choices they are given flow out of the limited alternatives established in these same places of power. This total circularity of choice-making in turn dominates the silent majorities in history.

Still, the mass is neither a subject nor an object. It bears no relation to any historical social referent—a class, a nation, a folk, or the proletariat.

Instead, it is a statistical entity that only appears in the social survey or opinion poll. Many smaller "psychodemographic" segments can be identified within the mass, but there are no real moral criteria available for guiding their actions. The silent majorities of the masses are perhaps even no longer representable in political terms or concretely identifiable in social terms. Their identity and unity are instead continuously redefined and remanufactured by psychodemographers intent upon perfecting even newer methodologies for the disclosure of their needs. Baudrillard argues that the complex coding of the media and the marketplace sets the outer boundaries of the mass in that "it only exists at the point of convergence of all the media waves which depict it." [50] Parodying McLuhan's "the medium is the message," Baudrillard suggests that the mass and the media are the same process today, or "the mass(age) is the message." Given this fact, Baudrillard claims, the historical resistance of the masses to social control by capital and the state now is turning into a hyperconformity, pushing the system into a hyperlogical practice of itself to abolish it. The only real possibility for radical action available to the masses boils down to subverting the tactics of consumerist overconsumption: "'You want to consume—O.K., let's consume always more, and anything whatsoever; for any useless and absurd purpose.'" [51] While traditional resistance "consists of reinterpreting messages according to the group's own code and for its own ends," the masses now "accept everything and redirect everything *en bloc* into the spectacular, without requiring any other code, without requiring any meaning, ultimately without resistance, but making everything slide into an indeterminate sphere which is not even that of non-sense, but of over-all manipulation/fascination." [52]

The System of Simulation. Baudrillard claims that modernity itself changes with the growth of this type of advanced capitalist society. A logic based upon simulation rather than representation constitutes the dominant organizing principle of this new era. "McLuhan's formula, *the medium is the message*," appropriately is "the key formula of the era of simulation (the medium is the message—the sender is the receiver—the circularity of all polls—the end of panoptic and perspectival space—such is the alpha and omega of *our* modernity)." [53] The masses no longer can act as effective, individual subjects in this new social and political context. Nonetheless, they cast an immense shadow as "silent majorities" that diffuse and deflect the circuits of corporate power and state authority.

Monopoly capital with state backing suspends the classical market dialectics of supply and demand, production and consumption, capital and labor in the formalized simulations of planning. To take this position is not to say that corporate capital has bridged all social contradictions or resolved all political conflicts. Everything does not exist or serve a function because of monopoly capitalism. Yet there is a tendency toward total administration in corporate capitalism that clearly differentiates it from entrepreneurial capital. Through mass education, professional counseling, or market research, human desires are abstracted and autonomized into needs that serve as a productive force. And the needs inculcated among individual consumers "are better defined as a *function* induced (in the individual) by the internal logic of the system: more precisely, *not as a consummative force* liberated by the affluent society, but *as a productive force* required by the functioning of the system itself, by its process of reproduction and survival."[54] The new managerial techniques for exerting "strategic control," or administering the "predictive anticipation" of these needs, displace those of crudely extracting surplus value through wage labor. "It means that one goes from a system of productive forces, exploitation, and profit, as in the competitive system dominated in its logic of social labor time, to a gigantic combinatory where all values commutate and are exchanges according to their operational sign."[55]

Therefore, the prevailing linguistic mode in advanced capitalist economies is the signal rather than the symbol. Corporate capital "puts an end to the superstitious fusion of word and thing. Anything in a determined literal sequence which goes beyond the correlation to the event is rejected as unclear and as verbal metaphysics. But the result is that the word, which can now be only a sign without any meaning, becomes so fixed to the thing that it is just a petrified formula."[56] The free-floating quality of such signifiers permits them to fuse arbitrarily with virtually any signifieds and referents. Corporate capital, in turn, can move beyond mere "use value" in selling goods and services. The individual's real or imagined use for commodities can be treated through advertising, fashion, or education with purposely coded signals. Usually counterintuitive and counterfactual kinds of signifiers are attached to particular commodities, coding the audience's reception of the message in the format of attributes assigned to the goods by the producer. Control of the code, rather than of the means of production, is the critical issue now. In the transmission of the codes, then, the imaging of denture adhesives promises social acceptance, security, and peace of mind; corporate-funded political candidates, standing in front of some forested ridge in the Rocky Mountains and claiming to be pro-environment, are accepted as being "quality" growth–oriented and ecology-minded conservationists; beer provides athletic fitness, fellowship, and sex appeal; automobiles pledge liberation, power, and sexual satisfaction; sugar-filled breakfast cereals offer health, the great outdoors, and cancer prevention. Language and its communicative function are changed in these new hyperreal uses, and "the more completely language is lost in the announcement, the more words are debased as substantial vehicles of meaning and become signs devoid of quality; the more purely and transparently words communicate what is intended, the more impenetrable they become."[57]

Coded signals are purposefully organized to override any rational, critical reception by generating these hyperrealities. This tendency simply continues the logic identified by Lefebvre, who suggests that "around the years 1905–10 the referentials broke down one after another under the influence of various pressures (science, technology, and social changes). Common sense and reason lost their unity and finally disintegrated; the 'common-sense' conception of absolute reality disappeared and a new perceptible 'real' world was substituted or added to the reality of 'well-informed' perception, while functional, technical objects took the place of traditional objects."[58] The substance of this newly perceptible real world is formed from images, which are mythological and spectacular expressions of capital's contradictory agenda for total commodification. Such images operate as self-contained and nearly irresistible signals, dictating their directions with little tolerance for independent personal decisions.

In the commodity structure, signal-based images guarantee that "there is *nothing*—whether object, individual or social group—that is *valued* apart from its double, the image that advertises and sanctifies it . . . imparting an ideological theme to an object . . . and endowing it with a dual real and make-believe existence. It appropriates ideological terms and links the salvaged signifiers to the re-conditioned signified. . . ."[59] Rather than being invited to question the coded signifiers' actual correspondence to the referent commodity, the audience is chosen or created to immediately accept the signals *as such* by purchasing the commodities. Demographic analysis frames particular groups and market niches in terms of those goods, qualities, or characteristics which have been discovered to be desired among the target populations. Once defined, specific types of products are encoded in accord with particularly differentiated signifiers. Certainly, such attempts at steering preferences or forming tastes often do not work; hundreds of new products fail every year. Yet entire industries are dedicated to market research, public opinion, product design, consumer psychology, and demographic targeting. And, more important, they are continuously improving the techniques of their still-inexact sciences. Therefore, these signals embody what are believed to be the desires of the occupants in the market's different demographic niches, but they also allow consumers considerable leeway in completing the circuits of the code. Continuously interwoven, these signal-driven codes now dominate virtually all aspects of everyday life.

Under competitive capitalism, the signifier arguably still referred formally to a signified and had some referent. Some distinctive opposition and formal difference tied the use value of signs to a lived distinction. With the code, however, the sign form marks this new organization of signs:

> The signified and the referent are now abolished to the sole-profit of the play of signifiers, of a generalized formalization in which the code no longer refers back to any subjective or objective "reality," but to its own logic. The signifier becomes its own referent and the use value of the sign disappears to the benefit of its commutation and exchange value alone. The sign no longer designates anything at all. It approaches its true structural limit which is to refer back only to other signs. All reality then becomes the place of a semiological manipulation, of a structural simulation. And, whereas the traditional sign (also in linguistic exchanges) is the object of a conscious investment, of a rational calculation of signifieds, here it is the code that becomes the instance of absolute reference, and, at the same time, the object of a perverse desire.[60]

As the following chapters maintain, the social and political implications of these observations are painfully evident in the everyday life of modern consumer society. To sustain the accumulation of capital, corporate capitalist modes of production have stressed the importance of product innovation and constant growth. New needs for new products for new consumers are continually developed to promote growth. Having satisfied real basic needs for many people, corporate producers cultivate new planned needs for status, community, style, or love in the marketing of goods and services. The consumer society serves as "the ultimate realization of the private individual as a productive force. The system of needs must wring liberty and pleasure from him as so many functional elements of the reproduction of the system of production and the relations of power that sanction it. . . . it is never an explosive liberation, but a controlled emancipation, a mobilization whose end is competitive exploitation."[61]

To justify its destruction of traditional needs and use value production, corporate capital often presents these transformations as a progressive social revolution. "On this basis," Baudrillard holds, "one could even argue (the *leitmotiv* of the ideologies of consumption) that its function is to correct the social inequalities of a stratified society: confronting the hierarchy of power and social origins, there would be a democracy of leisure, of the expressway and the refrigerator."[62] Yet life in these communities of consumption unfolds only a false liberation to consume. This programmed emancipation, in turn, renders corporate capital's programs of growth more productive. "Far from the individual expressing his needs in the economic system," as Baudrillard concludes, "it is the economic system that induces the individual function and parallel functionality of objects and needs." [63] The codes of planning for corporate growth and production ultimately produce both needs and need satisfactions for most individuals. Whereas competitive capitalism exerted social control through the coercive enforcement of production, coding effects control under advanced corporate capitalism through the collaborative mobilization of the subjects' code competencies in consumption: "For the system no longer needs universal productivity; it requires only that everyone play the game." [64] The codes work through their continual stylization in images of the consumers' roles, and the roles created by the codes make the game work as individuals adopt them into their own life-styles.

The Structural Law of Value. Since the mid-1970s, Baudrillard has completely moved away from a Marxian critique of symbolic exchange and the code into a more problematic and unsettling analysis of image and reality. In his *L' Echange symbolique et la mort* (1976), *A l'ombre des majorités silencieuses où la fin du social* (1970), and *Simulacres et simulation* (1981), Baudrillard maintains that "symbolic exchange is no longer an organizing principle; it no longer functions at the level of modern social institutions." [65] The industrial order's commodity law of value now has been absorbed into the cybernetic era's structural law of value, leading to a reality principle based on *hyperreal simulation,* rather than on substantive reality. In these later, less well-grounded studies, and in *Oublier Foucault* (1977), Baudrillard identifies the pure play of signs and simulacra, rather than commodities, as the linchpin of his analytical outlooks.

In this stage of his thinking, Baudrillard basically strays from the logic of commodification. Instead, the logic of simulation is broken free from social forces in the firm and state that anchor its operations. Consequently, Baudrillard often casts technology as an autonomous social force functioning almost as an end in itself. Today, "it is no longer a question of imitation, nor of reduplication, nor even of parody. It is rather a question of substituting signs of the real for the real itself, that is, an operation to deter every real process with its operational double . . . which provides all the signs of the real and short-circuits all its vicissitudes." [66] Having elaborated the logic of code, Baudrillard suggests that modern capitalist means of production have promoted the code's autonomous hegemony, sublating the logic of materially grounded exchange that underpinned Marx's critique of capitalism. Historically, the sign marked some referential value; it bore some designation of the signified. Now, as Baudrillard claims in *The Mirror of Production*, it is essential to comprehend how the new political economy imposes "a form of a general code of rational abstraction" that in turn anchors "the circulation of values and their play of exchange in the regulated equivalence of values."[67]

With these claims about the theory of value, Baudrillard clearly goes over the line of historical social analysis that he stayed behind in his earlier works. That is, he tends to ignore the nuts and bolts of actual social forces: class relations, group structures, market relations, institutional mechanisms, or political frictions. Any close rereading of Marx— as the entire post–1960 global Marxian culture industry illustrates— soon reveals that his allegedly careful analysis of how production and consumption relate to power, domination, and class conflict is in fact usually full of holes and quite contradictory. Still, Marx tends to set a standard in many people's minds for discussing these concerns. And, like Foucault's work, most of Baudrillard's project lacks Marx's attention to certain categories of historical detail and to all levels of social complexity. However, although Baudrillard's particular conclusions should not necessarily be accepted without reservation, his arguments are not hopelessly confused; they can be more firmly grounded in actual political and social conflict. Simulations and hyperreality, likewise, can still be tied back into the logic of commodification that is working its effects throughout the informationalization of society.

While keeping these doubts in our minds, Baudrillard also holds that a new theory of value grows along with advanced cybernetic modes of information. With the computerization of finance and commerce, the free flow of capital and labor in the transnational marketplace expresses the total relativity of value. The value of currencies is reduced to an hourly and daily "confidence game" based upon currency traders' faith in the future implications of transnational trade flows, national fiscal policy, new tax plans, or the basic direction of commodity markets existing now. Monetary signs dance nonstop around the clock in global stock, commodity, and monetary markets, often with little or no reference to real existing goods or services. Computerized program trading, as the October 1987 stock market crash illustrated, can even remove direct human action in real time from the loops of exchange. Money no longer has concrete grounding in the actual exchange of hard specie, like gold or silver. The gold standard has been replaced by the World Bank's SDRs (special drawing rights), free-floating currency rates, macroeconomic indices, and political risk analyses—all statistical simulacra—as the ephemeral standard of value. Such new monetary practices reveal how signs can interact and move more freely among themselves in exchange without direct reference to real substantive content other than the partly arbitrary and partly mathematically necessary values posited by the mathematical models that generate them. For Baudrillard, this is "the emancipation of the sign: released from any 'archaic' obligation it might have had to designate something, the sign is at last free for a structural or combinatory play that succeeds the previous role of determinate equivalence."[68] The loose steering of multiple demographic groups through sign flows projected within constant media broadcasting and polling had emerged as the new mode of social control and individual supervision. "Mandatory passivity" in this model of exercising power "evolves into models constructed directly from the 'active responses' of the subject, his implication, his 'ludic' participation, etc., and finally a total, environmental model made up of incessant, spontaneous responses, joyful feedback and irradiated contact."[69]

Discussing the logic of the code, Baudrillard speculates that it functions in accord with the structural law of value on the basis of simulation. He reifies the code and overspecifies its power, but he asserts that the structural law of value was preceded historically by two earlier forms. The first was the commercial law of value, tied to a dominant scheme of factory production during the industrial era, and the second was the natural law of value, based upon a logic of counterfeit in the artisan production of the preindustrial era. On the one hand, the natural law of value presumed a definite hierarchy and scarcity of signs in a world that prohibited their free production through caste and hierarchy. The natural law of values' forms, then, stressed imitation of the real and counterfeit via artificial materials to impose a synthetic core of meaning on the natural world. Therefore, social meaning stemmed from an artful imitation of the real. On the other hand, the commercial law of value assumed the abolition of hierarchy, scarcity, and control in the production of signs. In fact, its forms seem to accentuate an endless identical series of signs in its processes of reproduction to create an endlessly reproductive manufactured system of meaning and value. Meaning here flowed from mechanical reproduction of uniform products. With the structural law of value, however, social forms are predicated on the suspension of objective reality in a free play of totally relative referents. Its simulacra now constitute pure simulations substituting a play of signs for reality itself.

This imploding system presumes the sublation of traditional modes of reasoning in the domination of coding. Baudrillard claims that "the whole traditional mode of causality is brought into question: the perspective, deterministic mode, the 'active,' critical mode, the analytical mode—the distinction between cause and effect, between active and passive, between subject and object, between ends and means."[70] As perspective and panoptic space collapse in politics, society, and the economy, "one enters into simulation, and hence into absolute manipulation—not passivity, but the non-distinction of active and passive."[71] Regulation through the coding of options for the "silent majorities" by "quiet companies" and "secret government" grows in the indeterminacy of value. Values and goals are produced continuously in manufactured mathematical montages derived from polling and media signaling. Social and individual desires in terms of mass consumption, in turn, are artfully designed from the statistical results of analyses of innumerable psycho-demographic "focus groups." Reality becomes more code-intensive, embracing whatever can be stylized, modeled, simulated, gamed, designed. "At the conclusion of the process of reproduction," Baudrillard asserts, "the real becomes not only that which can be reproduced, but that which is always already reproduced—the hyperreal."[72] From these simulation games, the silent majorities of opinion and decision are discovered and tracked to ascertain the continually remanufactured "reality" of this new system of domination. Hyperreality promotes hyperconformity. A rational discourse about progress in the "new" in modernity increasingly slips behind hyperreal simulations of the "now."

To outline this case, Baudrillard elaborates his new theory of value for this new era. Following Saussure, he presents two perspectives on the organization of value: the structural and the functional. Saussure's approach to the exchange of language terms is analogous to the exchange of money. In structural terms, a piece of money can be placed in relation to all other terms in the monetary system. As such, it is both internally and externally referential, with its position in the general system also establishing its value. On the other hand, it can be exchanged for some real goods of value in a functional exchange, which it designates or signifies in monetary terms. Within the classical industrial order, Baudrillard argues, these two dimensions are differentiated, but they interoperate coherently within the commodity laws of value, "where the function of designation always appears as the goal or finality of the structural operation of language."[73]

Baudrillard makes Saussure's description of signification completely parallel to Marx's analysis of surplus value production. As Baudrillard suggests, "use value functions as the horizon and finality of the system of exchange value: the former qualifies the concrete operation of the commodity in (the act of) consumption (a moment of the process that is parallel to the sign's moment of designation); while exchange value refers to the interchangeability of all commodities under the law of equivalence (a moment parallel to the structural organization of the sign)."[74] The dominance of formal codes in bureaucratic planning, corporate management, and financial dealings, however, severs these two dimensions of value during the present phase of history. The determinate relation of terms to what they designate, of each particular signifier to its peculiar signified, or of abstract units to real fungible goods now are disarticulated. Baudrillard claims that *"referential value is nullified, giving the advantage to the structural play of value.* The structural dimension, in other words, gains autonomy, to the exclusion of the referential dimension, establishing itself on the death of the latter. Gone are the referentials of production, signification, affect, substance, history, and the whole equation of 'real' contents that gave the sign weight by anchoring it with a kind of burden of utility—in short, its form as representative equivalent. All this is surpassed by the other stage of value, that of total relativity, generalized commutative, combinatory simulation."[75]

Signs under these conditions, therefore, do not necessarily refer to any objective reality. Instead, the signifier can act as its own referent, making endless citations of itself. Like the well-known cola, the sign now can say, "It's the real thing," or simply, "It's it." These signs and signing are essentially simulations that do not really re-present anything. They are fabricated illusions that are accepted in the form of ideopolitical commodities as "the reality" of culture, ideology, politics, or national security in the absence of the real. Computer models, military spectacles, statistical indices, consumer goods design, corporate logos, or television images are all simulacra of the "society" now presented and accepted as social reality. Yet they too make reference only to themselves.

Television entertainments, for example, project an entire world of hyperreal persons, places, and things that are openly accepted as real and meaningful by millions of viewers who gossip away for hours talking over the latest trials and tribulations of their favorite "TV personalities." When the shows' initial runs are ended, periodic "specials" even allow viewers to revisit them at their fictional mediascapes and catch up on what has been happening there. Television personalities and characters actually serve as friends and neighbors for many viewers in electronic simulation of friends and community. They are hyperrealities, simulating intimate networks of emotional human activity for many alienated consumers in order to deliver the commodity of audiences to advertising producers and the advertised commodities of producers to the consumer audiences. The computer also perfectly exemplifies this mode of information: As a device programmed to simulate, manipulate, and approximate particular realities from diverse sorts of data in its coded software, the reductionist data of its processed outputs are commonly taken for what is "the real." Unfolding within its models, these cybernetic simulacra are commonly accepted as the shifting substance of the hyperreal world.

Simulation as an organizing principle assumes the purposeful substitution of the signs of the real for reality itself. Yet the tie to commodification clearly need not be broken. Hyperreality simply brings new forms of hyperreal commodification along with it. In democratic politics, as Chapter 5 argues, a simulated hyperreality of public life emerges from public opinion polls, whose mathematical indices are substituted in practice for "the public" itself. The ever-changing outcomes of daily, weekly, and monthly surveys continually span the gap between the opinion leaders and opinion holders. The mathematical montages of satisfaction and dissatisfaction from such polls, in turn, increasingly constitute what the contemporary public accepts as its sense of itself. Yet the entire process is one of hyperrealistically simulating reality in order to substitute it for the real. These artifacts are much more potent than traditional ideology as a mode of exercising power. Most historical forms of ideology entailed the betrayal or distortion of some actual reality with signs as "false consciousness," but simulation entails the complete "short-circuit of reality" and its "reduplication by signs"[76] in ways that suspend truth and falsity almost entirely in the fabric of hyperreality itself.

At the level of global politics, nuclear deterrence is "the apotheosis of simulation." The arsenals in nuclear arms races are the signs of hyperreality that neutralize the reality of actual nuclear war. Real nuclear war would annihilate the stakes at issue in global power struggles. Consequently, the superpowers devote their energies to the hyperreal simulations of preparing for such a war, which short-circuits that reality. However, this struggle reduplicates the conflict as a war of signs between the opposing superpowers. "The balance of terror is the terror of balance," as the simulations ensure that the real event of nuclear war will not disturb the equilibrium of the general system.[77] Baudrillard argues that this macrological system of deterrence also pervades the micrological dimensions of everyday life: "The same model of planned infallibility, of maximal security and deterrence, now governs the spread of the social," throughout the networks of social control.[78] Every effort is now being made, through constant simulations and resimulations of every conceivable eventuality in daily life, to guarantee that "nothing will be left to chance." The accidents that do occur, like the Chernobyl nuclear disaster discussed in Chapter 7, are so exceptional because they are rare incidents of purposive human error that are regarded as inconceivable and appear to be unsimulated. Once they happen, however, they become a new modeling scenario for innumerable fresh simulations. The deterrent engineering of existence ultimately guarantees an anticipatory control over any possible threat to this hyperreality: "Reality no longer has the time to take on the appearance of reality. It no longer even surpasses fiction: it captures every dream even before it takes on the appearance of a dream. The cool universe of digitality has absorbed the world of metaphor and metonymy." [79] While its connections to class contradictions or social conflict are plainly questionable, Baudrillard's treatment of "simulation" presents a useful account for grasping some of the mechanisms behind the strategies of social control embedded in the codes of contemporary culture. In turn, the following chapters will begin to trace out some of the class conflicts and social contradictions woven into the system of simulation.

Baudrillard sums up the state of society after the simulacra put an end to the social: "In this vertigo of serial signs—shadowiness, impossible to sublimate, imminent in their repetition—who can say where the reality of what they simulate resides? Apparently, these signs repress nothing. . . . even the primary process is abolished. The cool universe of digitality absorbs the worlds of metaphor and of metonymy, and the principle of simulation thus triumphs over both the reality principle and the pleasure principle." [80] For Baudrillard, needs increasingly have no autonomous basis in an authentic conception of humanity outside of commodity exchange. They are instead grounded in the prepackaged expectations of cultural codes conveyed to individuals as part and parcel of their aestheticized duty to consume. Consumers serve as the vital productive force of monopoly capitalism, while the code enforces their productive potential through a free-floating flow of signifiers and signs. Under this regime, art and industry continually "exchange signs" in order to keep "art productive" and industrial production masked in "esthetic signs of prestige." In the simulative dimensions of cybernetic hyperrealism, "we already live out the 'esthetic' hallucination of reality." [81]

There are, of course, considerable weaknesses as well as strengths in Baudrillard's system of analysis. Beyond the reservations expressed above, his lack of a consistent theory of the subject at both the individual and mass level makes it difficult to envision a way out of the political contradictions he describes. The "who" and "whom" of these power arrangements are never made concrete. Institutional mechanisms, group relations, and political conflicts all still need to be made more concrete in his analysis. There are no moral criteria elaborated for transforming the simulation regime into some more satisfying system of human organization. There is often no clear political direction or better sense of the ethical choices to be had from Baudrillard's analyses. His work promotes a deep distrust of collective action, while providing new categories to refine one's faculties of critique and analysis. Yet what must be (or, at least, might be) done to resist or contest the web of simulation largely is left unanswered. The future "now" will only be like the present "now," reiterating an endless play of signs in a never-ending simulation of hyper-real models.

POWER, TIME, AND SPACE: FROM NARRATIVE TO IMAGE

With their different perspectives, Barthes, Debord, and Baudrillard provide some promising insights into the basic mechanisms of power and domination as these have been changing with the rise of informational society. These transformations, which are described here provisionally through the ideal types of industrialism and informationalism, can be differentiated further by comparing and contrasting the possible constructions of power, time, and space under industrial and informational regimes. To puzzle through these changes, the organizing metaphors that might describe such different forces also can be tied back to some of the biases in their different modes of communication.

Industrial society is organized around institutional cultures with a different structure of cultural space and time than that found in informational society.[82] As Innis and McLuhan maintain, the metaphors appropriate for understanding industrial society largely tie back into the bias in its print-driven media, which were the first mass-production technologies for creating cheap, identical products.[83] These media essentially create a linear, panoptical or typographical mode of space. The personal sense and social sense of place are fixed in grids of class, status, or geographical distance. This "perspectival" space evolves with a particular sense of social time, grounded in diachronic concepts of "development-in-time" such as evolution, progress, or maturation. Change is marked by incremental measures of linear change; the "new" is the latest increment of diachronic development in time or space. The power exerted in linear, panoptical space presumes its own production by "power-ful" agents at the top of society, outside of or from within the center of established institutions, which mediate the production of power and its application to the "power-less."

Seen in this mode, power clearly is coercive, creating and policing its own subjects in the evolving procedures of civil institutions, social organizations, and parastatal discourses conducted in print and in writing. Without its strong oversight, the leadership of these institutions assumes everyone would repudiate its directions in complete revolt. Hence individuals often are seen as potential rebels, ready to cast off heavy coercive controls. The state places a high premium on obedience, loyalty, or full integration into its stuctures of hegemony. Ideologies tend to be a totalistic discursive program for transforming everything in accord with a fixed theoretical map. Power works through a logic of coercive detainment and continuous indoctrination, which finds expression in elaborate, extended narratives. A shift in social position within the perspectival scope of such space also assumes that some concomitant gain or loss of control over the power production process is experienced. As McLuhan argues in *The Gutenberg Galaxy,* "print exists by virtue of the static separation of functions and fosters a mentality that gradually resists any but a separative and compartmentalizing or specialist outlook." The sovereign agencies of the state—king, republican assembly, or bureaucracy—stand apart in these linear spaces as an *author,* who adopts and exercises a "fixed point of view" in its narratives of discipline and domination. Within such typographic fields, the state can be seen as a scribe or draftsman, scrolling power across its subjects as objects through discourses of visually anchored classification. Foucault's "disciplines" and "discourses of power," for example, can be seen emerging within the interstices of such procedures. A particular kind of individual subjectivity, typically grounded upon a "possessive individualism," is produced with such industrializing societies. Throughout these dimensions of power, as McLuhan observes, "the homogenization of men and materials will become the great program of the Gutenberg era, the source of wealth and power unknown to any other time or technology." [84]

From their panoptical perspectives, as Bentham proposed, powerful state agencies can normalize individual and mass behavior among their subject populations through a continuous regulatory gaze exerted through the police, schools, bureaucracy, health care system, and military. The spatiality of print, market exchange, and linear time sets out the expansive dimensions of the panoptical space in which those on top, outside, or at the center of society organize those at the bottom, inside, or margins of society. The analog clock perfectly exemplifies how these relations can be understood. The travel of its hands coterminously creates and regulates measures of time by moving continuously through an enclosed space from a central axis of representation, marking the twenty-four hours that represent one day on a calendar's grid. To a certain extent, social time can be measured or conceptualized under this logic as the duration or pressures of this kind of power traveling in "real time" through linear space from top to bottom. In turn, relatively clear relational-spatial distinctions of social status, cultural preeminence, and political authority develop in line with the print-bound, panoptical space in traditional industrial societies or industrializing agricultural societies.

Informational society, on the other hand, is framed by new structures of cultural space and time made possible by the bias in electronic networks of transnational exchange. Metaphors for interpreting it lock into images from telecommunication-based and computer-driven media, which can generate nonlinear, multiperspectival modes of space, containing innumerable hyperreal constructs of unique, nonidentical realities. The personal and social senses of place seem to become more mobile, defined by fluid changing connections into networks of information. One's ability to log on, call in, switch on, or tune in to cybernetic/electronic media overcomes many types of distance. Electronic transmissions allow for rapid shifts in focus between geographically and culturally unrelated places, either in time-sequence or simultaneously, through editing, directing, or split screening. If the average TV viewer, for example, is not pleased by the transmitted flow of images, then he or she can create his or her own "program" of rapidly changing and varied images simply by flipping through the channels. Participants in informational societies no longer live in tightly bounded ethnogeographic settings; they also inhabit a continuously changing mediascape of transnational scope and content with different regions organized around particular image flows or signs. Television does not "bring the entire world into our homes" as much as it moves everybody who is watching to the same place and into the same events. Such "screenal" space, likewise, builds a new sense of social time based upon *synchronic* concepts of "simultaneity," including those incompletely expressed in surrealism, postmodernism, or simulation. Change is marked by shifting permutations or passage between regions in the current constellation of signs, images, and appearances on synchronic screen displays. The "now" is simply an ephemeral existing configuration of particular images in a shifting sign flux at this or that point, discontinuously differentiated from many other "thens" in other sign fluxes.

The power exercised in nonlinear, screenal space, however, is more puzzling. It seems to require continuous *coproduction* by those with access to "behind the screens" and those without access "before the screens." Power here is essentially *seductive,* motivating its subjects with images to collaborate in reproducing or completing the codes' logic or sequence at their screens. Individuals recreate themselves continuously in the permissive coding of individual self-management. The institutional leadership of informational society recognizes that "rebelling" within such screenal spaces is not necessarily a serious threat to the social order. Given the complexity and rigorous demands of the codes of control, all can, at least in part, style themselves as something of a rebel. It even can become a central theme in selling goods and services. The organization of power, then, forces all to behave as *collaborators,* who fulfill their needs and desires by completing the outlines of constrained personal choices left partially unfinished in the available codes of commodification. As a result, states can set acceptable ranges of rebellion by putting an emphasis on containing the deeper roots of dissidence, resistance, or opposition existing beneath the constraints of collaboration. Even open rebellion can be tolerated because police technologies work out their own changing subcodes of interaction with dissidents, rioters, or rebels, designed to contain or deter their activities within specific regions or rituals of interaction. An ideology, if this notion retains its meaning in such hyperreality, often appears as a partial ad hoc routine pieced together from images or signs assigned to particular goods, behaviors, or styles in constantly changing codes. The final meaning of signs is never completely certain. They are never necessarily received as sent nor sent as received. Image production assumes their being continuously recoded or countercoded during their reception to complete the encoding of their transmission. Power, in turn, follows a logic of collaborative containment and constant deterrence, which exerts its influence through equivocal, ephemeral images.

The state, under informational conditions, largely is integrated into the loops of code circulation as a *systems operator,* that can range across and combine multiple points of view in an "interdisciplinary" or "networked" mix of different coding routines, options, and programs. Within these regions, the state can be seen as a scheduler, director, and programmer, constructing contexts for collaboration by its subjects or conflict among them with the assistance of business and industry, which also act as code-coprocessors in the codings of various reified scripts and packages that basically channel, but never totally control, behavior. Political conflict centers around who directs and whom is directed or what is coded where, when, and why. As Baudrillard asserts, under these conditions of power, in "the ecstasy of communication,"[85] audiences produce their own message displays and the message displays create their own audiences. Given these shifts, Poster argues, theoretical attention must now be paid to the "modes of information" interoperating between the state and capital rather than the "modes of production" in informational societies.[86] Who has and who does not have access, as well as who is behind and who is before the screens, for the most part varies with the shifting codes of control.

To a large extent, social time can be understood as a field of complete synchrony or as the simultaneous participation of diverse groups in coproducing their discrete networks of power. As McLuhan claims (following James Joyce), its reality (or hyperreality) is based upon "all-at-once-ness." In fact, culturally meaningful groups can and do emerge transnationally around the signs and images of successive discrete "nows," like the 1950s, 1960s, or 1970s, that differentiate themselves from each other by the reified insignia of their era's peculiar commodities. Movies, television programs, popular music, or the news clearly serve as means of creating space, defining identity, and forming group consciousness. Time also can be understood as being measured in the "machine time" of instantaneous communication or computation, which becomes so pivotal in creating codes of consent and consenting to code-creation. As its metaphor, the digital clock suggests how these forces are apprehended. Time simply reads out statements of its passage in continuously changing screens of LCDs or LEDs; what surrounds or coexists with that reading is that now-ness marked in its digital identity. "Now" is one digital display in the same place as "then," which was only another digital configuration of identical signs. There is no spatial sense of time, as was true with analog clocks, traveling in an enclosed but carefully measured space, only a constantly recirculating set of signs dictating its display of simultaneous readouts. Overall, social control in the screenal spaces of these mediascapes boils down to organizing attractive conditions for collaboration and using different forms of seductive, but nevertheless imposed, self-management in large social aggregates while aggressively containing those who challenge or fail to grasp the conditions of collaboration.

Of course, elements of panoptic linear space remain operant at the global level of transnational firms, banks, and superpower states. In the bureaucratic structures of oversight, these modes of power are critical tools of management for those persons with the highest, broadest, deepest points of access to these institutions. Notwithstanding the prophets of postindustrialism, like Alvin Toffler or John Naisbitt, who see high-tech electronics creating new, more equitable, "high-touch" global communities, advanced communications also can reinforce existing social barriers tied to language, class inequalities, education, or basic code competencies. The development of informationalism does not totally destroy the power of industrialism as much as it simply subsumes it: literacy and typographic consciousness have not been obliterated. They function as axial subcodes of the larger codes of cultural reproduction. In times of crisis the state always can activate a "fixed point of view" in the coercive powers of its bureaucratic, police, and military organs to scroll power directly across its subjects, forcing them to abide by direct bureaucratic dictates. The screens of power also act as a "screen" in the sense of sheltering, protecting, or concealing those with complete access from the view of those with partial or limited access or none at all. Here, for example, screens of power can hide many of the everyday routines of military or police containment operations in the ghetto, at the Iron Curtain, outside terrorist hideouts, or along the borders with the Third World, even as they apparently depict them in action. Screenable images of power, then, are always partial or indistinct. Like the swarming snow of pixels in television broadcasts, screens force viewers to project their own gestalts of completion into indistinct images of how "they," who have access to the networks of control, imperfectly steer the intertwined systems of collective choice.

From behind these screens, the basic expectations projected into the postlinear, multiperspectival, non-panoptic spaces of the electronic mediascapes are assembled imperfectly and incompletely by individuals in the sign systems of image-driven informational society. Those with less access listen to, read across, look through, and constantly watch these "screens," taken now in another sense as the many diverse surfaces upon which signs, images, or pictures are projected. From these circulating tokens with their partial, polyvalent meaning, diverse private codes with more total, univocal meanings enable individuals and groups to construct new personal and partial conventions of understanding for the mythologies of the spectacle. As Barthes maintains, the form and content of these projections are soaked with mythologies, which organize "a world without contradictions because it is without depth, a world wide open and wallowing in the evident."[87] With the growing hegemony of transnational corporate capital, the means of information become the critical force in modern modes of production. A new politics of image, in which the authoritative allocation of values and sanctions turns on the coding and decoding of widely circulating images by politicized "issue groups," arises alongside and above the interest-group politics of industrial society. Contesting these mythologies can expose some of the contradictions and hidden dimensions of image-driven power. But, on the whole, the endless streams of mythological images in turn bring together the flow of elite control, mass acceptance, and individual consent in a new informational social formation—the "society of the spectacle."

In work and play, or in public and private, everyone decodes these signs, giving them an individual slant or group style, because most commodities ultimately have a "do-it-yourself" dimension of fulfillment. Conventional culture and unconventional counterculture both rest on the same principles. Everyone's own needs are interpolated into the screens' partial, fuzzy images. Not all screens are as explicit as personalized junk mail that attempts to show addressees directly—referring to them by name—how a certain commodity fits into their lives, why they cannot live fully without the commodity, and how they are or must become what the customized commodity offers. Instead, the codes of commodification most often stipulate that each consumer/client/citizen complete his or her own script to match the fantasies partially promised on the screens. As discussed in more detail in Chapter 4, these are the key premises in the shallow ideologies of today's "permissive individualism."

By these actions, individuals can fuse their personal desires, at least in part, with the corporate goals of transnational capital and the state, co-producing power by creating their own unique styles of self-government in accord with the codes. Even revolutionary terrorists derive their limited powers from the codes of consumption, using bombs or machine pistols to countercode their victims' expectations of satisfaction (and the larger viewing public's vicarious consumption of the victims' terror through their expectations being violently denied) from airline flights, lunches in Paris cafés, or dances at Berlin discos. But in countercoding the conditions of consumption with random violence, they coproduce fresh commodified images for further consumption as political documents in the mass media, images which ironically can act as neutralizing barriers to contain their own radical intent. On the other hand, "those in charge," like the professional/technical experts, middle-level managers, or the critical intelligentsia, might have slightly greater freedom as code creators or sign managers within more restricted-access subscreens of the screen. Yet beyond the scope of such secured windows, which are defined by these individuals' special code competence or bureaucratic clearances to access gates, "those in charge" also remain among the code consumers and sign-managed.

The imperatives of government in screenal space are those of "indirect rule" as individuals "self-manage" themselves through the mazes of constant commodification. To fuel the growth of transnationalized capitalism, more and more of the everyday lifeworld must be colonized by the corporate coding system reducing autonomous noncommodified behavior to scripted/packaged choices projected on the screens of power. Despite the apparent "freedom" or "revolt" projected by many new cultural styles, the tokens of transnational informational capitalism still are hooked into all the behavioral scripts and material packages flowing across the screens. Moreover, those possibilities that are not yet penetrated soon will be as the codes of exchange absorb new contextual forms to sustain the instrumental substance of exchange. Individual and group resistance constantly works at countercoding or refunctioning these codes to suit each individual's or group's own immediate personal or social uses. Revolutionary changes in these hyperrealities, however, are often not abolitions of the existing regime. Instead, they frequently turn out to be limited affirmations of the regime's power to expand or contract the degree of freedom in collective choice within these transnational means of informational reproduction.

The following chapters will illustrate how transnational corporate capital has offered new kinds of "liberation" from the traditional drudgery of everyday life in agricultural or industrial society. Of course, the extent of, and opportunities for, such emancipation vary greatly across the world's various societies in relation to the growth of corporate markets. The consumer has had only to accept his or her unique place as a permanent client/customer of global commerce to enjoy the rewards of collaboration. Yet, in the bargain, collaboration also enforces new modes of domination over each individual's self-management through the ceaseless consumption of corporate capital's codes, scripts, and packages from screenal space. As Marcuse observes,

> Under the rule of a repressive whole, liberty can be made into a powerful instrument of domination. The range of choice open to the individual is not the decisive factor in determining the degree of human freedom, but what can be chosen and what is chosen by the individual. The criterion for free choice can never be an absolute one, but neither is it entirely relative. Free election of masters does not abolish the masters or the slaves. Free choice among a wide variety of goods and services does not signify freedom if these goods and services sustain social controls over a life of toil and fear— that is, if they sustain alienation. And the spontaneous reproduction of superimposed needs by the individual does not establish autonomy; it only testifies to the efficacy of the controls.[88]

Resistance or contestation is possible but is often difficult to organize and sustain beyond the threshold of weak, corrective forms of "artificial negativity."[89] Even rebellion and radicalism can become heavily encoded life-style choices lived out as conventionalized scripts of behavior in almost ritualized coexistence with government surveillance or police containment.

Resistance is very slow in coming, then, because individuals co-create the power that dominates them on these shifting mediascapes as they "liberate" themselves in a self-directed consumption montage of utopian moments. The material goods and symbolic codes of the corporate sphere can be refunctioned by individuals in their use and reception of them, but often only temporarily. The systemic utility and personal value of such commodified micro-utopias derives from individual consumers' psychic management of their own consumption as a perpetual rerun of image bits personally scanned off of the screens of power. The "utopia" of the consumer's countercoded personal "style" in popular culture simultaneously affirms the "ideology" of capital's overcoded "rationality" in collective choice. Transnational capital within each of its national markets, therefore, tries to provide the individual with the psychosocial means to indirectly rule himself or herself in screenal space, while permitting it to expand the culture and commerce of its electronic world system elsewhere, confident that most of its current clients basically will leave it alone or that their weak resistance may actually strengthen the flexible codes of corporate commodification.

NOTES

1. Georg Lukács, *History and Class Consciousness: Studies in Marxist Dialectics,* trans. Rodney Livingstone (Cambridge, Mass.: MIT Press, 1971), 149, 84.

2. Ibid., 83.

3. Ibid. Here, Lukács follows Marx's original definition of the commodity in *Capital,* vol. 1: "A commodity is therefore a mysterious thing, simply because in it the social character of men's labour appears to them as an objective character stamped upon the product of that labour: because the relation of the producers to the sum total of their own labour is presented to them as a social relation, existing not between themselves, but between the products of their labour. This is the reason why the products of labour become commodities, social things whose qualities are at the same time perceptible and imperceptible by the senses. . . . But it is different with commodities. There, the existence of the things qua commodities, and the value-relation between the products of labour which stamps them as commodities, have absolutely no connexion with their physical properties and with the material relations arising therefrom. There it is a definite social relation between men, that assumes, in their eyes, the fantastic form of a relation between things. In order, therefore to find an analogy, we must have recourse to the mist-enveloped regions of the religious world. In that world the productions of the human brain appear as independent beings endowed with life, and entering into relation both with one another and the human race. So it is in the world of commodities with the products of men's hands. This I call the Fetishism which attaches itself to the products of labour, so soon as they are produced as commodities, and which is therefore inseparable from the production of commodities." See Karl Marx, *Capital,* vol. 1, *The Process of Capitalist Production* (New York: International Publishers, 1967), 72.

4. Lukács, *History and Class Consciousness,* 84.

5. Ibid., 86.

6. Ibid., 88.

7. Max Horkheimer and Theodor W. Adorno, *Dialectic of Enlightenment,* trans. John Cumming (New York: Seabury Press, 1972), 121.

8. Although these works were written with many different intentions, some very useful examples of such decoding can be found in the following works: Peter Biskind, *Seeing is Believing: How Hollywood Taught Us to Stop Worrying and Love the Fifties* (New York: Pantheon, 1983); Noel Burch, *To the Distant Observer: Form and Meaning in the Japanese Cinema,* rev. and ed. Annette Michelson (Berkeley: University of California Press, 1979); Adrian Forty, *Objects of Desire* (New York: Pantheon, 1986); Richard Wrightman Fox and T. J. Jackson

Lears, eds., *The Culture of Consumption: Critical Essays in American History 1880–1980* (New York: Pantheon, 1983); Delores Hayden, *Redesigning the American Dream: The Future of Housing, Work and Family Life* (New York: Norton, 1984); Dick Hebdige, *Sub-Culture: The Meaning of Style* (London: Methuen, 1979); Bevis Hiller, *The Style of the Century 1900–1980* (New York: E. P. Dutton, 1983); Thomas Hine, *Populuxe* (New York: Knopf, 1986); Charles Jencks, *The Language of Post-Modern Architecture,* 4th rev. ed. (New York: Rizzoli, 1984); Chester H. Liebs, *Mainstreet to Miracle Mile: American Roadside Architecture* (Boston: Little, Brown, 1985); David Marc, *Demographic Vistas: Television in American Culture* (Philadelphia: University of Pennsylvania Press, 1984); Roland Marchand, *Advertising the American Dream: Making Way for Modernity 1920–1940* (Berkeley: University of California Press, 1986); Raoul Vaneigem, *The Revolution of Everyday Life* (London: Left Bank Books/Rebel Press, 1983); and Judith Williamson, *Decoding Advertisements: Ideology and Meaning in Advertising* (New York: Marion Boyars, 1984).

9. See Jonathan Culler, *Roland Barthes* (New York: Oxford University Press, 1983); Annette Lavers, *Roland Barthes: Structuralism and After* (Cambridge, Mass.: Harvard University Press, 1982); Philip Thody, *Roland Barthes: A Conservative Estimate* (Atlantic Highlands, N.J.: Humanities Press, 1977); and George R. Wasserman, *Roland Barthes* (Boston: Twayne, 1981).

10. See Roland Barthes, *The Empire of Signs,* trans. Richard Howard (New York: Hill and Wang, 1982); *Image-Music-Text,* ed. and trans. Stephen Heath (New York: Hill and Wang, 1977); *Roland Barthes by Roland Barthes,* trans. Richard Howard (New York: Hill and Wang, 1977); *S/Z,* trans. Richard Miller (New York: Hill and Wang, 1974); *Writing Degree Zero,* trans. Annette Lavers and Colin Smith (Boston: Beacon Press, 1970); *The Eiffel Tower and Other Mythologies,* trans. Richard Howard (New York: Hill and Wang, 1979); and *Mythologies,* trans. Annette Lavers (New York: Hill and Wang, 1972).

11. Horkheimer and Adorno, *Dialectic of Enlightenment,* 163.

12. Lukács, *History and Class Consciousness,* 91.

13. Barthes, *Mythologies,* 143.

14. Ibid., 110. This characterization of myth also echoes in Lefebvre's critique of advertising publicity: "This image *duplicates* not only an object's material, perceptible existence but desire and pleasure that it makes into fictions situating them in the land of believe, promising 'happiness'—the happiness of being a consumer. Thus publicity that was intended to promote consumption is the first of consumer goods; it creates myths—or since it can create nothing, it borrows existing myths, canalizing signifiers to a dual purpose: to offer them as such for general consumption and to stimulate the consumption of a specific object." See Henri Lefebvre, *Everyday Life in the Modern World* (New York: Harper and Row, 1971), 105.

15. Horkheimer and Adorno, *Dialectic of Enlightenment,* 163.

16. Barthes, *Mythologies,* 118.

17. Lukács, *History and Class Consciousness,* 91–92.

18. Barthes, *Mythologies,* 157.

19. For additional discussion, see Jean-Jacques Raspand and Jean-Pierre Voyer, *L'Internationale situationniste: chronologie, bibliographie, protagonistes* (Paris: Editions Champ Libre, 1972), and Ken Knabb, ed. and trans., *Situationist International Anthology* (Berkeley, Calif.: The Bureau of Public Secrets, 1981)

20. Guy Debord, "Report on the Construction of Situations and on the International Situationist Tendency's Conditions of Organization and Action," *Situationist International Anthology,* 17.

21. Ibid., 24.

22. Horkheimer and Adorno, *Dialectic of Enlightenment,* 161.

23. Debord, *The Society of the Spectacle* (Detroit: Red & Black, 1983), no. 1.

24. Lukács, *History and Class Consciousness,* 87.

25. Debord, *Society of the Spectacle,* no. 8.

26. Debord, "Report," 37.

27. Lukács, *History and Class Consciousness,* 89.

28. Ibid., 91.

29. Debord, *Society of the Spectacle,* no. 113.

30. Debord, "Report," 25.

31. Ibid.

32. Debord, *Society of the Spectacle,* no. 31.

33. "Translator's Introduction," *The Mirror of Production,* Jean Baudrillard (St. Louis: Telos Press, 1975), 1.

34. Lukács, *History and Class Consciousness,* 83.

35. Ibid.

36. See *Le Système des objets* (Paris: Gallimard, 1968); *La Société de consommation* (Paris: Gallimard, 1970); *Pour une critique de l'économie politique du signe* (Paris: Gallimard, 1972); and *Le Miroir de la production où l'illusion critique du matérialisme historique* (Tournai: Casterman, 1973).

37. Baudrillard, *Mirror of Production,* 123.

38. *Mirror of Production,* 18–19.

39. Ibid., 91.

40. Ibid., 20.

41. Lukács, *History and Class Consciousness,* 88.

42. Baudrillard, *Mirror of Production,* 117.

43. Ibid., 118.

44. Lukács, *History and Class Consciousness,* 89. For a similar discussion of commodification, see William Leiss, *The Limits of Satisfaction: An Essay on the Problem of Needs and Commodities* (Toronto: University of Toronto Press, 1976).

45. Jean Baudrillard, *For a Critique of the Political Economy of the Sign* (St. Louis: Telos Press, 1981), 29.

46. Baudrillard, *Mirror of Production,* 121.

47. Ibid., 129–30.

48. Jean Baudrillard, *Simulations* (New York: Semiotext(e), 1983), 27.

49. Ibid., 11.

50. Ibid., 30.

51. Ibid., 46.

52. Ibid., 43–44.

53. Ibid., 101.

54. Baudrillard, *Political Economy of the Sign,* 82.

55. Baudrillard, *Mirror of Production,* 127.

56. Horkheimer and Adorno, *Dialectic of Enlightenment,* 164.

57. Ibid.

58. Lefebvre, *Everyday Life,* 112.

59. Ibid., 105–6.

60. Baudrillard, *Mirror of Production,* 127–28.

61. Baudrillard, *Political Economy of the Sign,* 85.

62. Ibid., 58.

63. Ibid., 133.

64. Baudrillard, *Mirror of Production,* 132.

65. Jean Baudrillard, "The Structural Law of Value and the Order of Simulacra," in *The Structural Allegory: Reconstructive Encounters with the New French Thought,* ed. with introduction by John Fekete (Minneapolis: University of Minnesota Press, 1984), 54. Also see *L'Echange symbolique et la mort* (Paris: Gallimard, 1976); *A l'ombre des majorités silencieuses où la fin du social* (Paris: Cahiers d'Utopia, 1978); *Simulacres et simulation* (Paris: Galilee, 1981); and *Oublier Foucault* (Paris: Galilee, 1977). The latter three works are available in English translation from Semiotext(e) in the Foreign Agents Series. For some critical discussion of this turn in Baudrillard's project, see Kate Linker, "From Imitation, to the Copy, to Just Effect: On Reading Jean Baudrillard," *Artforum* 22, no.8 (1984): 44–48; Andre Frankovits, ed., *Seduced and Abandoned: The Baudrillard Scene* (Glebe, New South Wales: Stonemoss Services, 1984); and John Miller, "Baudrillard and His Discontents," *Artscribe International* 63 (May 1987): 48–51.

66. Baudrillard, *Simulations,* 4.

67. Baudrillard, ibid., 129–30.

68. Baudrillard, "Structural Law of Value," 60.

69. Ibid., 69.

70. *Simulations,* 55.

71. Ibid., 57–58.

72. Baudrillard, "Structural Law of Value," 71.

73. Ibid., 59.

74. Ibid., 59–60.

75. Ibid., 60.

76. Baudrillard, *Simulations,* 48.

77. Ibid., 60.

78. Ibid., 63.

79. Ibid., 152.

80. Ibid., 73.

81. Ibid., 72.

82. Also see Harry Braverman, *Labor and Monpoly Capital: The Degradation*

of Work in the Twentieth Century (New York: Monthly Review Press, 1974);
Michael Burawoy, *Manufacturing Consent: Changes in the Labor Process Under
Monopoly Capitalism* (Chicago: University of Chicago Press, 1979); Ralf Dar-
endorf, *Class and Class Conflict in Industrial Society* (Stanford: Stanford Uni-
versity Press, 1959); Bob Jessop, *The Capitalist State: Marxist Theories and
Methods* (New York: New York University Press, 1982); David Landes, *Unbound
Prometheus: Technological Change and Industrial Development in Europe
from 1750 to the Present* (Cambridge: Cambridge University Press, 1969); Ralph
Miliband, *The State in Capitalist Society* (New York: Basic Books, 1969); Lewis
Mumford, *Technics and Civilization* (New York: Harcourt Brace, 1934); and
Max Weber, *General Economic History* (New York: Collier Books, 1961).

83. See Elizabeth L. Eisenstein, *The Printing Press as an Agent of Change:
Communications and Cultural Transformations in Early Modern Europe* (New
York: Cambridge University Press, 1979); Harold Innis, *The Bias of Communi-
cation* (Toronto: University of Toronto Press, 1977); Harold Innis, *Empire and
Communications* (Toronto: University of Toronto Press, 1972); Stephen Kern,
The Culture of Time and Space 1880–1918 (Cambridge, Mass: Harvard Univer-
sity Press, 1983); Donald M. Lowe, *History of Bourgeois Perception* (Chicago:
University of Chicago Press, 1982), Marshall McLuhan, *The Gutenberg Galaxy*
(Toronto: University of Toronto Press, 1962); Marshall McLuhan, *Understanding
Media* (New York: Signet Books, 1964); Charles Newman, *The Post-Modern Aura:
The Act of Fiction in an Age of Inflation* (Evanston, Ill.: Northwestern University
Press, 1985); and Walter J. Ong, *Orality and Literacy: The Technologizing of the
Word* (London: Methuen, 1982).

84. McLuhan, *The Gutenberg Galaxy,* 126 and 127.

85. Jean Baudrillard, "The Ecstasy of Communication," *The Anti-Aesthetic: Essays on Post-Modern Culture,* ed. Hal Foster (Port Townsend, Wash.: Bay Press,

86. See Mark Poster, *Foucault, Marxism and History: Mode of Production
versus Mode of Information* (Cambridge: Polity Press, 1984), 146–69.

87. Roland Barthes, "Myth Today," *A Barthes Reader,* ed. Susan Sontag (New
York: Hill and Wang, 1983), 132.

88. Herbert Marcuse, *One-Dimensional Man: Studies in the Ideology of Advanced Industrial Society* (Boston: Beacon Press, 1966), 7–8.

89. See Paul Piccone, "The Crisis of One-Dimensionality," *Telos* 35 (Spring
1978): 43–54, and Timothy W. Luke, "Culture and Politics in the Age of Artifical
Negativity," *Telos* 35 (Spring 1978): 55–72.

PART III

*Power and Ideology in
Informational Society*

2

The Contradictory Capital of Culture: The Neoconservative Critique of the Cultural Contradictions of Capitalism

Despite the clear victories of neoconservative thought in politics, culture, and society since Ronald Reagan's first electoral victory in 1980, many neoconservative figures and thinkers continue to flog the dead horses of the liberal New Deal and the radical New Left in their criticism of American liberalism and the cultural contradictions of capitalism. Even after President Reagan's reelection in 1984, personal and corporate gifts to conservative think tanks, journals, and conferences have continued to subsidize a right-wing Kulturkampf against the national media, liberal universities, and secular humanism. The battle continues even though the driving forces behind the activities of the New Left largely dissipated long ago.[1] Secretary of Education William J. Bennett, for example, draws a direct connection between the open rejection of "the democratic ethic" on college campuses in 1986 and the New Left's "long march through the institutions" since the 1960s. Likewise, in *Commentary* magazine Balch and London caution those who disagree with Secretary Bennett to remember "the extent to which the practitioners of academic agitprop [in the 1960s] have vacated the quadrangles for more decorous and strategic roosts [in the 1980s] behind the lectern."[2] Today Kristol suggests that "our major universities seem to be living in some kind of a time warp, still casting their votes for George McGovern. The explanation is simple: These universities *are* living in a time warp, in a kind of self-imposed exile from American realities.... Never in American history have major universitites been so dominated by an entire spectrum of radical ideologies as today. Never in American history have these universities so militantly divorced themselves from the sentiments and opinions of the overwhelming majority of the people."[3] As a result, "university academic departments nowadays seek out feminists, Marxists, and others in whom the political impulse runs stronger than any other, to *teach their bias*—and to do so in the name of intellectual diversity."[4]

In these controversies over the cultural contradictions of capitalism, the real issue is not culture. It is instead this kind of politics, especially the "distemper of democracy" the neoconservatives have such distaste for, allegedly brought on by leftist teachings during the heyday of welfare state liberalism in the 1960s and 1970s.[5] As one enters these debates, the real issue must be kept constantly in mind; otherwise, many of the dubious premises, misattributed causations, and hasty conclusions that mar the neoconservatives' treatment of cultural crisis ultimately will confuse one's understanding of their case against modernism, aesthetic avant-gardes, and the left.

This chapter explores several new themes in these debates in order to rethink neoconservative approaches to the alleged cultural contradictions within capitalism. First, as the most influential source of these arguments, Daniel Bell must have his diagnoses of the contemporary cultural crisis dismantled for careful scrutiny. Bell clearly is *not* the typical neoconservative. He has summarized his basic stance as "a socialist in economics, a liberal in politics, and a conservative in culture."[6] Thus, Kristol describes Bell only half-jokingly "as the theoretician for what may be called our 'social democratic wing.'"[7] As a result, Steinfels observes, "to a certain extent, Bell has been labelled a neo-conservative because he runs with neo-conservatives."[8] It also must be kept in mind that Bell, like Daniel Moynihan, has disassociated himself completely from the more extremist and almost anti-intellectual positions taken by other neoconservative figures. Nonetheless, much of Bell's theoretical idiom has been appropriated by the neoconservative movement. And, more important, as an intellectual project taken separately from any ideological function, Bell's well-known, controversial treatment of America's cultural crisis provides a very useful analytical departure for this chapter's discussion of ideologies in informational society. Second, in the comprehending of Bell's model, many of the economic and political roots of the larger neoconservative appeal to tradition, religion, and authority can be identified and better understood. Third, the current revival of "traditional authority" and "religious faith," which the neoconservative thinkers celebrate as the cure for capitalism's cultural contradictions, can be explored more thoroughly as an ideological response of contempory conservatives, who seem to prescribe high-tech, telemythic nostrums as antidotes to the democratic distemper of welfare state liberalism.

Who are the neoconservatives? To a large extent, they are the cold war liberals of the 1940s and 1950s who were the architects of both *Pax Americana* abroad and the New Deal/New Frontier era at home. The extent of the neoconservative network today encompasses many well-known, well-placed, and well-connected intellectuals: Irving Kristol, Nathan Glazer, James Q. Wilson, Edward Banfield, Seymour Martin Lipset, Daniel P. Moynihan, Norman Podhoretz, Samuel P. Huntington, Aaron Wildavsky, Robert Nisbet, Midge Decter, Martin Diamond, and, to a certain extent, Daniel Bell. Before their deaths, Lionel Trilling and Herman Kahn also played important roles in the movement. Obviously, these figures are major forces in well-known intellectual journals like *Commentary* and *The Public Interest.* This short list of neoconservative luminaries also encompasses many of the best-known figures of American intellectual and policy debates since the 1950s.

These figures also are professionally well positioned. As faculty members at Harvard, MIT, Yale, Berkeley, Chicago, Stanford, or Columbia, and as affiliates of established think tanks like Rand, the Hudson Institute, the Heritage Foundation, the American Enterprise Institute, the Center for Strategic and International Studies, or the Institute for Contemporary Studies, neoconservatives have access to corporate and government decision-makers. Consequently, the neoconservatives' connections have shaped policy under Republican and Democratic administrations over the past decade and a half. As high scions in the policy analysis, nonprofit foundation, and research and development industries, neoconservative thinkers also have their work frequently circulating in White House briefing books, the mass media, journals of opinion, and even AT&T or Mobil Oil advertisements.

Since many neoconservatives, including Daniel P. Moynihan, Nathan Glazer, Seymour Martin Lipset, and Herman Kahn, were in the "liberal" managerial mandarinate in charge of steering the New Deal regime from 1932 to 1964, it is not surprising that their growing disillusionment with the realities of the years from 1965 to 1980 led to the credos of neoconservatism.[9] The rise of new social movements of popular protest from below after 1960 totally contradicted the political interests and social agenda of the present-day neoconservatives' traditional cold war liberalism. These range from the New Left to the civil rights and the women's liberation movements, from student protest and environmental activism to the anti-war and anti-nuclear movements. All of these groups in turn will be discussed in greater detail in Chapter 8. The 1960s, then, were a critical watershed for the neoconservatives. The basic precepts that unify these intellectual, organizational, and political interests are fairly simple: *anti-communism,* defined in terms of opposition to totalitarian, one-party states of Marxist or Marxist-Leninist derivation; *anti-modernism,* understood as a distaste for amoral personal hedonism that underpins the psychosocial motivations of the mass public in modern corpo-

rate capitalism; and *anti-populism*, constructed in terms of maintaining
the restricted power structures of democratic elitist pluralism.[10]

One must be cautious, then, with the neoconservatives. As their movement has mobilized, they have wrapped themselves in ancient symbols:
the flags of Authority, the robes of Religion, and the wreaths of Tradition.
In evoking these powerful symbols in today's social discourses, which
are totally suffused with the spectacular codes of telegenic image and
commodified myth, neoconservatives have found that their supporters
and detractors often mistake them for the "real conservatives" that America always has lacked as a postfeudal, liberal "fragmentary polity."[11] In
truth, the distorted mythological discourses of contemporary American
society promote such ad hoc reconstitutions of history and society. In
such texts, the tumultuous 1960–80 era can be redescribed as the corrupted "modernity" of modernist avant-gardes, while the comparatively
halcyon 1945–60 period is redefined as the last days of a relatively un-
corrupted epoch of "traditional authority," "individual morality," and "collective unity."[12] The politics of neoconservatism, in turn, are often not so
much about what is "new" in modern American society as much as what
is "now" in its mythological discourses.

Moreover, many of the neoconservatives, speaking today in their journals, conferences, and think tanks as the arrière-garde of cold war liberalism, are the same technocratic experts and elite policymakers that have
opposed, for a generation, the many new forms of resistance from citizens living under the present corporate capitalist regime. As the architects of corporate modernization, state intervention, and scientific progress in America since the 1940s, the neoconservatives were confronted
by the unintended politicization and unexpected acculturation of new
classes, groups, and interests among the mass public in the 1960s and
1970s. The neoconservatives' intellectual efforts over the past decade,
then, have sought to generate a type of *neo-tradition, neo-religion,* and
neo-authority as the means of dampening this resistance, which they
have identified with avant-garde modernism and recent progressive political movements.

THE CULTURAL CONTRADICTIONS OF CAPITALISM

Before reviewing additional evidence for the neoconservatives' case on
the death and disappearance of America's cultural consensus, words of
warning are needed. Complaints to the authorities about "the cultural
crisis of late capitalist societies," brought on by the destruction of tradition, religion, and authority, have been a recurring commonplace in modern social criticism for many decades. In this century, Max Weber as-

serted before World War I that the spreading affluence of modern industrial capitalism had crushed the idea of moral duty in one's economic calling, leaving only a faint specter prowling "about in our lives like the ghost of dead religious beliefs." [13] Musing about how the instrumental logic of capitalist economic exchange had consumed the substantive values of cultural ethos, Weber saw the "tremendous cosmos of the modern economic order" turning into "an iron cage." [14]

This same tradition of theoretical ghostbusting, however, continues to find cultural clients and social subscribers today among American neoconservatives, even though Weber's concerns have preoccupied Bell since the 1940s. [15] Fifteen years after Daniel Bell's 1970 *Public Interest* article, "The Cultural Contradictions of Capitalism," this neoconservative thematization of cultural crisis is still winning a major market share in the polemical exchanges of many advanced capitalist societies. [16] The endurance of this neoconservative product, in turn, can be traced to some of Bell's peculiar ghostbusting techniques. During his fascinating autopsy on the puritan body of America's dead religious beliefs, and in his thorough interrogations of the ghosts of America's religious morality past, Bell allegedly uncovers hard evidence as to who and what killed cultural consensus, moral duty, and traditional authority in America's advanced capitalist society.

Modernism as Bolshevism/America as Petrograd

Given the political profile of the neoconservatives, as Steinfels notes, "the formative political experience for these men, was the rise of totalitarianism and the failure of socialism in the face of that threat. This experience was to determine their attitudes and give all their later work its political impetus." [17] In Bell's narrative on America's twentieth-century cultural crisis, *The Cultural Contradictions of Capitalism,* these cold war liberal attitudes, unconsciously or consciously on Bell's part, cast modernism and aesthetic avant-gardes in the role of an underground revolutionary insurgency. Here, a politics of image becomes interesting as Bell superimposes the conceptual syntax of Leninism and Bolshevization on the cultural conflicts of American capitalist society.

The cold war liberal subtexts of Bell's neoconservative narratives are overpowering. Modernism is communism; aesthetic avant-gardes are Red Guards, fellow travelers, Old Bolsheviks; the adversary culture is the Bolshevik party center; bourgeois capitalism is the Old Regime; the Protestant Ethic is the America's "true" ethno-national soul; mass hedonism is atheistic collectivism; and the new class is the corrupt ruling *nomenklatura.* In a sense, Bell reads these events of the twentieth-century American cultural crisis as if they were plotted out of a communist-style revolution won after a long march through American institutions. A god-less, anti-moralistic, personalistic hedonism, grounded in the demonic dark side of humanity, entrenched itself in power during a period of po-litical, cultural, and economic bewilderment. The vanguard party of pro-fessional New Class revolutionaries allegedly broke down the stalwart defenses of bourgeois capitalism with wave after wave of aesthetic avant-garde movements, forcing life to imitate their art. Finally, the old reli-gious order and bourgeois capitalist regime collapsed as the masses ac-cepted the demonic hedonism of modernist revolution in the capitalist marketplace.

Consciously or unconsciously, Bell casts modern American society as Petrograd in 1917. And now with this revolution "won," modernism proves to be a soulless, amoral, spiritless gulag that is incapable of further dynamic transformations. In Bell's analysis, modernity is summed up in "the autonomous man who, in becoming self-determining, would achieve freedom. With this 'new man' there was a repudiation of institutions (the striking result of the Reformation, which installed individual conscience as the source of judgment); the opening of new geographical and social frontiers; the desire, and the growing ability, to master nature and to make of oneself what one can, and even, in discarding old roots, to re-make oneself altogether. What began to count was not the past but the future."[18] While the bourgeois entrepreneur championed these ideals in the economy, the independent artist pushed these principles in the cul-tural sphere. "In the development of culture," Bell argues, "this search for independence, the will to be free not only of patron but of all conven-tions, finds its expression in modernism and, in its extreme form, in the idea of the untrammeled self."[19]

According to Bell, this intense preoccupation with the self soon de-cayed into demonic immoralism as the bonds of convention, ethics, and law dissolved in the marketplace and in art. "In effect, the culture—par-ticularly modernist culture—took over the relation with the demonic," actually beginning "to accept it, explore it, and revel in it, seeing it as a source of creativity."[20] Here Bell reduces much of the emancipatory thrust of modern art, literature, and culture to a selfish sympathy for the devil, totally opposed to the industry, morality, and sobriety of Protestant Ethic–based bourgeois capitalism. Modernism is anti-bourgeois, anti-religious, and anti-traditional. Indeed, "modernism has thus been the se-ducer. Its power derived from the idolatry of the self. Its appeal stemmed from the idea that life itself should be a work of art, and that art could only express itself against the conventions of society, particularly bour-geois society."[21]

However, modernism—as a cultural road to serfdom and immorality—

needed human agents, which Bell found in the "adversary culture" of aesthetic avant-gardes. The new sensibilities of modernism, "and the new styles of behavior associated with them, are created by small coteries which are devoted to exploring the new; because the new has value in and of itself, and meets with so little resistance, the new sensibility and its behavior-styles diffuse rapidly, transforming the thinking and actions of the cultural mass (if not the larger masses of people), that new, large stratum of the intelligentsia in the society's knowledge and communications industries."[22] The avant-garde is the anti-bourgeois vanguard, the fellow-traveling shock troops and Red Guard militia of the party center, or the adversary culture that sought to crush bourgeois society. Bell suggests the aestheticism of avant-gardes is actually a new mass ideology, which is "consciously accepted by the artist, that art will lead the way, will serve as the avant-garde. Now the very idea of an avant-garde—an advance assault team—indicates that modern art or culture would never permit itself to serve as a 'reflection' of an underlying social structure but, rather, would open the way to something radically new. In fact, as we shall see, the very idea of an avant-garde, once its legitimacy is accepted, serves to institutionalize the primacy of culture in the fields of manners, morals and, ultimately, politics."[23] With these tools of power, the adversary culture emerges from its underground insurgency to assume establishment power, dominating and remaking the populace as it suits its demonic modernist program:

> The adversary culture has come to dominate the cultural order, and this is why the hierophants of the culture—the painters, the writers, the filmmakers—now dominate the audience, rather than vice versa. Indeed, the subscribers to this adversary culture are sufficiently numerous to form a distinct cultural class. Compared to the society as a whole, the membership in this class is not large. No statistical estimates are possible, and the figure could vary from a few hundred thousand to a couple of million. But size alone is meaningless, for, . . . perhaps most important, the protagonists of the adversary culture, because of the historic subversive effect on traditional bourgeois values, substantially influence, if not dominate, the cultural establishments today: the publishing houses, museums, and galleries; the major news, picture, and the cultural weeklies and monthlies; the theater, the cinema, and the universities.[24]

Bell sees this cultural coup d'état by the radical adversary culture during "the 1950s, a decade of political conservatism and cultural bewilderment," as political radicalism wilted under "the threat of a foreign communist foe."[25]

The radicals of the adversary culture, after burrowing into many social institutions during the "end of ideology" era, have come to dominate modern corporate society as part of its new professional/managerial/technical classes, especially since the 1960s. Indeed, they have even successfully steered modern capitalism away from its productivist economic ethos, or the Protestant Ethic, down the treacherous channels of a post-bourgeois, modernist ethos of hedonism. Chapter 4 will suggest that the growth imperatives behind modern corporate capital's own agenda of mass production tore down the restraints of tradition to ensure that mass consumption would absorb the output of this technologically intensified new system of production. Bell, in contrast, argues that modernist ethics mainly caused this change. The aesthetic avant-garde completed its revolutionization of life through art by using fifth columns hidden among the marketing departments of major corporations. Hedonist psychosocial norms demand "that what was previously played out in fantasy and imagination must be acted out in life as well. There is no distinction between art and life. Anything permitted in art is permitted in life as well."[26] For Bell, "the break-up of the traditional bourgeois value system, in fact, was brought about by the bourgeois economic system—by the free market, to be precise."[27] Therefore, by the 1950s and 1960s, "American culture had become primarily hedonistic, concerned with play, fun, display and pleasure. . . . what this abandonment of Puritanism and the Protestant Ethic does, of course, is to leave capitalism with no moral or transcendental ethic."[28]

A Gosplan of Geist?

At this juncture, then, Bell believes that a solution for these problems must and can be found. From the excesses of modernist revolution, the shorings of spiritual stability can be rebuilt and recovered. We often are told that Minerva's owl can only fly at dusk; in the case of Bell's arguments, it is obvious the owl has not flown by Next Day Air. Instead, it seems to have just deplaned from a long, slow transoceanic flight on the China Clipper. Bell's solution is simple: "I will risk an unfashionable answer—the return in Western society of some conception of religion."[29] Yet, after nearly three generations of secularizing modernism, one must ask where this revitalized religion and its adherents will be found. As Chapter 3 will argue, it will not easily be found in the words of Pat Robertson or the sermons of Jimmy Swaggart. If hedonism is, in fact, the hegemonic cultural force in contemporary America, then Bell's answer might be more impossible than unfashionable. After the turmoil of permanent revolution in modernist America, under the guidance of aesthetic avant-gardes and adversary culture/new class groups, it would appear that this crisis could only be ended through a type of spiritual

Stalinism—the forced resurrection of traditional faith, the central planning of psychosocial authority, and the rapid de-hedonization of individual everyday life. For Bell, "the real problem of *modernity* is the problem of belief. To use an unfashionable term, it is a spiritual crisis, since the new anchorages have proved illusive and the old ones have become submerged."[30]

This spiritual crisis crops up most destructively in the psychosocial economic ethos of modern American society. Under the traditional psychosocial economics of bourgeois capitalism, "the Protestant ethic had served to limit sumptuary (though not capital) accumulation. When the Protestant ethic was sundered from bourgeois society, only the hedonism remained, and the capitalist system lost its transcendental ethic." Consequently, "even the ability of the system to provide for economic growth is now questioned—the lack of a transcendental tie, the sense that a society fails to provide some set of 'ultimate meanings' in its character structure, work, and culture, becomes unsettling to a system."[31]

With the rise of hedonistic mass consumerism, Bell argues, this vital tie between the instrumental management of the *economy* (constant investment, instrumental rationality, capital accumulation, continual growth) and the cultural *ethos* of society (values of work, sacrifice, morality, order) has been broken. Modernism and its hedonistic psychosocial economics are largely responsible for "the disjunction between the kind of organization and the norms demanded in the economic realm, and the norms of self-realization that are now central in the culture. The two realms which had historically been joined to produce a single character structure—that of the Puritan and of his calling—have now become unjoined."[32] In Brick's estimation, "the real problem of culture, as far as Bell is concerned, lies not in modernism *per se* but in 'postmodernism,' the extension of the anti-social self-aggrandizing impulses of classic modernism to a mass attitude, sustained by the regime of mass consumption. . . . In sanctioning an insatiable search for innovative experience," as Bell's argument goes, "mass culture turns nihilistic and disintegrates the bonds that tie a community together."[33]

This disruptive division of economic needs and cultural imperatives by hedonism and modernism has led to "Department II" (consumer goods and their production) dominating the growth and strength of "Department I" (producer goods and their production). Likewise, in the psychosocial economics of most individuals, Department I virtues, such as hard work, thrift, diligence, sobriety, constant sacrifice, respect for authority, and personal contributions to growth, are eclipsed by Department II ethics, like leisure, spending, irresponsibility, license, constant indulgence, disregard for authority, and debt-driven personal consumption. To rearrange the psychosocial priorities of modernist economies and hedonist individuals, Bell points toward the central planning of faith through a neo-religious reformation.

Bell admits, "I do not believe in religion as a patch for the unraveled seams of society.... Religions cannot be manufactured. Worse, if they were, the results would be spurious and soon vanish into the next whirl of fashion. ... Religions grow out of the deepest needs of individuals sharing a common awakening, and are not created by 'engineers of the soul.'"[34] Still, as the possible foundation for revitalizing ethical life, Bell cites Geertz with approval; that is, religion might tune "human actions to an envisaged cosmic order" in addition to projecting "images of cosmic order onto the plane of human experience."[35] While denying that such continuity can be manufactured or engineered, Bell and other neoconservatives, who cut their professional teeth in the social engineering ethos of the New Deal/New Frontier era, recommend that what "religion can restore is the continuity of generations, returning us to the existential predicaments which are the ground of humanity and care for others."[36] Religion, however, is not necessarily the universal, univocal force called for here. It also can be a particular and contradictory institution, particularly in postmodern mediascapes that often retain only its images and surfaces. And the neo-traditional, neo-religious, neo-authoritative basis of this neoconservative revival of "religion" seems to be aimed at returning today's postmodernist generation to the continuity of cold war vigilance. It also aims at solving the existential predicament of opposing communism, modernism, and populism—the task that forms the basis of a neoconservative American humanity's caring for others.

Tradition and religion, at this juncture, then, are to be mobilized in neoconservative reforms as new productive forces in the postmodernist psychosocial economy. Yet—as the discussion of televangelism in Chapter 3 holds—given the all-intrusive character of modernist culture over the past several decades, one must question whether or not there truly are real traditions to "return" to or religious fundamentals to "resurrect" from beyond the pale of modernity. Instead, the nearly complete colonization of the everyday lifeworld by the commodification of corporate capitalism arguably has so twisted, turned, and toppled the "traditional" practices of pre-modernist religion, tradition, and authority that only memories, traces, and fragments remain. Yet among neoconservatives like Bell, this is not a problem. From beneath the rubble "the recurrent underground theme is the salvation of man through the resurrection of traditional faith."[37]

THE OUTLINES OF A TELETRADITIONALISM

Unless there is an unpredictable intervention of true moral charisma from some new religious prophet, it is still unclear as to how and when "traditional faith" can be resurrected within modern American capitalist society. Today, as Bell admits, "the cultural, if not moral, justification of capitalism has become hedonism, the idea of pleasure as a way of life," because over the past few decades "the system was transformed by mass production and mass consumption, by the creation of new wants and new means of gratifying those wants."[38] Yet, given this logic in Bell's analysis of modernity, the transformed system of American corporate capitalism *only* can resurrect traditional faith by turning the need for religion into "new wants" and then manufacturing the "new means" of gratifying those wants. If "the problem of *modernity* is the problem of belief,"[39] then the magic of the corporate marketplace can package and deliver neo-traditional product lines to deliver neo-religious solutions—Soul-Care, Nu-Faith, Spirit-Gard—to the untidy spiritual problems of disbelief and doubt.

Most neoconservatives are not really selling first-run faith or original-equipment tradition. On the contrary, as the polemics of the neoconservatives and politics of the New Right ultimately illustrate, they are vending images fabricated out of *recycled/remanufactured modernity,* rather than *pre-modernity,* as the substance of resurrected traditional faith. The "tradition" of neoconservative discourse is composed of bits of Progressive, New Deal, cold war codes from modern 1890s–1950s America. Similarly, the "faith" of neoconservatism is the familiar possessive individualist belief in the Protestant Ethic, free markets, scientific progress, limited government, and superior firepower from America's "golden days of yesteryear." Yet, for the neoconservatives, these cultural codes were the anchor of "modern" post–1945 America before it allegedly was crippled by the democratic distemper induced by welfare state liberalism and the Vietnam syndrome. A mythical (and now past) "then" is projected televisually as the fresh sociopolitical foundation for improving the "now" of informational society. At this juncture, as Chapter 3 claims, the practical mediations of this mythic ideological resurrection of "traditional America" can be observed most clearly in the images circulating throughout New Right political and religious discourses.

Teletraditions encapsulate the sociocultural meanings of "America past" as television, radio, and movies have packaged and repackaged them for the past fifty years. "America," its "traditions," and its "national interests" are all reduced to mere signifiers in search of referents, which

are in turn continually reassigned televisually. The manufacturers of televised spectacle can integrate almost anything into the media matrices of
commodification, including historical time, ethical norms, national traditions, social customs, and cultural community. The myths of unity,
codes of community, and signs of solidarity, which in society usually constitute the conventional understandings of particular social groups binding the generations of that society together, do exist in advanced capitalist America. Still, in the final analysis, these understandings also can be
increasingly organized by corporate designers, managers, or spokesper-
sons to suit the market imperatives of corporate production or public
opinion management.

In fact, as product ads for peanut butter, automobiles, running shoes,
soft drinks, laundry detergents, or hand soap suggest with their appeals
of "remember when," America is now on the threshold of passing its "traditions" televisually to a third generation. As the major networks continue to generate new packagings of culture and custom with each new
season's programming, cable systems, independent local stations, and
videocassette vendors selectively rebroadcast and reaffirm older "classic"
packagings in the rerun markets. Thus, in the late 1980s, virtually any
viewer can revisit the mediascapes of the 1950s, '60s, '70s, and early '80s
by zapping through the "teletraditional" lore of the rerun channels. And
the demographics behind the corporate production and presentation of
televised images clearly have created a teletraditional matrix of myths,
codes, and signs, which bears less and less relation to the organic traditions of premodern lifeworlds or to the actual process of historical modernity. The components of the matrix can be, and are, continuously
reconstituted to express the needs and desires related to the present, but
always changing, market conditions.

To a large extent, such teletraditions serve as the conventional understandings, manifest in act and artifact, of definite individuals and groups
in particular media markets, local, national, and international. Chapters
4 through 7 will explore some of the implications of teletraditionalism
for religion, the family, democratic politics, and the public's understanding of its own history. As fragments composing, in part, the internalized
psychosocial consensus shared by definite individuals and expressing, in
part, the approved hegemonic cultural codes of dominant groups, teletraditions organize the meaning, purpose, and value of actions and artifacts in the phantom objectivity of corporate society. Teletraditional society continually codes and recodes the activity of everyone's electronic
neighbors down Hill Street, on Walton's Mountain, in Mayberry, R.F.D., or
around Mayfield, U.S.A., in terms of an ever-changing corporate product
demographics or national policy agendas.

According to the teachings of these teletraditions, the "America" behind these idealized electronic neighborhoods basically is strong, productive, unified, and moral, even if it has a few flaws. The conflicts and contradictions that were part of the real America from 1890 to 1960 are usually suppressed through the teletraditions' alibis for traditional social cleavages, political struggles, or economic crises. This must be the case because, in part, these teletraditional interpretations and innovations occur under the constraints of corporate capitalist mass production and consumption. In part, these polyglot raw materials are reprocessed into image-mediated forms to present social consensus as the most "middle-of-the-road" and "least objectionable" programming for the teletraditional society. Moreover, as with all traditions, its fables, images, and signs are polyvalent in order to capture complex aspirations and serve simple needs for many diverse viewing groups. But in the end, "teletraditions" recycle only some aspects of *modernity* as "tradition," remanufacturing the meanings, values, and purposes of an attractive "modernity past" in the context of a disappointing "modernity present" that might guide individuals and groups to a promising "modernity future."

Televangelism

This tendency for "America," "tradition," and the "past" to become a mutable, multi-thematic commodity, remade continually to relate directly to changing market conditions, also can be witnessed in televised religion. Although Chapter 3 will address this subject in more detail, the diverse religious teachings packaged in "televangelism" all seem to have a teletraditional inspiration. As consumers and their corporate cultivation became the primary productive force in the post–1945 advanced capitalist base, many new forms of consumerist superstructure emerged in teletraditional guise from within the electronic mass media. The electronic church is one response to this consumer culture. Indeed, a new and unique consumerist confession has developed in the "religious programming" of this re-born Christian fundamentalism. Televangelism plainly is not designed by "engineers of the soul." Instead, it is more like a variety/vaudeville show of a common awakening, hosted by several neo-traditional "masters of cermonies."

In the teletraditional codes of consumer culture, the profession of religious faith has become an audiovisual cult, deriving its form and substance from the same master codes of consumption endlessly reproduced in "secular programming." Televangelism celebrates, however, a theology based not so much on personal liberation as upon collective integration. In societies based upon commodified spectacles, the intense importance of communal religious belief can be reduced through teletraditionalism to an extensive sign system of personal image consumption in passive, isolated watching. As with daytime quiz shows, most viewers leave televangelist spectacles feeling that they now have "some lovely parting gifts" after participating in their mythological production. The unique position of televangelical fundamentalist religion in contemporary American society, then, is also expressive of neoconservatism's teletraditional answer to the cultural contradictions of corporate capitalism. Given Bell's support for religion, such televangelical cults could provide the broadest possible presentation for projecting "images of cosmic order onto the plane of human experience," even though their entire operational logic is shot through with notions of consumerist private choice.

"Japanization"

Neo-traditionalism is also evident in the frantic campaigns to "Japanize" U.S. workers, managers, and businesses in which Japan continually is represented telegenically in U.S. media markets as today's most "successful," as well as its most "traditional," advanced industrial system.[40] Japan's economic strength frequently is attributed to its surviving quasi-feudal cultural traditions, including strong commitments to family, mass subservience to the state, individual acceptance of corporate patrimonialism, and low material standards of living. Strangely, however, this often xenophobic, homogenous culture is prominently positioned in the American mediascape as a worthy model for other more open and heterogeneous pluralistic societies—like the United States in the 1980s. As Japan increasingly pushes for dominance in world financial, technological, and industrial circles, its image also is being imperfectly and incompletely reprocessed to serve as a model for America's future modernization. Transnational capital admires Japan's strong neo-Confucian ethics, business domination of government, and relatively lower material standard of living in contrast to America's "secular humanist" normlessness, government regulation of business, and debt-driven profligate consumerism. Thus Japanese diligence, self-effacement, group consciousness, and unflagging industriousness are tagged as the new benchmarks of ego identity and personality formation after decades of permissive individualism in America. The material foundations of the American dream have crumbled; hence, to reclaim them from South Korea, Taiwan, or Japan, teletraditional narratives are teaching that Americans must "Japanize" their culture, state, and society simply to halt their decline, and then perhaps the U.S. will fully regain status as a core nation.

Japanization, on one level, ideologically represents the current state of a world in which the former hegemonic core state (the United States) is no longer politically hegemonic, nor economically the uncontested core, nor militarily unchallenged as the most powerful state. Since Japan's economic strategy has been identified as a major cause of America's declining hegemony, Japanization represents a vague set of policies for the other advanced industrial nations to gain new comparative advantage over each other and potentially become the new hegemonic power. The management of American and transnational corporate capital, in turn, now is encouraging U.S. society and its government to come to terms with Japanization in order to retain or improve the United States' current global position. The relentless growth of the Japanese, Korean, and Taiwanese economies and their expansion into the global marketplace is also often tied directly to neo-Confucian values and their transmission within strong Asian family structures.[41]

On another level, the Asian drives to succeed and to sacrifice for the family are being made into exemplary teletraditional models for Western society. Everything that "fails" in the American welfare state is seen as "succeeding" in the typical Japanese household, which apparently always stresses discipline, self-sacrifice, druglessness, reverence for the aged, education, and the subjection of women to male prerogatives. Since most Americans have no direct, personal knowledge of Japan and see it only as a montage of preprocessed news images, Japanization can serve many ends in constantly shifting applications. Although "Japan, Inc." is highly successful, the material living conditions of most Japanese are far below those of American or European societies. This down side of the Japanese worker's incredible hard work is, of course, usually ignored. Japanization is an ideal teletradition, wrapping up highly desired traditional American values into a new cultural package together with threatening images of a foreign competitor, presented as becoming "Number One" economically by using old-time Yankee virtues to do America one better.

As a political strategy, Japanization can also stand for a new corporatist fusion of labor, capital, and the state in self-sacrificing cooperative arrangements competing with aggressive foreign rivals to capture the leadership of world export markets, high-tech innovations, and efficient capital accumulation. Ordinary redistributive politics and welfare state services are to be reduced, as Thatcherism and Reaganism originally advocated, as a means of rationalizing greater capital accumulation. Some slack in the safety nets might be picked up by corporate paternalism, but most of it, as in Japan, should be shoved off onto the family or it will simply no longer be performed. In other words, Japanization is a more acceptable, socially satisfying form of collective adjustment to diminishing expectations of combating narcissistic consumerism. (Ironically, then, Japanization became one of corporate capital's strategies in the Reagan Era for realizing what Carter tried to sell as traditional American puritan enterprise by inviting Christopher Lasch and Bell to the White House to moan and groan over the "culture of narcissism" and the "cultural contradictions of capitalism.")[42]

Japanization gives transnational corporations a concrete, albeit politically and materially regressive, model for coping with the transition in America to modern informational production. Following the example of paternalistic Japanese firms, American corporations can assume a new guise of "community involvement" or "social activism" as management intervenes through corporate human resources or personnel programs in employees' private lives. Personal fitness regimens, quality circles, anti-smoking clinics, corporate aid to schools, workplace democracy, drug counseling, maternity and paternity leaves, corporate day care, retraining leaves, and creative sabbaticals are all efforts to reconstruct a family life or social tradition that makes industrious, dedicated workers out of present-day Western consumers.[43] Within these frameworks corporate capital can try to resurrect or simulate a neo-traditional culture, teletraditionally modeled in part on Japan and in part on corporate management's own ethics of law-and-order Sunbelt suburbanism.

Reaganism

Reaganism also can be seen, in large part, as a form of teletraditionalism. It perhaps best expresses the form and content of the neo-tradition, neo-religion, and neo-authority behind the neoconservatives' political project. As the teletraditional account of his career holds, Ronald Reagan, a bona fide New Deal Democrat, shocked by the excesses of Big Government (welfare state liberalism of the Great Society), regretfully left his party. In other words, the New Deal "went wrong," forcing good citizens to oppose it. While serving as a professional "spokesperson" for General Electric, he joined the nascent cause of the Opportunity Society (cold war liberalism, individual self-reliance, corporate-managed "free" markets). As the state-run New Deal soured in the 1960s, Ronald Reagan and other good citizens of like mind had to turn to the "private sector" and "corporate world" for answers to "today's complex problems." After allegedly cleaning up one of the worst nests of avant-garde "modernism" in the United States (namely, California, and especially its government, welfare system, and state universities), the candidate campaigned for many years during the 1960s and 1970s to get national power in order to "straighten out" Washington. That is, he did not just criticize the statist and modernist corruption of America, he *did something* "positive" and "constructive" in the hope of spreading his ideas nationwide. Evoking the "traditional America" he had worked to construct in the telemythic memory of America's mass electorate as a film, radio, and TV personality, Reagan could continue to outline and redefine his "neoconservative" political program in teletraditional terms.[44] Like his conflation of World War II B-movie scripts with actual wartime heroism in his remarks at many White House medal-award ceremonies, Reagan could believe in this teletraditional America, because he helped build it and still resided there most of the time.

To re-rationalize American markets and bureaucracies, collective capital in the Reagan era essentially returned to earlier versions of modernity, which it now labels "traditional values," and endorsed new teletraditional values, like privatization, entrepreneurialism, and local self-reliance. On the global level, transnational capital has often found recalcitrant economic nationalism in the private and public sectors to be an irrational barrier to progress. Such nationalism in developed economies, like that of the United States, usually rests upon entrenched coalitions of centralized state bureaucracies, jobs-oriented national labor unions, and large national industrial monopolies. Since the transaction costs of steering such transition-era social formations are excessive, the coalitions can be faulted for inefficiency, overtaxation, overregulation, or unresponsiveness, or for creating inequalities by giving everyone an equal share of less and less. The newly attained and still-limited "opening to free markets" in China under Deng Xiaoping, and in the USSR under Mikhail Gorbachev, is only the most recent indication of this mythology's power to motivate economic change under difficult political conditions.

For example, to produce and enjoy more, it is claimed by Reaganism, the social surpluses consumed by the state during its period of social welfare expansion must be returned to the marketplace for use by individual entrepreneurs. Yet this appeal is directed mainly at national capital to decentralize and diffuse ownership and control to more local levels. Such developments would not eliminate large transnationals. In fact, corporate "entrepreneurialism" also is expressed as hostile takeovers, leveraged buy-outs, and friendly acquisitions with the aim of creating stronger, more concentrated transnational industries while reducing the autonomy and market share of smaller national firms. With the reduction of these middle-level, national firms, the major transnationals can work more effectively with hundreds or thousands of smaller entrepreneurs at the subnational/local level as suppliers, vendors, or franchisers. Meanwhile, the health of the consumer-driven economy is sustained with massive new programs of private and public spending based upon borrowed money from Japan, the Middle East, or Europe.

In the abstract, Reaganism makes teletraditional appeals on the basis of individual emancipation from "tax and spend" statism because it allegedly overbureaucratizes and overregulates society to the point of stagnation. Anyone who reflects on these appeals for a moment, however, soon recognizes that "tax and spend" traditionally has meant taxing wealthier individuals and large corporations in order to spend public monies on the joint welfare of the many, who are less wealthy and powerful. Under Reagan, teletraditional entrepreneurialism was aimed at assisting wealthy individuals and large corporations evade state taxation and regulation, while pushing the costs of paying for collective goods down into the lower tiers of society. As far as the 1988 presidential campaign went, it appears that President Bush plans on continuing many of these same policies.

At the same time, teletraditionalism makes the nation-state much less significant as a means of social control. In the age of ICBMs, global communications, and electronic banking, nation-states can no longer easily guarantee their populations' security, national identity, or monetary stability. Corporate capitalism works to create its own ideal personalities and uniform social needs on a transnational scale through new, constantly changing style regimes and advertising sophisticated and new consumer goods in the global marketplace. The normalization politics of national bureaucracies are no longer as necessary to produce these standardized outcomes because consumers in Japan, Europe, and North America all volunteer, on their own terms and at different times, to catch many of the same waves of personal identity in product consumption. State elites, in turn, are encouraged to reprivatize social services that once were nationalized. Hence opportunities for private enterprise and local self-reliance spring from the state's relinquishing of responsibility for providing housing, education, police protection, firehouses, hospitals, schools, prisons, asylums, orphanages, and basic utilities. Since the welfare state is defined as an impediment to growth, privatizing these state services removes them as barriers to local and transnational economic development.

These tendencies toward privatization are actually limited in their inspiration and implementation. Even after eight years of Reaganism the American welfare state survives in many ways intact. The intent of Reaganist policies is not to introduce true capitalist competition in free markets—that would be too disruptive. Instead, these shifts continue the re-rationalization of the state apparatus by trying to reduce its overall responsibilities for providing personnel, high-quality services, or new funds for social welfare. This is part of Reaganism's teletraditional strategy for freezing or slowing government growth, but, practically speaking, the state will still provide considerable funding and ensure that the entrepreneurs serving the state really assume few market-driven risks. Save for outrageous abuses, they have guaranteed government contracts. It is simply their role to continually deliver more service with less funds as state monies remain at old levels or at slightly decreasing rates of growth. Private-sector prisons or fire departments are not competing with each other to provide better services, faster rehabilitation, new technologies, or improved effectiveness in a struggle with other firms. They are instead established to counter Parkinson's laws of bureaucratic growth by using private sector tools to contain costs and keep benefits stable, while the state still assumes the risks and pays the bills.

In the final analysis, this Reaganist program can work this magical mobilization of consensus probably only in a teletraditional society. As Wills concludes, "If one settles, instead, for a substitute past, an illusion of it, then that fragile construct must be protected from the challenge of complex or contradictory evidence, from any test of evidence at all. That explains Americans' extraordinary tacit bargain with each other not to challenge Reagan's version of the past. The power of his appeal is the great joint confession that we cannot live with our real past, that we not only prefer but need a substitute. Because of that, we *will* a belief in all his stories." [45] Indeed, under few other existing political systems could such a leader, who is a former Hollywood film actor, advocate such contradictory policies to so many diverse audiences. Reagan's multifaceted appeal proves that "the triumph of advertising in the culture industry is that consumers feel compelled to buy and use its products even though they see through them." [46] In teletraditional discourse, Reagan, the lifelong service-sector worker, can urge average steelworkers to stay the course in their decaying mill towns; the big-business TV shill can tout the holiness of small-time, mom-and-pop enterprise; the divorced head of a blended fast-lane family can support the sanctity of traditional nuclear family living; the former film-colony playboy can denounce the pleasures of secular humanism; the small-town midwestern farm boy can sketch the contours of the USSR as an "evil empire" and then five years later appear in Red Square with the CPSU General Secretary to lift his curse saying it "really" only applied to another long-gone era; the non-combatant World War II motion picture officer can visit SS graves at Bitburg believing they hold the remains of Hitler's victims; the infrequent church attender can assert the imperatives of following God's constant guidance; the father of an associate editor of *Playboy* who danced in his underwear on late-night television spoofing his parents in the White House can censure the spread of pornography in America; and the star of several B-grade cowboy movies can demand virtually unlimited funds for the Pentagon's war chests. In the telegenic narratives of American teletradition, Reagan "remembers," for himself and the nation, what suits the political exigencies of the hour. He is the ultimate icon, unifying the free-floating signifiers of teletraditional America with the mythical referents of everything his viewers want their nation to be or become. But, at the bottom line, teletradition recalls a mythic pre–1960 United States that allegedly had no racism and enjoyed constant growth, happy families, humming factories, soldiers willing to make the ultimate sacrifice unquestioningly, global respect, not much poverty, and neat little towns of WASPs living in well-kept homes with white picket fences—on the right side of the tracks from well-behaved minorities that knew their place in the back of the bus, across the Rio Grande, in the closet, or out in the kitchen.

CONCLUSIONS

"In all ideology," as Marx notes, "men and their circumstances appear upside-down as in a *camera obscura.*"[47] Not surprisingly, then, the recent wide-ranging inquest into "the cultural contradictions of capitalism" conducted by neoconservative investigators must be seen instead as their disappointed deposition on "the contradictory capital of culture." Indeed, they believe that the reserve assets of the Western social ethos have been excessively depreciated with virtual criminal intent during the expansive growth of society's cash flow under advanced industrial capitalism, leaving both accounts now overdrawn and society morally bankrupt. While their inquest did not turn up a smoking gun, the usual suspects have been rounded up and charged in this major indictment, entitled "The Cultural Contradictions of Capitalism."

The culprits are well known. That is, the left-leaning "new class" of an adversary culture, and its avant-garde modernism, dealt a death blow to cultural consensus. This class allowed cultural, economic, and social overdraft privileges in the form of modernist, individualistic hedonism on the reserve assets of traditional morality in the working capital accounts of technological productivity. No longer demanding deferred gratification from cultural assets to dynamicize instrumental rationality in Department I of the psychosocial economy, a final frenzy of explosive growth erupted during the last generation in Department II on the overextended credit of hedonistic excess. Resultantly, today there are no legitimate motivational funds to drive technological productivity and growth in the midst of global economic crisis except for the greedy bankruptcy of personal pleasures.

In an inversion of their "cultural contradictions of capitalism" arguments, the neoconservatives now have constituted themselves as a traditionalist arrière-garde to win a cultural war of maneuver against the modernist avant-garde. Rather than touting the hedonist utopias of an untrammeled self, they support alternative images of a revitalized American puritan discipline drawn from a new moralistic televangelism, a Japanized neo-Confucian work ethic, and teletraditional Reaganist myths, to be embraced in the 1990s by patriotic American/Christian citizens. All along, they have ignored or downplayed the critical corrosive role that capitalist exchange in and of itself has played in the destruction of existing social institutions. Their program denounces the adversary culture of the new class by celebrating a more mutable mainstream ethos allegedly shared by the silent majorities behind teletraditional/televangelical demographics. In turn, ironically, the neoconservatives now use their well-placed and well-connected professional positions to spread their messages in today's cultural establishments—publishing houses, museums, news services, the cinema, television networks, the universities, the cultural weeklies and monthlies.

To oppose the spread of communism, to reindustrialize the ailing national economy, and to contain secular humanist culture, many neoconservatives enjoin all citizens of advanced capitalist America to embrace their newfound but still-old mediation of valorization: the "traditions" of religious faith. The meaning, purpose, and values that modernist secular humanism has robbed from everyday life will be restored at full value with a recharge from "the faith of our fathers." Yet the bridge of restorative remembrance is largely teletraditional in form, and the road of religious rebirth seems mainly televangelical in its course. As Chapter 3 illustrates, televangelism resurrects personal sacrifice, unquestioning obedience, and disciplined labor. These valorizing forces, however, are not embraced as absolute moral goods. Rather they are touted as essential new psychosocial inputs into the means of production of embattled America, whose global economic, political, and technological hegemony is allegedly eroding under rising waves of Japanese imports, Soviet arms, and Third World debt. In the final analysis these teletraditionalist narratives simply use religion, authority, and tradition as the instrumental means to reaffirm the meaning, purpose, and values of the neoconservatives' real substantive ends: cold war liberalism, traditional morality, productivist supply-side economics, and elitist polyarchy.

NOTES

1. See Stephen H. Balch and Herbert I. London, "The Tenured Left," *Commentary* 82, no. 4 (1986): 41–51. Secretary Bennett argues that in America we have a "common culture," which consists of "the democratic ethic, the work ethic and the Judeo-Christian ethic." See David Wagner, "Bill Bennett's Dilemma," *National*

Review 34, no. 11 (1987): 28. Similarly, William E. Simon sees the "intolerant" left of the 1960s totally entrenched in today's academic community: "How ironic that academic America could be transformed into a great bastion of intellectual rigidity and reaction, and that this reaction could be rooted not on the right, but the left, as encrusted elites become more belligerent—at times, hysterical—in their determination to dominate the ivory towers of our leading colleges and universities." Therefore, he argues, corporate and private donors, as college alumni, should take "the time to identify, reach to and support scholars and intellectuals who are committed to freedom, men and women who understand the nexus between economic freedom and political freedom, the link between capitalism and democracy, and who also know the intellectual job that needs to be done." See William E. Simon, "Give to the College a Choice," *The Wall Street Journal,* July 8, 1988, 16.

2. Balch and London, "The Tenured Left," 46. Irving Howe also has noticed this peculiar mean-spiritedness among the neoconservatives: "There's something grotesquely comic, almost Dickensian, about these people. They have more political influence today than any other intellectuals, but they indulge in more self-pity also, complaining about being outside of, and scorned by, the cultural 'establishment.' By that I suppose they mean certain magazines like *The New York Review of Books.* But when it comes to real influence and even power—the ability to mold policy in the Department of Education, the National Endowment for the Humanities, *The New York Times* and even, partly, the State Department—the neoconservatives are doing rather well for themselves. And this, quite apart from their plushy connections with foundations, magazines, corporations, etc. Yet they feel unloved. Indeed, they think of themselves as a beleaguered minority guarding the pass against spineless liberals who are preparing the downfall of Western civilization." See Irving Howe, "The Spirit of the Times: Greed, Nostalgia, Ideology and War Whoops," *Dissent* 33, no. 4 (1986): 413.

3. Irving Kristol, "American Universities in Exile," *The Wall Street Journal,* June 17, 1986, 28.

4. See Joseph Epstein, "A Case of Academic Freedom," *Commentary* 82, no. 3 (1986): 39.

5. See Daniel Bell, *The Cultural Contradictions of Capitalism* (New York: Basic Books, 1976); Michael Crozier, Samuel P. Huntington, and Joji Watanuki, *The Crisis of Democracy* (New York: New York University Press, 1975); and Irving Kristol, *Two Cheers for Capitalism* (New York: Basic Books, 1978).

6. Bell repudiates the label "neoconservative" because, "in its own terms, such a designation is meaningless, for it assumes that social views can be aligned along a single dimension. . . . In the larger historical context, the phrase makes no sense because the kind of cultural criticisms I make—and I think of similiar criticisms by Peter Berger and Philip Reiff—transcends the received categories of liberalism, and seeks to treat the dilemmas of contemporary society within a very different framework." See Bell, "Modernism and Capitalism," *Partisan Review* 45, no. 2 (1979): 206.

7. For Bell, "Economic policy can be efficacious as a means; but it can only be

as *just* as the cultural value system that shapes it. It is for that reason I am a socialist in economics. For me socialism is not statism. . . . It is . . . a judgment on the priorities of economic policy. It is for that reason that I believe that *in this realm,* the community takes precedence over the individual in the values that legitimate economic policy" (ibid., 208).

8. Peter Steinfels, *The Neo-Conservatives: The Men Who Are Changing America's Politics* (New York: Simon and Schuster, 1978), 165.

9. See Gillian Peele, *Revival and Reaction: The Right in Contemporary America* (Oxford: Oxford University Press, 1984); Thomas Ferguson and Joel Rogers, *Right Turn: The Decline of the Democrats and the Future of American Politics* (New York: Hill and Wang, 1986).

10. See Jürgen Habermas, "Neo-Conservative Culture Criticism in the United States and West Germany: An Intellectual Movement in Two Political Cultures," *Telos* 56 (Summer 1983): 76–89.

11. See Louis Hartz, *The Liberal Tradition in America: An Interpretation of American Political Thought since the Revolution* (New York: Harcourt, Brace and World, 1955); Hartz, "A Comparative Study of Fragment Cultures," in *Violence in America: Historical and Comparative Perspectives,* ed. Hugh Davis Graham and Ted Robert Gurr (New York: Bantam, 1969), 107–27.

12. See, for example, Irving Kristol, *Reflections of a Neoconservative Looking Backward* (New York: Basic, 1983); Kristol, *Two Cheers for Capitalism* (New York: Basic, 1978); Norman Podhoretz, *Why We Were in Vietnam* (New York: Simon and Schuster, 1982); and Podhoretz, *Breaking Ranks, A Political Memoir* (New York: Harper and Row, 1979).

13. Max Weber, *The Protestant Ethic and the Spirit of Capitalism* (New York: Charles Scribner's Sons, 1958), 182.

14. Ibid., 181.

15. As early as 1949 Bell was looking for some sort of spiritual unifying force to bridge the growing contradictions in American capitalism. He sought "some new sense of civic obligation . . . strong enough to command the allegiance of all groups and provide a principle of equity in the distribution of rewards and privileges of society." See Daniel Bell, "America's Un-Marxist Revolution: Mr. Truman Embarks on a Politically Managed Economy," *Commentary* 7 , no. 2 (1949): 215. Secretary Bennett also sees religion playing this role: "He wants values derived from religion, and he wants recognition of the positive role of religion in American history. He means these as civil goals; indeed, he understands them as civic needs" (Wagner, "Bill Bennett's Dilemma," 31).

16. Daniel Bell, "The Cultural Contradictions of Capitalism," *The Public Interest* 21 (Fall 1970): 16–43.

17. Steinfels, *The Neo-Conservatives,* 26.

18. Bell, *The Cultural Contradictions of Capitalism,* 16.

19. Ibid.

20. Ibid., 19.

21. Ibid., 20.

22. Ibid., 34.

23. Ibid.

24. Ibid., 40–41.

25. Ibid., 42–43.

26. Ibid., 53–54.

27. Ibid., 59.

28. Ibid., 70–71.

29. Ibid., 29.

30. Ibid., 28.

31. Ibid., 21.

32. Ibid., 15.

33. Howard Brick, *Daniel Bell and the Decline of Intellectual Radicalism: Social Theory and Political Reconciliation in the 1940s* (Madison: University of Wisconsin Press, 1986), 207.

34. Bell, "Modernism and Capitalism," 221.

35. Clifford Geertz, *The Interpretation of Cultures* (New York: Basic Books, 1973), 90. Quoted in Bell, *Cultural Contradictions of Capitalism,* 28.

36. Bell, 30.

37. Ibid.

38. Ibid., 21–22.

39. Ibid., 28.

40. See, for example, Ezra F. Vogel, *Japan as Number One: Lessons for America* (Cambridge, Mass.: Harvard University Press, 1979); Zbigniew Brzezinski, *The Fragile Blossom: Crisis and Change in Japan* (New York: Harper and Row, 1972); Herman Kahn, *The Emerging Japanese Superstate: Challenge and Response* (Englewood Cliffs, N.J.: Prentice Hall, 1970); William Ouchi, *Theory Z: How American Business Can Meet the Japanese Challenge* (Reading, Mass.: Addison-Wesley, 1981); Ouchi, *The M-Form Society: How American Teamwork Can Recapture the Competitive* Eage (Reading, Mass.: Addison-Wesley, 1984); Chalmers Johnson, *MITI and the Japanese Miracle—The Growth of Industrial Policy* (Stanford: Stanford University Press, 1982); Rodney Clark, *The Japanese Company* (New Haven: Yale University Press, 1979); Kevin P. Phillips, *Staying on Top: The Business Case for a National Industrial Strategy* (New York: Random House, 1984); and Richard Bolling and John Bowles, *America's Competitive Edge—How to Get Our Country Moving Again* (New York: McGraw-Hill, 1982). Japan's traditionalism here is its key cultural attribute. As Bell argues, "the debasement of modernity is the emphasis on *self*-expression. . . . to have significance, a culture must transcend the present, because it is the recurrent confrontation with these root questions whose answers, through a set of symbols, provide a viable coherence to the meaning of existence. And since the appreciation of tradition in culture, and judgment in art (and a coherent curriculum in education), has to be learned, authority—in the form of scholarship, teaching, and skilled exegesis—is a necessary guide for the perplexed" ("Modernism and Capitalism," 210). This imaging of Japanization, of course, embodies all of these qualities—respect for authority, strong cultural traditions, rigorous norms of cultural judgment, and repression of *self*-expression—in its teletraditional construction and circulation.

41. See James M. Zimmerman, "Schools Are My Business," *Newsweek*, May 11, 1986, 6–7. Mr. Zimmerman, an executive with an Atlanta department store, discusses how his firm began a remedial training program to educate ordinary public school students, who have failed to learn anything in Georgia schools, in order to obtain trained workers competent enough to work in his stores. He asks, how can we compete with the Japanese, Taiwanese, or Koreans with this sort of educational system? Most of corporate America echoes his concern.

42. See Christopher Lasch, *The Culture of Narcissism: American Life in an Age of Diminishing Expectations* (New York: W. W. Norton, 1978); Jack W. Germond and Jules Witcover, *Blue Smoke and Mirrors: How Reagan Won and Why Carter Lost the Election of 1980* (New York: Viking, 1981).

43. See Martin K. Starr, ed., *Global Competitiveness: Getting the U.S. Back on Track* (New York: W. W. Norton, 1988), 12–42.

44. See Garry Wills, *Reagan's America: Innocents at Home* (New York: Doubleday & Co., 1987), 1–4.

45. Ibid., 387.

46. Max Horkheimer and Theodor W. Adorno, *Dialectic of Enlightenment*, trans. John Cumming (New York: Seabury, 1972), 167

47. Karl Marx, "The German Ideology: Part I," in *The Marx-Engels Reader*, 2d ed., ed. Robert C. Tucker (New York: W. W. Norton, 1978), 154.

3

From Fundamentalism to Televangelism

The ongoing rebirth of Christian fundamentalism in the United States since 1945 must be acknowledged as one of the key shifts in the post–World War II American political scene. Every president from Truman to Reagan in one way or another has recognized the power of Christian symbolism and values as a legitimating animus for the *Pax Americana* underwritten across the globe by American technology, military force, and corporate commercial culture. While Christian religiosity figured prominently in the classic republican myths of America's puritan founding and its divine writ of manifest destiny, the United States of America did not offically pledge itself to be "One Nation, Under God" or collectively in "In God We Trust" until the mid–1950s, following congressional action in the era of Ike and Senator McCarthy. As Chapter 2 initially suggested, with the development of an informational society in the United States, the venerable icons of traditional churchly Christianity quickly were reformated as the ideological infrastructure of conservative cultural codes.

This revitalization of "Christian faith" (usually meaning a vague and largely Protestant credo) can be traced to several sources: the economic crises of the 1930s, the destructiveness of World War II, the rise of "atheistic" communism in Eastern Europe and Asia, and the massive cultural shocks induced in the 1940s and 1950s by nuclear arms, television, regional migration, suburbanization, and the consumer economy. Under these pressures, and despite the reputed "end of ideology" in this era, a diverse and deep reawakening of religious faith spread throughout American society, cutting across class divisions, racial groups, geographical regions, and many denominational lines.

Contemporary analyses of this religious revival—and, in particular, the rise of Christian fundamentalism—differ sharply over its social significance and political implications. One interpretation associates the reborn fundamentalists, in some organized sects and persuasions, with the quasi-fascist, right-wing underside of American populism. Another view sees how other Christian fundamentalist sects and groups have sided with progressive forces in the postwar struggles for civil rights, nuclear disarmament, and human rights in Third World societies. Evidence can be cited in favor of both outlooks. At this juncture, however, the depth and diversity of this latest "great awakening" stands in the way of making any definitive final judgments on these issues.

Yet, in the context of this debate, a number of troubling issues have emerged with this rebirth of Christian fundamentalism, particularly since the 1960s, as the severe cultural contradictions contained in consumer-driven corporate capitalism have been challenging a "Christian" way of life. As the consumer society of advanced American capitalism displaced the traditional social ties of the nation's diverse regional cultures, corporate producers and mass advertisers in the 1940s and 1950s presented individuals with vast new arrays of preprocessed behavioral scripts and commodity packages, which Chapter 4 addresses in greater detail. Equipped with these correctly encoded scripts, and given access in the marketplace to the attractively packaged commodities of modern life, individuals were charged with exchanging their autonomous producer-ship for dependent consumership and clientage. In exchange for the destruction of their traditional identities, communities, and freedoms, consumers were urged by corporate capital and mass advertising to find new ones in the accumulation of commodities, the practice of stylized scripts, and the consumption of professional services.

Through television, radio, and movies, which became the primary technologies for managing mass consumption, corporate producers urged consumers to base their identities on their Buicks, find community in those rock-and-roll classics of the '60s, and gain emancipation through the enjoyment of their favorite cigarettes, beer, and soft drinks. Values, meaning, and purpose no longer were communicated through the intricate rituals of the family, neighborhood, church, or workplace. Instead, advertising, the electronic media, and mass publications assigned vital new meanings to commodities, new values to the symbolically enriched packages of material life, and new purposes to the conventionalized scripts of personal improvement in advanced capitalism. At the same time, as consumers and their corporate cultivation became the primary productive force in this new advanced capitalist base, new forms of consumerist superstructure emerged from the electronic vacuum of mass media. In response to this consumer culture, an electronic church (a "tele-evangelism" or consumerist confession) developed out of "religious programming" staged by re-born Christian fundamentalists.[1] In the codes of consumer culture, corporate capital has successfully transposed even religious faith into an audiovisual cult—deriving its form and substance from the same master codes of consumption that are reproduced in "secular programming"—which celebrates a theology not of personal liberation, but rather of collective integration.

Still, a clear distinction must be drawn between the televangelists, who have gained increasing visibility and influence over the past thirty years, and previous "great awakenings" of American religiosity before the advent of electronic mass media, and also the fundamentalist revival among many contemporary Christians, who still come to their faith authentically in rural backwoods churches, ramshackle chapels on the wrong side of the tracks, or revival tents at the county fairgrounds. In the latter two instances, a strong case can be made that fundamentalism, as Marx once observed, is still the sigh of the oppressed creature, providing solace to the last outsiders, the real losers, and the truly oppressed through the opiates of religious ritual. Some viewers may even derive spiritual guidance from the televangelists, especially from the low-budget productions of small-time local preachers. With regard to the audiovisual cults of televangelism, however, an equally strong case can be made that these mass-marketed devotions are the sigh of the confused consumer. Like the fans of Reverend Ed Young's "Fellowship of Excitement" in Houston, Texas, they are bored with the demanding credos of traditional churchly practices. These new converts seek a less painful, more entertaining road to salvation. The major televangelists, who have practiced their ministries in the mass media, like Jim and Tammy Bakker of the "PTL (Praise the Lord) Club," Pat Robertson of "The 700 Club," Robert Schuller and his "Hour of Power," Jerry Falwell of the "Old-Time Gospel Hour," and Oral Roberts of "Oral Roberts," all spread the uppers of success, healing, and fulfillment to the troubled and to the upwardly mobile people who are going through "tough times" in the corporate marketplace. Most of the televangelists' adherents, except for the truly faithful in the studio audiences, experience their epiphanies electronically, coming to their faith artificially after flipping the channels through the morning game-shows, the afternoon soaps, and the evening sitcoms.

FUNDAMENTALISM AS A CONSUMPTION COMMUNITY

The development of an audiovisual cult, defined almost wholly in the meta-codes of commodification used in corporate capitalist society, is the troubling problem posed by Christian televangelical fundamentalism. Even before the lurid exposés in 1987 and 1988 of Jimmy Swaggart's sexual misadventures or Jim and Tammy Bakker's misappropriation of church funds and high-flying personal spending, the contradictions between televangelism's spiritual mission and its show-biz style plagued many of these operations. Indeed, in the society of spectacle, as it has formed from the standardized scripts of teleplays and the pleasing packages of the electronic marketplace, the intense significance of communal belief can be quickly subsumed within the existing sign system of personal consumption as it is expressed in passive, isolated watching.

Neither an ineffable god, the unknown mysteries, nor limitless good can be revered or celebrated fully in such practices of bureaucratically controlled consumption. The electronic mediations of Christian fundamentalism destroy these auras of faith in order to produce an electronic image. Animation, cosmic sound scores, computer graphics, or telegenic talking heads all can and will reduce limitless good to a light-show image; the mysterious unknown to a haunting rift of organ or synthesizer chords; and the ineffable godhead to an uplifting cartoon animation. The codes of televisionary ministries (in that television is the consumption experience par excellence) necessarily must attractively package and completely commodify even the Divine to effectively integrate an unseen, diverse, and passive audience.

During the 1950s and '60s, an entire generation came of age in the United States under the horizon of a mass media–borne corporate culture. The broadcast and rebroadcast of images from certain movies, television series, and celebrity actors, as Chapter 2 asserted, laid symbolic foundations for an entire teletraditional culture. The election returns, World Series, Oscars, Emmys, World Cup Games, Olympics, party nominating conventions, Miss America and Miss Universe spectacles—watching them all is part of a national, and in some cases, a transnational ritual. Every holiday is marked by the replay of particular movie classics. Every year has its ritualistic cycle of television events ranging from the January football bowl games to the December New Year's Eve broadcast parties. Each day has its familiar replay of fresh releases, old reruns, news programming, and late-night entertainment. Film stars and TV personalities are constantly available as cultural ideals, figures of authority, and important role models. Electronic images have constructed genuinely meaningful cultural communities, via videotape delay, across the nation's four time zones. Carefully coded video morality plays assign and reassign new meanings to the conventionalized scripts of everyday life. And incessant commercial messages cue consumers, young and old, into the "really important things in life." Following the line of Durkheim's theory, then, it is not surprising that televangelical fundamentalism is an alienated projection of corporate consumer society reflected back to itself as electronic imagery. Nor is it startling that televangelists have assumed the guise of televised talking heads. Thus, average American consumers, as they matured and sought to know God, flipped the channel from "Mister

Rogers' Neighborhood" to "Oral Roberts," quit "The Mickey Mouse Club" to join "The 700 Club," and dropped Ted Mack's "Amateur Hour" to tune in to Jerry Falwell's "Old-Time Gospel Hour." In consumer society, Jesus or God, like Wonder Bread or Geritol, is sold telegenically as a product that heals bodies, mends lives, renews health, and changes attitudes. Faith is presented as "a piece of the rock," "going to the source," and "reaching out to touch someone." As this system of bureaucratically controlled consumption slowly has colonized the everyday lifeworld of American consumers, the cross has followed trade and the flag to imperialize its own domain in the electromagnetic consciousness of contemporary society.

In these electronic churches, the aura of faith, the intense spirit of communion, and the shared consciousness of humanity's transcendent ends or original sins largely are effaced in the electronic media's codes of consumerist communication. In such televangelical broadcasting, religious ritual (in keeping with the logic outlined in Chapter 1) decays into an electronic simulation: an existing "church" often becomes a studio with its own built-in live audience as up-link antennas join the steeple on the roof, or an artificial studio set and its broadcast audiences become "the church." The institution of services or worship devolves into watching a breezy Christian talk show, complete with gospel-rock interludes, "man on the street" interviews and in-depth reports on the vital issues facing Christians today. Similarly, the codes of consumerism reduce the clergyman or reverend to an amiable quizmaster, a talk-show host, or a variety special master of ceremonies. Confession, communion, and conversion, for instance, are redefined as calling a Christian phonebank, finding God's mission for oneself in selling more used cars, or slapping a 700 Club bumpersticker on one's diesel truck trailer. The word of God is conveniently packaged on ten audiocassettes for the convert/consumer's personal enjoyment in the car or out in the workshop. Even Calvary is recreated on videotape for constant broadcast throughout the viewing day as sixty-second spots admonishing viewers to "get to know Jesus," in accord with the same code of product promotion that sells laxatives, the prevention of forest fires, and more life insurance. Taking this logic to its ultimate conclusion, Jim and Tammy Bakker even built— before their fall—an amusement theme park called Heritage, U.S.A., in Fort Mill, South Carolina, which was billed as a "Christian Disneyland," to round out their televangelical consumer product line and prove that fundamentalist faith can be "fun."

It appears that no substantive system of values can escape commodification completely in societies with corporate-planned consumption. Worship, reverence, and devotion are repackaged electronically into special events rather than continuing as habitual communal practices. These events, in turn, fit into the corporate society of spectacle as telecast or teleprompted rallies, crusades, conferences, and revivals that can be mass-marketed like the Superbowl and passively experienced on endless rebroadcasts in many media markets by their loyal viewers. Televangelism, then, necessarily transforms its sect into a market, its believers into consumers, and its messages into products. An entire industry of Christian products, services, and merchandisers has emerged with televangelism, marketing Jesus as a product that works and God as a service that delivers. The overhead for these enterprises, however, is very steep. As a result, the major televangelists are continually promoting their message and image in an endless telethon, soliciting contributions, pledges, and financial support to spread their gospel.

The cross, the dove, the fish, and Jesus are no longer merely icons or holy symbols; they are mass-marketed insignia of Christian consumption. Indeed, in the "K-Mart Kultur" of corporate capitalism, these signs mark the boundaries of only one segment in corporate capital's evolving master code of product demography. As the drug culture must have its marijuana leaf T-shirts, coke spoons, and roach clips, or the suburban gentry must acquire its preppie wardrobe, squash racquets, and barbecues, Christian televangelists must have their expensive bibles, Christian greeting cards, and lithographs of Jesus for the living room. The consumption of these objects, or "Christian supplies," gives the televangelicals new tangible signs of their identity, community, and values in the correctly coded conventions of telecast consumerism. Just as "country music" is now merely a genre of commodities—produced in the city of Nashville, packaged with the full array of high Hollywood hype, and promoted in a massive Madison Avenue fashion—so too is fundamental Christian faith devolving into a standardized kit of services and symbols devoid of much of its original substance. While it may not be truly "authentic," it is presented as "the real thing" or the latest "what's happening now." Clearly, cowboys, woodsmen, and farmers no longer produce "country music" in the society of spectacle; therefore, it is not surprising that talk-show entertainers, audio technicians, teleprompter operators, and studio producers now produce the commodified electronic surrogate for devotional services. Televangelism is "lite religion," just like "real religion," only better, because it is less filling and even more satisfying.

With this syncretic fusion of a ministry with marketing, televangelists openly act, talk, and dress like entertainment stars or corporate salesmen. The three generic codes of Christian programming cast their content in the form of an afternoon talk show, like "The 700 Club" or "The PTL Club," a low-budget variety show with well-known stars, musical groups, and talented soloists, like the "Old-Time Gospel Hour" or "Day of Discovery," or an intense public service announcement, like "Oral Roberts" or "It Is Written." These programs and formats totally diverge from those of old-line churches' established service broadcasts of their rites, like "The Lutheran Hour" or "Mass for Shut-ins." In televangelical programming, the televangelist is a star, working to sell his or her line of "power passages," "Championship of Christ," or "healing through faith." The program's object is to build audience share, gain contributions, and create a need for the "faith products" marketed through images, telephone hot lines, and special literature. Traditional churches' denominational liturgies, arcane rituals, or theological doctrines often are derided as worthless, obsolete, or ineffective. Such claims stick because these traditional forms of worship are presented as "bad TV"—no sizzle, no action, no excitement. All that counts is the video viewers' continuing "faith" in the televangelist, expressed in watching the program and pledging monetary support to the unending telethon of the ministry.

In keeping with this logic, televangelists build broadcasting or production studios, not churches. Instead of forming synods, wards, or dioceses, electronic evangelists organize the Christian Broadcasting Network and Liberty Broadcasting System. The word of God no longer arrives every generation on the wings of angels or in the infrequent manifestation of miracles. Rather, the imperatives of televangelical market building ensure that the word of God arrives daily in the homes of millions from a CBN satellite and that Miracle Day is a permanent feature of televangelical broadcasts in order to celebrate new conversions to the fold. Likewise, each televangelist, as a star, directs the attitudes of his or her share of the fundamentalist audience through the codes of entertainment marketing. In turn, their constant orchestration of conversions, healings, and testimonials for the viewers' edification meshes perfectly with the corporate-based code of telegenic proof through product endorsements, which also show consumers switching decisively from one deodorant to another, gaining quick relief from packaged nostrums, and swearing that the new, improved product tastes best.

If Christian fundamentalism were merely an audiovisual cult thriving only on the distant margins of contemporary society, then it might be safely ignored. However, the pure professionalism of its most persuasive packaging has garnered televangelism considerable support.[2] In the society of corporate-controlled consumption, the marketplace becomes a voting booth. Popular packages and products win votes of favor when they are consumed by isolated, passive consumers. By participating in the televangelists' shows, the faithful are often seeking to send and receive the right sign meanings with other consumers in an ideopolitical movement. The growth of televangelism's following, along with the increasing politicization of its special events, such as Pat Robertson running for the Republican presidential nomination or Jerry Falwell's elevation of Oliver North to sainted martyrdom in 1988, indicates an important ideological role in televangelical fundamentalism that needs to be examined in more detail.

TELEVANGELISM AS AN IDEOPOLITICAL FORCE

The unique position of televangelical fundamentalism in contemporary American society is expressive of the cultural contradictions of corporate capitalism. Everyone in the 1950s did not immediately or completely subscribe to the new consumer ethic of affluence in the advanced corporate economy, particularly many of those Christian fundamentalists who now find satisfaction in televangelism. The real insiders of American society—or the mainstream participants in middle-class culture who had enough income, status, or leisure—did shift their identities and purpose from being producers to consumers. At the same time, the national planning of the federal welfare state and the transnational productivity of corporate capital worked throughout the 1950s and 1960s to include as many groups, interests, and subcultures as organizationally possible. Hence, as Chapter 2 illustrated, a major contradiction erupted in the cultural underpinnings of American society. While the traditional productivity of American industry assumed the unquestioning adherence of its workers and consumers to the frugal discipline of the Protestant ethic, the new model of corporate consumer society demanded a headlong leap into the more unrestrained hedonism of the psychedelic bazaar, made possible by commodities in the corporate marketplace. The traditional culture's injunction to "wait for your just rewards" was replaced by an electronic call to "go for the gusto." Yet, in urging consumers to pursue their consuming fantasies in the short run, corporate capital may have caused the long-run productive potential of the American economy to suffer as capital, technology, expertise, and labor were channeled into the production of goods for personal leisure and consumption.

As the consumer society unfolded in postwar America together with these underlying cultural contradictions, an entirely new industrial infrastructure also formed, tied to knowledge-intensive informational production with an unprecedented kind of truly national culture knitted together by CBS, NBC, ABC, interstate highways, and AM-FM radio. Yet the old moral verities, nationalistic virtues, and optimistic values that the America of puritan producers held to be true prior to the rise of consumer society doggedly held on among the most marginal elements of mainstream society. Either as aspirants to the attractions of consumerist leisure or as poorly adjusted parvenu participants in suburban consumption, these semi-insider elements are the most familiar followers of the televangelists' electronic churches. Working in industrial parks scattered around interstate highway interchanges, the agribusiness tracts of the Sunbelt states, or the regional shopping malls dotting modern urban sprawl, these men and women turn to televangelism for the credo of success, healing, and faith in old-fashioned values that it exalts.

Christ, these parvenus are told by televangelism, chooses a mission or ministry for each of us; hence, televangelists assure their viewers that Jesus wants us to be exactly whatever we are: aerospace workers, truckdrivers, check-out girls, salesmen, or hog growers. The "spirit of God," they are told, is running through their places of work; pushing their employers' products in the marketplace, therefore, is "ministering" to God's flock. Similarly, whatever consumer goods, job promotions, good health, or financial prosperity these arriviste consumers acquire is all part of God's "master plan" for their lives because they are "champions of Christ." In a society of bureaucratically controlled consumption, the have-not followers of televangelism consume their scripts of faith and packages of success as though they were downpayments on having material commodities for consumption. God, in turn, creates miracles that usually are expressed in getting, having, or keeping the most sought-after goods of the corporate marketplace. At the same time, however, subscribing to televangelism also can provide prepaid spiritual care for life's tough times. Here the televangelists recognize that consumer society excites individuals to buy too much, to play too many games, or to go too far in chasing personal pleasures. Unable to cope, these poorly adjusted consumers may need the guidance, solace, and hope that only Jesus or God can give. Through telecast counsel, phonebank prayers, or pre-recorded audiocassettes, televangelists intervene electronically in their viewers' lives to act as psychosocial therapists, dispensing God's reassurance with their ministries' pledge cards.

The message of these sessions on "The Christian Family," "God, Sex, and Marriage," or "Divorce, Remarriage, and Faith" is that of discipline, sacrifice, success, and work. Pleasures are allowed, but not the unlimited, unchecked, unbalanced pursuit of any pleasures anytime. The latter type of advice is the work of secular humanists, pornographers, and abortionists aiming to break up the traditional American family and destroy its economic prosperity. To counter the commodified utopias of corporate capital projected in beer, automobile, perfume, and soft drink ads, televangelical therapy projects its own commodified utopias of happy families, secure finances, certain faith, and Christian living to its viewers. Ironically, however, even these invocations to work harder with more Christian discipline are vended electronically to the televangelical viewers in consumerist advertising codes.

As an ideopolitical force, then, televangelism constitutes itself as one response to the cultural contradictions of capitalism. Having seen the collective crises of consumer society explode in the 1960s and 1970s, televangelists electronically advocate a rediscovery of the good old days of the 1940s and 1950s, prior to the 1960s psychedelic bazaar, when women knew their proper role, blacks stayed in their place, men wore the pants in the family, kids were not on dope, the Japanese exported low quality goods, the United States was Number One, and things just overall worked. Although much of this image is myth, CBN reinforces it by broadcasting a schedule of old 1950s sitcoms and 1940s cowboy movies, sprinkled with wholesome recent reruns to prove it is "in touch" with today. In such electronic texts, the video consumer does not suffer the obscenity of Lucy and Ricky Ricardo sleeping in the same bed, but rather can celebrate the glory of Randolph Scott blowing away ten Comanches without reloading his six-gun. The televangelists' response to the artificial revolution of "sex, drugs, and rock-n-roll" begun in the 1960s is to mount an equally artificial counterrevolution against the corporate capitalist advertisers and national welfare state planners that have aided and abetted these crises of the past two decades.

In the 1980s, the ideopolitical importance of televangelism interlocks with the right-wing revivals of the Reagan era.[3] Televangelists have little regard for the separation of church and state: proselytizing and politicking tend to merge in their programs. Having packaged recent history as a series of dismal failures that are attributable to a meddlesome welfare bureaucracy or immoral coporate management, televangelical fundamentalists support the dismantling of government services, the encouragement of private entrepreneurialism, and the rollback of atheistic Soviet communism. As a carefully packaged form of self-administered support, televangelist programming would substitute its faith and healing for public welfare services. Criticizing big business, international banks, and transnational capital for stealing jobs from Americans by moving to Asia, televangelism sells the virtues of self-employment, exemplified in faith-based salesmanship, and Christian discipline in the workplace as a means of fighting the more dedicated neo-Confucian sweatshop labor of Asia. Similarly, in decrying the rise of communist expansion, televangelists assure their audiences that Jesus, if he were around today, would support building new nuclear weapons systems. Calling on the God-fearing, Bible-toting America of old, televangelical fundamentalists urge Washington to launch "search and destroy" sweeps in Central America,

Africa, Asia, and the Carribbean to mete out fire and brimstone to communists, crazies, and other infidels threatening America. In addition to Jerry Falwell's well-publicized comments on everything on today's political agenda from AIDS to South Africa to abortion clinics, Pat Robertson organized a grassroots movement with his own political action committee to run for the 1988 presidential nomination from within the GOP. Although he was unsuccessful in the wake of the various ethical scandals involving Jimmy Swaggart, Oral Roberts, and the Bakkers, he has not ruled out future attempts at winning political office. Robertson implied that God was his campaign coordinator and chief advisor when he, like Ayatollah Khomeini, assured his followers that "when I pray, I get answers." While Robertson's 1988 campaign ran out of gas after winning only a handful of convention delegates and Falwell's attempts at organizing effective chapters of the Moral Majority nationwide largely have failed, their efforts illustrate the deeper political ambitions of many televangelical organizations. In many respects, these institutionalized electronic churches function every day as political action committees for cultural conservatism, pressuring mass media, elected officials, social institutions, and their followers to acknowledge the importance of televangelism's ideopolitical agendas.

Christian fundamentalism, as an audiovisual cult, has acquired ideopolitical importance today because it strongly opposes the consumerist cultural consensus of the 1960s and 1970s. As a weak negative oppositional force articulating the social criticisms of an electronically generated community of religious adherents held together across several time zones and demographic niches by their watching of televised images, televangelism allegedly shows consumer soicety, with its excesses and false licenses, as a culture of narcissism. Yet at the same time, televangelism's codes and packaging are denominated in the same basic signs of corporate capitalist consumerism. As the 1987 PTL scandal transparently revealed, it is the same logic of capitalist exchange with its peculiar dynamics of corporate concentration and relentless growth that has guided the various televangelists' quests for bigger market shares, not to mention their defensive moves against hostile outside takeovers by their competitors.

Ironically, even in the wake of the Jim and Tammy Bakker scandals, no televangelist has yet recognized the inherent contradictions in their new gospel of wealth. They continue to mistake the sociopathologies of consumerism for "secular humanism," while urging their followers to seek more and more material prosperity to please Jesus and keep the 700 and PTL Clubs on the air. Televangelism, then, has gained more visibility and influence only as it has dropped the trappings of religious ritual and more closely embraced the average consumers' secular talk-show/game-show/variety-show consciousness in its productions. The growth of televangelism illustrates how power can be created and exercised on today's mediascapes within the prevailing modes of information. Hence, televangelism's powers as a teletraditionalist theology may become even more significant in the 1990s, particularly if the central televangelists can once again regain legitmacy and renew their financial support in the aftermath of the scandals in their ranks during the 1980s. No longer content to merely preach from the pulpit (or the teleprompter), televangelists and their followers still are mobilizing political power at all levels of government to redirect society in the 1990s toward their mythical vision of America's "traditional ways of life."

NOTES

1. See Jeffrey K. Hadden and Anson Shupe, *Power and Politics on God's Frontier* (New York: Henry Holt and Company, 1988); Hadden and Charles E. Swann, *Prime Time Preachers: The Rising Power of Televangelism* (Reading, Mass.: Addison-Wesley, 1981); and Ben Armstrong, *The Electronic Church* (Nashville, Tenn.: Thomas Nelson, 1979).

2. See George Gerbner et al., "Religion and Television: A Research Report by the Annenberg School of Communications" (University of Pennsylvania and the Gallup Organization, April 1984).

3. For additional discussion, see Richard G. Hutcheson, Jr., *God in the White House: How Religion Has Changed the Modern Presidency* (New York: Macmillan, 1988).

4

Regulating the Haven in a Heartless World: The State, Firm, and Family under Advanced Capitalism

Anyone who has noticed the tremendous shifts over time in America's mass media markets cannot ignore how sitcom and teledrama manufacturers have been repackaging their images of everyday family life over the past generation. These transformations in media program packaging hieroglyphically seem to sum up a major cultural contradiction in contemporary advanced capitalism; namely, the tension between an *ideology* of the traditional family that was vital to the emergence of capitalism in its entrepreneurial phase and the *utopia* of the permissive individual, which has proven decisive in the consolidation of advanced capitalism in its current corporate phase. From these social hieroglyphs, one can begin to decipher how the family mediates social and political control in the United States today. In particular, these signs tentatively indicate how ideological the usual distinctions between "public" and "private" have become as private-sector firms have teamed up with the blessing of public-sector state agencies to regulate the consumption of goods and services of private individuals in the privacy of their homes as part of the larger public interest of constant economic growth.

At one time, the small-town family image (posed in the "capitalist realism" tradition of Norman Rockwell) of a harmonious household of mother, father, sister, brother (prospering in the privacy and sanctity of their single-family dwelling on a tree-lined street over from the church and across town from grandma and grandpa) safely legitimized the emergent industrial order of entrepreneurial capital. These satisfying images of the family as a haven in a heartless world provided the members of many families with a secure ideology that defined their productive roles, moral goals, and sources of emotional support in the brutal nineteenth-century struggles of urbanization, secularization, and industrialization.[1]

Once America *was* industrialized, secularized, and urbanized, however, this set of domestic images proved to be an ideological fetter upon the further rationalization of the corporate order. Through state intervention and corporate integration from the 1920s through the 1960s, the allegedly private sphere of the family—grounded in an autonomous civil society and in rational market exchange—slowly came to be put under the "public administration" of the fused "public" and "private" sectors. In turn, new utopian images of personal life arose in the sprawling metroplex (initially articulated in the "narcissistic expressionism" of Hugh Hefner and Helen Gurly Brown) that were tied more to the broken households of SSWD's (the single, separated, widowed, or divorced, his or her own particular forms of "happiness," "liberation," or "professional achievement" in the urban hustle). These new images have begun to underwrite, in a determinant way, the privatized consumption of corporate capitalism.[2]

Despite the imperfections of its representation, the family image being packaged and broadcast on the major media networks continues this contradiction between ideology and utopia. These images cannot be ignored. In today's mobile and rootless cities, Ralph Kramden, Lucy Ricardo, Opie Taylor, Mary Richards, Hawkeye Pierce, Bones McCoy, Thomas Magnum, and Frank Furillo are much more reliable friends and neighbors than the people who live next door for far too many real American families. Indeed, apparently believing that American family life once was or should again be like it was in "Ozzie and Harriet," "Leave It to Beaver," or "Little House on the Prairie" (or should again be like that), many "typical families" and "average consumers" today want to defend the powerful ideology of the traditional family as it has been indelibly impressed in the "silent majority's" consciousness in "Happy Days," "The Waltons," or, better yet, "Father Knows Best." So strong has the ideology become that even the possibility of historical alternatives has been effaced, as this ideological consciousness would have everyone indeed believe that the middle-class nuclear family represented by the Andersons on "Father Knows Best" directly descended from "The Flintstones" and is slowly evolving into "The Jetsons." Of course, today, the family is in the stage exemplified by the Huxtables on "The Cosby Show." Therefore, Christian fundamentalists, for example, have cast this universal kind of "traditional family" beseiged by "secular humanists," "liberals," and "pornographers," who whip up "permissiveness" and "moral decline."[3] Unless the massive middle-class majority acts now, such groups assert, the "obscenity" and "pornography" being beamed in episodes of "Dallas," "Dynasty," "Soap," "Three's Company," or "One Day at a Time" into America's living rooms will surely destroy the "free enterprise system."

Unfortunately for those drawing the battle lines in this fashion, only 7 percent of all American households in the 1970s and 1980s fit the "traditional" domestic model allegedly favored by the silent American majority. At the same time, over 22 percent, or three times as many households, are composed of SSWDs seeking the elusive satisfactions of "permissiveness."[4] In fact, it is not the destruction, but rather the continued development, of America's "free enterprise system" that requires the further elaboration of "permissiveness" or, more important, of the "consummativity" which advanced capitalism requires to grow.[5] In an economy in which two-thirds of the GNP per annum is generated by consumer spending and in which highly mobile, domestically unattached, and professionally motivated individuals turn over much of that spending, it is no accident that "frugal" households of traditional nuclear families are exploding almost exponentially into many more "consummative" SSWD households, or that in television programming the media marketers are trading upon image packages that legitimate such cultural developments.

For corporate marketing departments, this sociological issue is simple. One can sell one toaster to mom, pop, sis, and junior as a family unit, or one can sell one each to separated mom, swinging pop, single sis, and indepedent junior and his college roommates. Essentially, the planned productivity of corporate capital needs more and more people to need more and more products (or more costly products) to maintain its programs for economic growth. Utterly destroying the fabric of existing social institutions such as the family of local neighborhoods or even high-density cities is, in the short run, a low-risk, high-benefit strategy for meeting this goal of "growth." Thus the ideological apparatus popularizes new values, norms, and practices that do little to forestall the internal collapse of one unit of consumption—the nuclear family—in order to multiply its consummative potential by providing new goods and services to the more numerous, surviving individual fragments of such nuclear families. In the last analysis, the continuous development of corporate capitalism seems to require the planned reconstitution and rational regulation of a new haven, in an even more heartless world, such that the domestic certainties of "Father Knows Best" can be continually reconstituted as the basically privatized insecurities of "One Day at a Time" or as the temporarily collectivized wants of "The Brady Bunch."

This chapter, then, critically explores the origins and processes of the contemporary family's ongoing reconstruction during the transition from entrepreneurial to corporate capitalism to today's more transnational and disorganized capitalism. Obviously, there are many irrationalities and discontinuities in the networks of capitalist reproduction. Not everything that exists in the media or marketplace can be identified as playing an important function in the reproduction of society. Even so, the imperfect, but still planned, management of aggregate and specific demand for goods and services exercised by corporate capital and the service state in advanced capitalism[6] clearly has necessitated the socialization and rationalization of domestic reproduction, just as entrepreneurial capitalism had earlier required the socialization and rationalization of domestic production.[7]

The basic logic of "consummativity" that anchors this entire system needs to be analyzed. Instead of maintaining the irreducible tension between the "public" and "private" spheres implied by conventional economic and legal theory, capitalist exchange increasingly has pressed the public and private into becoming identical under consummativity as the collective goals of the state and the firm are internalized by individuals in the family, the firm, and the mass public.[8] These identity linkages, in turn, allow the state and firm to regulate individuals, albeit imperfectly, to the extent they actually accept the "needs" extended to them as reified "scripts" of normal behavior by the media, mass education, or professional experts and as "packages" of material satisfaction by corporate manufacturers. From these scripts and packages, individuals often are struggling constantly to refunction, countercode, or subvert these larger imperatives in their own personal practice of resistance to these micrologies of power. Still, these "needs" of individuals simultaneously are required by the state and firm inasmuch as the aggregate economic growth and specific commodity claims implied by these needs are a productive force guaranteeing the further development and legitimacy of the state/corporate system.

By defining certain behavioral and material needs for particular groups of "private individuals" to internalize, the more "public authorities" of the state and firm can "liberate" new demographic segments—women, children, teenagers, blacks, senior citizens, gays, Latinos—to expect and acquire need fulfillments once mainly reserved for straight, middle-aged male WASPs. Specific prepackaged need fulfillments can be defined by various kinds of consciousness engineering—advertising, formal schooling, or the entertainment media, for example—and, in turn, the aggregate access of individuals to their need satisfactions can be mandated through legal entitlement or job creation. To deny that such consciousness engineering occurs, one must ignore the obvious; namely, the careful manufacture, marketing, and manipulation explicit in such highly processed cultural packages as New Age music, public school curricula, *Saturday Night Fever,* Mustangs, "baby boomer" television programming, heavy metal rock, "Sesame Street," network news programs, "thirtysomething" life-styles, *E.T.,* "Miami Vice," or the constant retooling of weekly play lists in urban FM radio markets. In closely monitoring these need definitions and need satisfactions through market research surveys or focus group studies, corporate capital and the service state, in effect, can attain a considerable degree of social regulation through the "freedom of choice" in market exchange.

A familiar point of faith in the contemporary American debates over "the crisis of the family" is that it, of all social institutions, remains the most resistant to change. But, almost in the same breath, these debates also note how constant change in the content, form, and process of family relations has dogged American family life for generations. This chapter's analysis has moved beyond such contradictory debates, indicating how institutional continuity, change, and crisis in the family have been, in part, instrumentally regulated to more effectively rationalize the consolidated workings of corporate capital and the service state.[9]

FROM ENTREPRENEURIAL TO CORPORATE CAPITALISM

Entrepreneurial capitalism, which so decisively transformed much of Western European and North American society through the creation of modern commerce and industry after the Reformation, largely fueled its productive cycles *extensively.* That is, entrepreneurial capitalism, as it emerged in the modern bourgeois city, transformed economic and social relations by extending its rationalizing commercial exchange logic into economic activities, social institutions, or geographic regions that were hitherto precapitalist.[10] As this exchange-based logic of commodification generated in the workingplace penetrated the private living space, the city penetrated the countryside, the market dominated the farm, the mind-worker subordinated the hand-worker, and the capitalist metropole imperialized the precapitalist periphery. With the advancement of this process, the bourgeois family system formed to cushion family members against the ravages of commodity exchange relations. In particular, women and children were slowly taken out of productive economic activity and put more into the domestic reproductive sphere of creating and maintaining the emotional haven of the household.[11]

Yet, as Chapter 1 claimed, the dynamic of this productive cycle under the commercial law of value continually implied its own inherent limits. Beginning in the fourteenth and fifteenth centuries, capitalist entrepreneurs acquired power by extending the reach of their markets to areas outside their cities, into adjacent villages, farms, and regions. With the growth of nation-states, entrepreneurial commerce (often accompanied by evangelistic churchmen) extended across continents to win new conquests in Asia, Africa, and the Americas. By the late nineteenth-century, however, the easy pickings in the precapitalist societies of the Western and Southern Hemispheres had been largely divided among the competing entrepreneurs and nation-states.

In the 1880s, as the Congress of Berlin oversaw the final subdivision of Africa, as the Romanov czars finally subdued Central Asia and Siberia, and as the wide-open American frontiers rapidly closed, entrepreneurial capitalism lost the precapitalist underpinnings of its *extensive* commerical logic. Although political premonitions of this crisis can be found, for example, in the organizational response of German, Italian, and Japanese industrializers to a world market largely dominated by England, the decisive shift to intensive commercialization and industrialization from the extensive entrepreneurial mode of capitalism did not become general until American capitalism constituted the urban consumer society as its structural response to the synchronized great depression of the 1890s.[12]

The Bourgeois Family System

Several historians of the family have observed that the domestic order was wholly transformed under entrepreneurial capitalism. As Zaretsky suggests, "with the rise of industry, capitalism 'split' material production between its socialized forms (the sphere of commodity production) and the private labor performed predominately by women within the home."[13] Initially women were not completely divorced from capitalist exchange because the family units, with their own productive agricultural, commercial, or industrial property, contributed to larger processes through middlemen, rural factors, or urban entrepreneurs. But as the scale of production increasingly necessitated larger concentrations of capital, the workingplace split from private living space, along with work splitting from leisure, men's labor from women's labor, and the market from society. These trends toward the socialization of production in turn combined themselves with tendencies toward the privatization of reproduction.

Multiple nuclear households formed from the looser extended kinship order of precapitalist society. As the production of commodified goods for exchange became "man's work," the provision of everyday needs used in households almost exclusively became "woman's work." Age-old patriarchy found yet another expression in the exchange logic of capitalism by playing this new double standard against women, who came to be "simultaneously degraded and exalted"[14] in the bourgeois family. With the expropriation of production from the household, women were protected from joining—and prevented from enjoying—the thrills of victory and agonies of defeat in the capitalist marketplace. Still, in being shielded, women were entrusted with "new responsibility for maintaining the emotional and psychological reality of personal relations."[15]

By creating these new behavioral worlds of childhood and womanhood,[16] the bourgeois family system assigned women ambiguous new roles in the market economy; namely, as the primary subcontractor within this new child-centered family in charge of manufacturing new psychic identities in sync with market competition and as the emotional fix-it shop for menfolk and little ones who might be roughed up by "the invisible hand." As the sayings went, women truly were angels of consolation, whose hands rocked the cradle and thereby ruled civilization. Bourgeois-style families, then, captured in the privacy of their socially isolated homes, "created psychological conditions favorable to the emergence of a new type of inner-directed, self-reliant personality—the family's deepest contribution to the needs of a market society based on competition, individualism, postponement of gratification, rational foresight, and the accumulation of worldly goods."[17]

To accumulate capital and to preserve themselves for production, bourgeois families, in turn, developed new social rituals for self-discipline, delayed satisfaction, and material sacrifice. Only in the privacy of the home and under strict rules of propriety could psychic, physical, and emotional needs be gratified, but just to the point of not weakening one's productivity by excess. Building up one's business, career, or estate demanded frugal discipline, and the child-centered family virtually transmuted the child into a market "future" whose character had to be properly managed and invested in so that the child might also become productive. The aristocratic ideals of intimate romantic love, which continually mystified the rules for bourgeois courting and marriage with its present-oriented, adult-centered vision of love, caused tremendous sexual, personal, and emotional estrangement as they were twisted in the future-oriented, child-centered bourgeois family to allow the *men* to build fortunes, professions, and reputations "for" the women and children. These cold concessions by the family to the outside forces of the market eventually overloaded the spouse/spouse and parent/child relationships in the family.[18]

The artificially inflated psychic income paid to women and men in the privacy of the family for centering their lives on the children first and, perhaps, on their spouses second, was soon found to provide inadequate compensation for the rising psychic taxes exacted by the trivialization of men's work by machines and of women's work by men. With the increase of affluence in the nineteenth century (an extensive function of entrepreneurial capital's world economy of scale in colonialism), the devalued emotional wage of man's and woman's work coupled with the excessive personal price of privatized family life began to distort the psychic balance of payments in the bourgeois family system. As the sexual frustration, family violence, and emotional repression of the Victorian home clearly indicated, the bourgeois-style family was no unspoiled paradise. Instead, and in spite of its mystifying guise of sentiment and affection, the bourgeois family was more often an authoritarian patriarchy centered upon cultivating "civilized" children and controlling women's alleged "uncivilized" sensuality.[19] Having been economically and emotionally bankrupted in the unequal exchange between men and women, parents and children, and families and firms imposed by entrepreneurial capital, many families found that the myth of private happiness before the family hearth had crumbled under the tremendous revolutionary blows that came both from within and without the household.

Invading the Haven in a Heartless World

With advancing urban industrialization, many women rebelled within the entrepreneurial capitalist family against the deforming demands of subservient domesticity. The growing cities increasingly afforded many women consumer goods and services they could buy rather than produce themselves, giving them a new responsibility for informed, rational consumption. In the 1890s, for example, 90 percent of urban households switched to baker's bread, 65 percent sent out some laundry for finishing, and commercially processed food decisively displaced home-processed foods.[20] Since men remained preoccupied by their roles in modern production, most middle-class women, and many working-class women, basically acquired the role of modern consumers, turning this opportunity into new forms of extra-domestic assertiveness in the spheres of feminist politics, cultural reform, and social agitation. At first many women did not press decisively for expanded participation in the work force; instead, they internalized the instrumental rationality of industry assigned to their roles in household reproduction as these duties were being redefined by consumer goods producers.

As Catherine Beecher exhorted women in the 1870s and 1880s, woman was to gain "appropriate *scientific and practical training* for her distinctive *profession* as housekeeper, nurse of infants and the sick, educator of childhood, trainer of servants and minister of charities."[21] Plainly, these "feminist" rebellions boiled down to women—in terms of emotional caregiving—exchanging their special female "sensibility" for a more rationalistic "sense" of managing consumption. With "leisure time" and "discretionary income" increasing in society, industrial capitalism slowly provided women, and later children and teenagers, with weapons to resist their subjugation to unpaid, unrewarding domestic drudgery as guerrillas of modern consumerism. After all, baking the daily bread or doing the weekly laundry was "the white woman's burden ... the bane of the American housemother's professional life."[22] Hence, the feminist quest for liberation—mediated by market exchange as extra-domestic consumption against subservient domestic production—aided the corporate professional's invasion of the backward household economy by urging women to accept consumption rather than production as their major relation to capital.

But, as partisans of mass consumption, women largely gained only a particular form of liberation—one that the industrial system needed to intensify its exhausted extensive order—becoming "consumers, not producers, of the new technology."[23] Even the independent practical activity implied by "homemade" eventually was degraded to new forms of dependent passivity as advertising and education steered tastes toward "store-bought" goods and services. In aiding and abetting these transformations, women began changing their status and role in the family, but still "a very special ideology defined women's proper social roles in narrow and restricted ways."[24]

Of course, women asserting themselves outside of the home after the 1880s helped launch new trends—the rise of "permissiveness," falling birth rates, a growing female work force, and rising divorce rates.[25] Nonetheless, these trends never proceeded at rates which corporate capital or the service state could not adapt to. In fact, these agencies helped to define these new female roles in narrow, restricted ways suitable to the marketing strategies of corporate firms and the policy interventions of the state. The "home" may remain the "woman's kingdom,"[26] yet this feminine monarchy has been largely a comprador state ultimately propped up by regular infusions of Campbell's Soup, Tide, Geritol, "Sesame Street," Hoover Floor Sweepers, and Oldsmobiles shipped in from the corporate imperium. No longer content to flit about on missions of mercy in the privacy of their homes, the angels of consolation found unique new places in the public sphere—either on the productive topside or in the consumerist underside of the satanic mills of industry and commerce.

This revolution in morals against the classical entrepreneurial family, then, did not spring from a vacuum. From outside the family, the nearly exhausted imperial logic of entrepreneurial capital gained a new lease on life as the serene secluded privacy of the bourgeois family was revealed to be hiding a backward, primitive social sphere needing to be "modernized." Having "underdeveloped" the family earlier by lifting production out of the household, industrial capitalism now sought to more rationally "develop" family relations by socializing reproduction as well.[27] Because the family, even in its bourgeois capitalist form, "was associated with the 'natural' processes of eating, sleeping, sexuality, and cleaning oneself, with the agonies of birth, sickness, and death, *and* with the unremitting necessity of toil,"[28] it easily was portrayed as backward, primitive, and underdeveloped. Given that entrepreneurial capital had largely imperialized most of the outer world by the 1880s, corporate capital in its formative era launched into the commercial colonization of this final inner frontier—armed with the faith of psychoanalysis and bearing consumerist trade goods.

The more progressive commercial and industrial elites of entrepreneurial capital recognized that *extensive* capitalist expansion with its emphasis on accumulation, productivity, and building the "supply side" had to be augmented if not replaced. By mobilizing scientific research to technically inform and managerially guide industrial production, the entrepreneurs slowly concentrated their market shares and capital holdings through oligopolistic organization into large capital combines that could obviate market forces by creating a planned system of production.[29] *Intensive* capitalist administration, with a new stress on organization, consummativity, and managing the "demand side" of industry, presented itself as the most rational path out of the tangled maze of entrepreneurial capital's limits.[30]

Just as entrepreneurial capital slowly grew into a world market by integrating disparate points of production into a unified whole, so did corporate capital tend toward total administration in its regulatory assault on the family. In the workingplace and private living space, professional managers divorced skill from activity, planning from doing, theory from practice, and thought from action.[31] By integrating capital, technique, material, energy, labor, and markets into corporate concentrations, the managerial classes and owners purposely alienated the workers from their family-accumulated property and personally acquired skills, as well as from the basic natural materials, simple energy, communal crafts, and local markets to which the entrepreneurial family had tied itself. With this economic reconstitution of the family, then, corporate capital could intensify its rationalization of everyday life by means of increased state regulation, the technical reorganization of labor, and the scientific management of all spheres of social interaction.

Developing the Corporate Family System

As large firms claimed a monopoly upon planning purposive rational action in the workplace, families increasingly accepted corporate capital's definitions of their individual needs and private goals. The organic need for air, drink, food, clothing, shelter, praxis, and affection, hitherto defined by the "homespun" organic crafts of the entrepreneurial household, underwent commercial redefinition as the commodified "need" for purchasing air conditioning, Coca-Cola, Wonder Bread, coats and ties, suburban split-levels, a college degree, and a flesh-and-blood approximation of some cinematic sex symbol in the corporate marketplace.

In commercially colonizing the traditional roles and rituals of domestic reproduction, as Chapter 2 maintained, neither the large firm nor the modern state has accepted the sanctity, privacy, or autonomy of the family. Bourgeois notions of frugality, sexual propriety, personal trust, parental authority, private property, family status, and household autonomy placed irrational limits and inefficient constraints before the total commodification of personal relations. The bourgeois family system necessarily has been dismantled from without as professional experts in the areas of health care, childbirth, nutrition, education, fashion, morality, elder care, shelter, leisure, and mortuary and funeral services expropriated these functions from the family, where they had been provided naturally as use values, to return them in exchange as commodified goods and services. These rationally designed interventions, in turn, have enabled the aggregate planning system of corporate production "to organize the entire society in its interest and image."[32]

Having made the real decisions about how these goods and services would be provided, corporate capital turned to the state to make acceptance of exchange-based domestic reproduction compulsory through coercion and legislation. As a result, an entire new administrative regime formed to provide public health regulation, minimal nutritional requirements, mass education, mandatory retirement, urban planning, and national recreation areas, as well as a bevy of other public welfare services and payments.[33] Starting first in the affluent middle-class surburbs of the major industrial cities and then spreading into more marginal market zones in inner-city ethnic neighborhoods, racial ghettos, small towns, and rural areas, the corporate family form emerged from the wreckage of the bourgeois family system. Corporate capital and the state decided what particular material "packages" and behavioral "scripts" could be produced and provided along a spectrum of quality- and quantity-graded alternatives to the consumer. The consumers would exercise their *free choice* over the alternatives, which would deliver the need-satisfactions required to fulfill the consumers' need-definitions—as consumers had been socialized to define them—while boosting GNP growth rates healthy percentages per annum.

In this fashion, the individual personality becomes an integral element of the collective means of production, and the family becomes yet another service delivery system of the modern corporate state. Seemingly, the corporate family serves as a "half-way house" that inculcates the formal skills of adaptive role performance in its members, but which leaves the substantive definition of those roles to the school, television, specialty magazines, the workplace, peer groups, or professional societies.[34] As these other agencies psychosocially define the child and the parent as they "grow" or "develop" as "persons," it is the family, or at least its income, that provides people with access to food, drink, shelter, and clothing.

Along these same lines, Lasch observes that

> by providing the child with emotional security in his early years and then by giving him a high degree of independence, the isolated nuclear family trains a type of personality ideally equipped to face the rigors of the modern world. Permissiveness, which many observers mistake for an abdication of parental responsibility, actually amounts to a new way of training achievement. It prepares the child to deal with an unpredictable world in which he will constantly find himself faced with unstructured situations. In dealing with such exigencies, he has little use for hard-and-fast principles of duty and conduct learned from his parents. He needs the ability to take care of himself, to make quick decisions, and to adapt quickly to many types of contingencies. In a slower world, parents could act as role models for their children, but the modern parent . . . can hope only to provide his children with the resources he needs to survive on his own. We should not be deceived by the "leeway" granted to their children by American parents. . . . Modern parents fulfill their obligations to the young precisely by refraining from the attempt to inculcate precepts and standards that would prove useless in a world where nothing is fixed. What looks like "abdication" is simply realism.[35]

Lasch slightly overstates his case inasmuch as corporate capital does remain permanently fixed in its collective organization of the contemporary family system. Nonetheless, one need only refer again to the innumerable commercial media texts ceaselessly beamed into the home, for example, to witness how corporate consciousness management can structure personal roles around ignoring one's parents, forgetting moral duty, dropping personal loyalty, and developing quick thinking in a continually changing world. Every ad for floor wax, patent medicine, junk food, or laundry soap that pits grandma, mom, and granddaughter against each other in pitched battles over the different virtues of the same household product, "renewed" and "improved" every generation to meet "new needs," leaves the granddaughter arrogantly castigating her elders for their obsolescent product loyalties or sternly rehabilitating the oldsters' consumer consciousness with new cultural cues for adapting to the rapidly changing contingencies of detergent technology.

Having briefly surveyed the structural transition from the bourgeois to the corporate family system, the underlying logic of "consummativity," with its ethic of personal development, needs to be further examined as the basis of the corporate family. The discussion that follows tentatively analyzes how consumption might serve as a means of social, political, and economic regulation.

CONSUMMATIVITY AND PERMISSIVE INDIVIDUALISM

Most conventional empirical analyses of consumption regard the creation and appropriation of consumable objects as a function of humankind's technological relationship to the environment. People supposedly manipulate the environment to create objects and processed materials that satisfy their innate human needs for material goods and services. Yet in actuality, this entire theory of consumption (if it is scientific theory and not pure ideology) grows out of a global tautology inasmuch as the objects (material goods and services) are defined completely by the subjects (innate human needs) and the human subjects are understood in terms of these material objects. In complex economies, therefore, humans conveniently realize that they need exactly what is manufactured and delivered to the "markets of free enterprise." At the same time, the manufacturers and sellers (amazingly) produce and ship those objects and services that fulfill the precise needs of the buyers.

Regrettably, these scientistic parables tautologically mystify the actual social logic behind these accounts. Clearly, such conventional sociological, psychological, or economic explanations of needs falsely "naturalizes the processes of exchange."[36] Thus the mode of consumption and production—which is always historically contrived, culturally guided, and economically controlled for the benefit of one group at the expense of other groups—is reduced to an ahistorical, noncultural, apolitical, and extra-economic "natural" process. In these economic myths, consumption consequently is like respiration: just as one must breathe, one must consume goods and services to satisfy needs that are as innate and uncontrollable as the body's need for oxygen.

Nothing could be further from reality. To counter such conventional explanations that naturalize the process of exchange, one must instead adduce interpretations of how politically fabricated systems of exchange commodify natural processes. At this point, sociology, psychology, and economics usually must be doubted because they serve as "both a dupe and an accomplice" by taking "the ideology of consumption for consumption itself."[37] Consequently, one must explore how corporate capital has reconstituted consumption itself as an ideology and a politics of consummativity, which pivots not upon the possessive individualism of entrepreneurial capital but rather upon the new forms of "permissive individualism."

The Basis of Permissive Individualism

The underlying social logic of consummativity under corporate capitalism never openly manifests itself. Instead, it is masked as a democratic social and economic revolution "rooted in the democratic alibi of universals" like religion, egalitarian humanism, or democratic populism. As Baudrillard suggests, consummativity presents itself "as a function of human needs, and thus a universal empirical function. Objects, goods, services, all this 'responds' to the universal motivations of the social and individual anthropos. On this basis one could even argue (the leitmotiv of the ideologues of consumption) that its function is to correct the social inequalities of a stratified society: confronting the hierarchy of power and social origins, there would be a democracy of leisure, of the expressway and the refrigerator."[38] In a sense, corporate capital poses as a sort of Jacobin vanguard presuming to speak on behalf of all oppressed consumers. In this guise, it challenges the stratification, inequality, and material deprivation of entrepreneurial capital with the promise of complete economic democracy, social equality, and material abundance—a pledge knit together from many skeins of new material goods, cultural objects, and social services.

The directing elites of corporate capital organize this democratic universalism within the framework of the service or welfare state to preserve their particular authority. Here "one only pretends to universalize the criteria and values of consumption in order to better assign the 'irresponsible' classes (without the power of decision) to consumption and thus to preserve the exclusive access of the directing classes to their powers."[39] The classic bourgeois public, stripped of its property and productive power in the collapse of competitive, local entrepreneurialism, thus loses its decision-making role as a political aggregate of private citizens, but acquires a new place as a passive corporate public exercising its power of choice in the democracy of consumption.

As a result, corporate capital generates new hierarchies in the economic democracy of mass consumption by developing different "consumption communities"[40] around distinct grades of material objects and services. Corporate capital increasingly produces very similar goods and services by using very similar techniques and structures planned out on a massive scale. This increasingly homogenized object world concomitantly is invested with rich, new heterogeneous symbolic/imaginary differentiations in order to distinguish the various relative grades within these consumption communities. In the final analysis, this highly politicized process of differentiating identical goods and services wholly pre-occupies the engineered consciousness of corporate capitalist production. As Baudrillard observes, "Thus the fetishization of the commodity is the fetishization of a product emptied of its concrete substance of labor and subjected to another type of labor, a labor of signification, that is, of coded abstraction (the production of differences and of sign values). It is an active, collective process of production and reproduction of a code, a system, invested with all the diverted, unbound desire separated out from the process of real labor. Thus, fetishism is actually attached to the sign object, the object eviscerated of its substance and history, and reduced to the state of marking a difference, epitomizing a whole system of differences."[41] Therefore, under corporate capital, consciousness-engineering industries spend millions of dollars and hours to carefully differentiate in sign values, for example, Cadillacs, Continentals, and Mercedes from Chevrolets, Fords, and Toyotas—objects that ultimately are artificially defined and symbolically differentiated identical products of corporate capital—that produce and reproduce this symbolic code of privilege in consumption.

By fabricating distinctive consumption communities, corporate capital also

> distinguishes those who are *in addition* privileged consumers, those for whom the prestige of consumption is in a way the usufruct of their fundamental privilege (cultural and political), from those who are *consecrated* to consumption, triumphantly resigning themselves to it as the very sign of their social relegation, those for whom consumption, the very profusion of goods and objects, marks the limit of their social chances, those for whom the demands for culture, social responsibility, and personal accomplishment are resolved into needs and absolved in the objects that satisfy them. In this perspective, which is not legible at the level of the apparent mechanisms, consumption and the *values* of consumption are defined as the very criterion of a new discrimination: adherence to these values as a new morality for the use of slaves.[42]

Consumption communities, then, internalize and reproduce the symbolic differentiation propagated by corporate capital in the familial, social, and cultural understandings of the community. A Cadillac or Mercedes community is markedly distinguishable in sign values from Mercury, Chevrolet, and Toyota communities. Those having Cadillacs or Mercedes display their sociopolitical decision-making power, expressed as wealth in consumption, which under this logic virtually requires them to own a luxury car as their special sign of power. Yet, those who only get to "choose" to buy (Mercuries, Chevrolets, or Toyotas) must be content to *enjoy* their highly structured choice, believing that it fills their needs and does so better than their neighbor's choice. In these mythological spaces, "all are free to dance and enjoy themselves, just as they have been free, since the historical neutralization of religion to join any of the innumerable sects. But freedom to choose an ideology—since ideology always reflects economic coercion—everywhere proves to be the freedom to choose what always is the same"; therefore, in accepting these symbolic alternatives, certain classes consign themselves to "finding their salvation in objects, consecrated to a social destiny of consumption and thus assigned to a slave morality (enjoyment, immorality, irresponsibility) as opposed to a master morality (responsibility and power)."[43] And in accepting these packaged forms of imposed consumption that are directly tied to "discretionary income" and "leisure time," which also are provided by the state and corporate capital, individuals purposely accept new kinds of responsibilities. In an important sense, they closely control themselves (or serve as complements of the administrative state), and they almost ceaselessly consume (or function as predictable units of production for the corporate sector).

Corporate capital purposely stimulates the propagation of consumption not as the rewarding outcome of material abundance in an affluent society, but rather as a constant investment in a new productive force. "The *consumption* of individuals," as Baudrillard states, "mediates the *productivity* of corporate capital; it becomes a productive force required by the functioning of the system itself, by its process of reproduction and survival. In other words, there are only these kinds of needs because the system of corporate production needs them. And the needs invested by the individual consumer today are just as essential to the order of production as the capital invested by the capitalist entrepreneur and the labor power invested in the wage laborer. It is *all* capital."[44] Under corporate capitalism, all individuals as "consumers" become capital assets in that their consummative mobilization directly boosts the productivity, profitability, and power of corporate capital's increasingly intensive industries.

Corporate capital, then, does not need to expand immediately into India or China or Africa as entrepreneurial capital did in order to sell simple goods to satisfy one set of unchanging organic needs for every individual there. Instead, it totally capitalizes these more "artificial" needs of affluent North American and European individuals by selling them three times, five times, ten times what they really need to survive as human beings. In America, 5 percent of the world populace uses nearly 35 percent of the world's material resources per annum because needs here have been "liberated" by advertising, planned obsolescence, organized waste, and regulated fashion to be six times as "consummative" as they should be in strictly equitable material terms. These changes express the shift from a "manufacturing base," in which factories sell only what they produce, to a "marketing base" under corporate capitalism, in which factories produce as much as their sales forces can successfully market.

In the consummative order of corporate capitalism, social "permissiveness" and the increasingly individualistic permissiveness which mediates the rationally organized exploitation of needs to increase productivity, acquire as much importance as that implied by ascetic self-discipline, personal frugality, and individual sacrifice under entrepreneurial capital. With "permissiveness," corporate capital finds

> the ultimate realization of the private individual as a productive force. The system of needs must wring liberty and pleasure from him as so many functional elements of the reproduction of the system of production and the relations of power that sanction it. It gives rise to these private functions according to the same principle of abstraction and radical "alienation" that was formerly (and still today) the case for his labor power. In this system, the "liberation" of needs, of consumers, of women, of the young, the body, etc., is always really the mobilization of needs, consumers, the body. . . . It is never an explosive liberation, but a controlled emancipation, a mobilization whose end is competitive exploitation.[45]

Under the logic of consummativity, as Marcuse also has noted, the individual's private space "has been invaded and whittled down by technological reality. Mass production and mass distribution claim the entire individual, and industrial psychology has long since ceased to be confined to the factory."[46] Instead, new technified forms of community and subjectivity are formed through the consumption of commodities, and the proper administration of this consumption allows the simultaneous management of many of the communal, emotional, and psychological relations between consumers.

For example, the contemporary organization of personal identity, group solidarity, and social history around the popular music, movies, television, or news events (which were rationally manufactured, consumed, and managed) of "the twenties," "the fifties," or "the sixties" has become a common means of turning everyday corporate life into communal ideology in order to lay claim to the consciousness of the individual members of these commodified temporal tribes. Increasingly, it is these corporate cultural mediations rather than the individuals' church, family, neighbors, or vocation which prescribe the correct behaviors, attitudes, values, and emotional styles for survival in a permissive, consummative society. As Marcuse sees, the consummative ideology eventually allows only the practice of more or less "one-dimensional" modes of thinking and behaving:

> The productive apparatus and the goods and services which it produces "sell" or impose the social system as a whole. The means of mass transportation and communication, the commodities of lodging, food, and clothing, the irresistible output of the entertainment and information industry carry with them prescribed attitudes and habits, certain intellectual and emotional reactions which bind the consumers more or less pleasantly to the producers and, through the latter, to the whole. The products indoctrinate and manipulate; they promote a false consciousness which is immune against its falsehood. And as these beneficial products become available to more individuals in more social classes, the indoctrination they carry ceases to be publicity; it becomes a way of life. It is a good way of life—much better than before—and as a good way of life, it militates against qualitative change. Thus emerges a pattern of one-dimensional thought and behavior in which ideas, aspirations, and objectives that, by their content, transcend the established universe of discourse and action are either repelled or reduced to terms of this universe. They are redefined by the rationality of the given system and of its quantitative extension.[47]

When put in this light, the impact of consummativity on family relations under the regime of corporate capitalism acquires new significance, particularly as one recognizes that contemporary "permissiveness" basically boils down to the packaged "liberation" of new needs for minorities, women, children, and oldsters as they are mobilized as new productive/consummative forces. Consummativity, then, implies the rise of permissive individualism; the commodification of needs transforms them into a dynamic productive force; and their elaboration and sophistication ramifies into new dimensions of goods and services that communicate the consummative ideology to new consuming groups. These new groups have been created by restructuring domestic reproduction to reveal new markets for the new objects and services "demanded" by these new consumers. Whereas entrepreneurial capital concentrated its consumer goods production on the child, the married or marriageable woman, and, most important, the man of the house, corporate capitalism, by its "expropriation of child rearing by the state and by the health and welfare professions,"[48] has constructed many new marketable needs to dynamicize productivity.

As one matures in the consummative society, professional experts and corporate provisions indicate that different needs exist for distinct phases of life. Since your "mother never told you" or your father never had that "man-to-man talk" with you, corporate capital constructs suitable codes to guide your behavior by and through commodities. Commercial media texts encourage us daily to "take care of yourself" because "you're worth it." Thus, investing correctly in the life cycle means acquiring the proper product packages and adopting the correct behavior scripts that guarantee "happiness" during all stages of consumer existence: infancy (which must be preceded by proper prenatal care from one's parents and the therapy industry), the preschool years, childhood, teenagerdom, young adulthood, young marriedness (or divorcedness, separatedness, singleness), productive maturity, new parenthood, middle-agedness, pre-retirement, retirement, the golden years, and, finally, death. Each segment of natural reproduction has been sliced up scientifically by marketing analysts and reconstituted as a field of consumer objects planned to satisfy the "innate needs" inculcated in the individual—in order to energize the industries that produce the requisite objects of satisfaction. Living and working in urban sprawl, people can fulfill many of these needs in the "commercial strips" lining the highways and byways of any metropolitan area. Yet each individual existence is ultimately reduced to a personal "strip of commerce" irregularly delimited in these chronologically and demographically defined regions of needs.

From Fordism to Fondaism

Within the corporate commodity system, human needs, as defined under this system, ultimately constitute the psychosocial character of the individual under corporate capitalism; "that is, the historical concept of a social being who, in the rupture of symbolic exchange, autonomizes him/herself and rationalizes his desire, his relation to others and to objects, in terms of needs, utility, satisfaction and use value."[49] In the last analysis, permissiveness can be closely equated with this tendency toward individuals forsaking the more symbolic moral exchange of the traditional bourgeois family in favor of corporate society's encouragements to "think of yourself," autonomizing the self and rationalizing its desire for material goods and services. Gaining liberation from the antiquated cultural, moral, religious, or symbolic expectations attached to the roles of being a "worker," a "farmer," a "woman," a "man," a "child," an "oldster," a "husband," a "wife," a "black," a "Latino," a "straight," or a "gay" allegedly enables individuals to act as "autonomous" persons "developing" their own unique identity and purpose.

Ironically, this peculiar developmental ethic, or "looking out for number one," could not be further from autonomy. Developing a unique personal identity and purpose under this cultural horizon essentially boils down to this: taking the prepackaged purposes imputed by one's income level or job or material possessions as an individual behavioral map for loosely programmed personal development. This development is defined in terms of accumulating standardized objects or consuming conventionalized experiences. "Far from the individual expressing his needs in the economic system," as Baudrillard argues, "it is the economic system that induces the individual function and parallel functionality of objects and needs." [50] The individual—whether the original emancipated one of liberal bourgeois "male liberation" or one cast in the more corporate capitalist forms of "minority group" liberation—ultimately remains "an ideological structure, a historical form correlative with the commodity form (exchange value), and the object form (use value)." [51]

Gradually mobilized individual needs permit corporate firms to mobilize human instincts simultaneously in "a kind of totally consuming immorality in which the individual finally submerges himself in a pleasure principle entirely controlled by production planning." [52] The processes of this submergence may begin with Disneyland, Bloomingdale's, or suburban malls, which are scientifically engineered to mobilize the play and pleasure instincts for profit. Yet in the absence of "antiquated" moral restrictions, production planners can as easily design more exciting packages like Club Med, Plato's Retreat, or *The Love Boat* to help modern individuals "find themselves," "get inside their heads," "explore their own space," "grow as persons," or "develop attitude." Nonetheless, real autonomy or true individuality has little to do with these highly administered forms of permissive individualism, which take their rationalized practical forms from the leisure industry and draw their theoretical legitimation from the ideology of mental health, sexual adjustment, and therapeutic intervention. [53]

Rather than upholding some universal standard of morality, responsibility, or authority, the professional experts adhere to their permissive therapeutic coda which releases children, mothers, and fathers from any strict moral discipline in favor of looser standards of personal behavior more loosely dictated by one's peer groups, commercial fashions, or flexible expert opinions. In turn, these new authoritative sources for guiding personal behavior key individuals into those conventionally acceptable needs that they can use both to liberate and dominate themselves simultaneously. By allowing outside forces to define and direct human instincts in a rational fashion, the family expedites the consummation of consummativity by abandoning its more locally or communally derived moral dictates, social organization, and expectations of responsibility. In submitting to the permissive directives of leisure planners, family psychologists, pediatricians, marriage counselors, home economists, and teachers, the family inculcates an individualist consciousness in its members that presumes personally instrumentalized choices in favor of individually rationalized goals. Consequently, "the family serves the social order even in the dissolution of its authority. It teaches the child his first lessons in the corruption of authority and thereby exposes him, at an impressionable age, to prevailing modes of social control."[54]

These tendencies toward passivity, dependence, and submission perhaps show up nowhere so well as in modern attitudes toward sexuality and the body. Gramsci, for example, recognized that this revolutionization of social control, which he called "Americanization,"[55] required new psycho-physical structures for personally allocating energy, commitment, and will. The crucial variable for organizing this transformation was sexuality. Specifically, "the formation of a new feminine personality is the most important question of an ethical and civil order connected with the sexual question."[56] Although Gramsci admitted that creating "a new sexual ethic suited to the new methods of production and work" would be "extremely complicated and difficult," he still argued that "the new type of man demanded by the rationalization of production and work cannot be developed until the sexual instinct has been suitably regulated and until it too has been rationalized."[57] Gramsci also foresaw that "Fordism"—or the consciously planned attempts by Henry Ford to authoritatively regulate his workers' lives in accordance with puritan bourgeois ethics through moralistic education, corporate inspectorates, and ethical policing—would fail because of its heavy-handed external direction of the working-class household.

Under the developmental logic of consummativity, as Gramsci anticipated, Americanization continues as an ongoing, evolving process. However, beyond Fordism, an even more subtle and effective means of rationalizing sexuality and regulating the use of the body has been constituted: by educating individuals to view themselves as appreciating or wasting "capital assets" in the corporate economy. The usefulness of individuals to the corporate system as a productive force also structures their responsibility for themselves as the ethics of permissiveness stipulate that above all else individuals must make "good" or "effective" use of themselves. While Fordism may have been appropriate for the productivist era of heavy industrial expansion, today's informational economy requires a more comprehensive approach. It might be best defined as "Fondaism," after Jane Fonda's well-known and widely imitated rational programs of comprehensive, individually tailored "workouts" that use specially designed, video-communicated diet, exercise, and mental-discipline techniques to manage one's mental, emotional, and physical assets rationally. With Fondaism, even the deepest personal insecurities and self-doubt can be reified, labeled, and then subjected to the commodified therapies of disciplinary retraining programs. Succinctly stated, through Fondaist physical- and mental-training philosophies, the logic of corporate capital unexpectedly provides its clients with a revolutionary form of worker and consumer "self-management" based on these new codes for personally managed sexuality, physical refinement of the body, and individually conducted psychic reeducation.

"*In the process of satisfaction*," Baudrillard maintains, the individual "valorizes and makes fruitful his own potentialities for pleasure; he 'realizes' and manages, to the best of his ability, his own 'faculty' of pleasure, treated literally like a productive force." [58] Thus, to use the asset of ourselves, we must successfully identify our productive capacity for physical pleasure and effectively manage our potentialities by acquiring the requisite technical skills and experience. With ultrasexualized and physically trained bodies, as self-managers we can plan our own needs, program our own goals, acquire the most efficient techniques, and realize our own personal profits after investing the necessary time and energy in the symbolic economy of commodified sexuality.

It perhaps is no accident that this peculiar "rediscovery" of the body comes with the consolidation of transnational corporate capitalism. The collectivization of tangible capital assets in corporate conglomerates attends the privatization of the body as personal capital, just as the scientific management of work rises hand in hand with the self-management of sexuality. In fact, the most powerful impetus toward male and female "sexual liberation" developed from the 1920s through the 1970s—as part of the new ideology of beauty, health, and romantic companionship[59]—following the contraction of the individual family's control over productive property in industry and commerce.

Sociologists, family psychologists, and moralists ironically have directed individuals to find true satisfaction in their "productive property," namely, the body and its sexuality. For example, Ernest Burgess could have been talking about private property and its personal satisfactions during this period when he declared that "love and marriage are essentially *personal* and *private* and are, perhaps, even more than other aspects of life to be *controlled by the individual*." [60] Actually, with the consolidation of corporate capital, individual sexuality has become the major aspect of life that individuals still can control, individualize, and manage—yet even that freedom has been intruded upon by the counseling and guidance of professional medical and social psychological experts.

Corporate capitalist womanhood and manhood, like any modern managerial appointed position defined in rational terms, necessarily evolved into "professions" demanding gradual mastery of proper techniques. Women were not to train as angels of consolation as much as they were to study as attractive enchantresses. Concentrating upon the personal accumulation of material objects and the individual enjoyment of capital-intensive experiences as a way of life quickly placed a material disincentive on raising large costly families; hence, the purpose of sexuality shifted from familial procreation to personal recreation. Avoiding the responsibilities of becoming a parent or the commitment of bearing a child, in turn, obviously demanded the intervention of medical experts to oversee the scientific planning of parenthood and the technical control of birth to allow individuals maximum utilization of their corporeal capital.

Womanhood especially proved quite demanding, since sociologists and psychologists essentially placed the ultimate responsibility for the sexual satisfaction of males on their female partners.[61] Nonetheless, as Gramsci forecasted, this new mode of female activity gained complete formal rationalization only as scientific, moral, and marketing experts generated the efficient techniques, proper procedures, and operating manuals for women to deal with childrearing, lovemaking, homemaking, and self-improvement in the consummative corporate order. Liberated from the arduous morality of the Victorian hearth, women now were encouraged to do exactly those things that their fathers had forbidden them or that their mothers had told them not to enjoy, all in order to dynamicize the corporate family system with planned pleasure and productive permissiveness.

Premarital sexuality and romance, then, once totally taboo, gained respectability as brief ventures of short-term capital utilization to prepare woman for the obligations of a long-term investment in marriage, which demanded sophisticated technical acumen to contine "the preservation of beauty under the penalty of emotional insecurity, the rendering of ego and libido satisfaction to the husband, the cultivation of social contacts advantageous to him, the maintenance of intellectual alertness, [and] the responsibility for exorcising the demon of boredom."[62] As the use of this new corporate capitalist formula for realizing life, liberty, and the pursuit of happiness has spread and developed, technical sexuality and the capital-intensive body have emerged as the vital means of profitably commodifying natural processes formerly left underdeveloped in the bourgeois family. Even the herpes and AIDS panics of the 1980s still have not really changed these trends; they simply have refocused their ends and means. As the newfound celebrity of condoms in the United States illustrates, new venereal disease plagues have further rationalized technical sexuality, imposing new imperatives of protection, screening, and therapy, which consumers must scrupulously heed in their sexual self-management. New dating services, singles' clubs, and certification procedures already are springing up to guarantee HIV-free partners to interested clients. While celibacy has been touted as the best policy in the late 1980s, public service ads depict the contents of a liberated woman's purse as including condoms among the car keys and checkbook—the caption, "Don't Go Out Without Your Rubbers."

As this new sense of private property has been extended to individuals for their enjoyment, the consummative order necessarily has had to provide increasingly looser writs of authority for their operational expansion and technical intensification in the cosmetic, health, diet, drug, leisure, and entertainment industries, and even through certain liberal segments of modern feminism. Sexuality itself ultimately has been submitted to a Taylorist logic of time/motion/energy analysis to maximize orgasmic potential and personal realization. Even though these technical refinements were launched originally within the confines of marriage, they are now being permissively liberalized for use with any possible partner of any sex, age, race, or class in order not to, of course, waste any individual's unique potential as a person. Moreover, once refined to such an extremely rationalized technical art, the sexual experience increasingly becomes ensnared in a pure exchange of mutual individual use. Under this horizon of personal self-management, for example, the marriage contracts of yuppies might specify how many times per week each partner is entitled to intercourse; gay males would score with multiple partners in one evening in urban bathhouses (at least until the AIDS panic finally took hold); and single female professionals might buy donated sperm to enjoy the "personal peak experience" of pregnancy and motherhood. Hence, in the era of Masters and Johnson or Dr. Ruth Westheimer, Henry Miller's classic goal of unencumbered "organ grinding" or Erica Jong's "zipless fuck" (arranged such that "no one is trying to prove anything or get anything out of anyone"[63]) seem to emerge as exemplary moments of permissive individualism under corporate capitalism. Clearly, the AIDS epidemic will modify these expectations; however, the remedies employed up to now emphasize still more rigorous "screening" and complex rigorous "personal protection" rather than the abolition of permissive individualism.

In the 1980s Fondaism and its many derivatives take these tendencies to their logical conclusion. Not only is sexuality reduced to a Taylorist logic of the time/motion/energy analysis, one's entire physical being, including all of its emotional and mental aspects, is fitted into physical-workout grids, cosmetic-surgery plans, stress-reduction routines, and power-thinking exercises. Scientific control and improvement of the body's physical appearance and structure at all ages places responsibility for a piece of society's collective capital on both men and women. To meet the rigorous demands of the global marketplace every personal asset must be mobilized and put into optimal operational condition. The proliferation of high-energy diets, weight-control exercises, beauty guidelines, "dress for success" codes, inspirational videos on entrepreneurialism, mental-training hints, stress-management technologies, pregnancy-training workouts, super-baby nuturing techniques, and emotional-management philosophies all reflect corporate capital's program for extending the logic of self-management into the deepest recesses of personal life under informational conditions of production. The scripting of behavior and the packaging of needs in the codes of commodification deploy these many complex Fondaist options to loosely fuse the conduct of each individual's everyday life with the agenda of corporate capital and the state. Thus, in the age of informationalism, even the United States military is forced to make slickly packaged, Fonda-like appeals to its potential male and female recruits, urging them to tap hidden personal potential by "aiming high" or to "be all that you can be" by joining the Army, Air Force, Navy, or Marines.

PERMISSIVE INDIVIDUALISM IN A CONSERVATIVE AGE

These means of cultivating passive consumption, social dependence, and cultural submission through the controlled emancipation of personal self-seeking and sensual fulfillment serve, in part at least, as the regulatory apparatus for managing personal and family life under corporate capitalism. The logic of consummativity effectively enables corporate marketing departments and the state's fiscal policy-makers to plan the level of aggregate demand and to manage the scope of specific demand for goods and services by turning the psychic need for these satisfactions into a dynamic productive asset.

By usurping much of the real decision-making power once held by families in entrepreneurial capitalist production and reproduction, professional experts employed by the firm and the state are increasingly able to regulate mass and individual behavior by reducing group autonomy and personal liberty to sets of highly structured, predetermined choices between varied menus of prepackaged material goods and conventionally scripted behavior options. In the choices they make, individuals collaboratively participate in their own social regulation as they seek to construct personal zones of expression as their escape. Again, turning to the mediascape, one can see telegenic expressions of such professional steering in the "disease of the week" or "psycho-socio-pathology of the week" docudramas depicting an "average American family" as it deals with breast cancer, Alzheimer's disease, incubator babies, leukemia, euthanasia, incest, abortion, drug addiction, religious cults, AIDS, wife abuse, birth defects, street crime, or alcoholism. The experts define for the family a range of correctly coded alternative choices and also refine the individual's choice-making ability, in terms of mastering these codes, through counseling, education, therapy, marketing, and gatekeeping. Accepting these choices amounts to submitting by default to the broad outlines of corporate and state regulation. Resistance is possible by creatively contesting the conditions of collaboration in one's personal zones of activity—or "the choices." Still, in the end, making the choices in accordance with the ideological management embedded within the pre-processed options continually reaffirms the values and practices of the new "consumption community" made possible by corporate capitalist production, in addition mobilizing the individual as a capital asset in the industrial cycle.

To allow the classic entrepreneurial family, with its peculiar organic ties and problematic emotional loyalties, to obstruct this regulatory logic ultimately becomes unacceptable for advanced corporate capitalism. When the continued productive elaboration of advanced capitalism might require greater emphasis on the "supply side" rather than the "demand side" in order to curtail consumption and augment capital accumulation, the culture industry can shift gears and partially rehabilitate traditional family values. Even as corporate advertising and marketing departments redefine psychosocial identities and personal goals from a "me generation" in the 1970s to a "we generation" in the 1990s, the productive system can continue the consummative logic of need definition by slightly refocusing its assumptions.

With no other substantive alternatives either within the prevailing regime (like antagonistic lower classes) or without (such as alienated outsiders), further progressive advance into the future has been keyed upon a selective recall of the *past*. The ongoing revision and reconstruction of modernity here can assume its own particular televisual forms of "premodern" traditionalism. Such teletraditional values are the matrix of an imperfect design for going "back to the future." And, as the mythic outlines of Reaganism have suggested, it is a "retro" past—formated in terms of Gilded-Age robber barons, social Darwinism, roaring-twenties economic booms, emergent industrial super-monopolies, and Calvin Coolidge's night-watchman state—which represents fragments of the old as new "traditional values" for a society intent upon building Stealth bombers, space stations, and the Strategic Defense Initiative.

In celebrating unrestricted capital accumulation and business power, this New (Gilded) Age—perhaps, more appropriately, the Era of the Platinum American Express Card—also has resurrected some of the more overt racist, sexist, class-biased, homophobic, and anti-environmental values that were deemphasized during the emancipation of outsiders in the 1960s and 1970s. Having destroyed the basic foundations of region-alistic entrepreneurial capitalism because they were limiting its opera-tions, transnational monopoly capital now tries to revitalize some of the cultural subassemblies from the traditions of liberal entrepreneurialism that always opposed mercantilist statism. Yet it must be remembered that such traditions are not entirely "traditional." They are unfolding as a new recombinant mix of neo-traditional beliefs that is much more suitable to the growth of transnational commerce in the coming century rather than to the interests of local petit-bourgeois entrepreneurs of the last century.

This shift back to entrepreneuralism and self-reliance redefines the im-portance of the family. Whereas modernist social engineering foresaw the eventual elimination of the family as an organic unit of social/financial/material reproduction, contemporary capital and the state ironically seem more committed to its resurrection. This commitment directly fol-lows from re-rationalization: if the state is no longer responsible for pro-viding jobs or key social services, and if the corporate sector can provide them only to those with the requisite skills or the funds to pay for them, then the family is again crucial as a center of moral education and a means of funding social infrastructure. In the 1960s and 1970s, the family suffered tremendous damage as a "swinging singles" life-style of permis-sive individualism was fostered in the marketplace in response to wom-en's liberation and the increasing inability of male wage earners alone to provide materially for a family. Of course, these conditions have not im-proved radically in the 1980s, but a number of social trends and media-driven campaigns all point back to a resurrection of the family in this new "we generation." Indeed, these tendencies seem certain to survive the Reagan era itself. As President Reagan's second term closed, both George Bush and Michael Dukakis sought to ride this wave of renewed cultural conservatism in adopting the rhetoric of "the family" during the 1988 campaign for the White House.

In the United States, the Age of Aquarius has turned into the Age of AIDS. Secular humanism, corporate consumerism, or state intervention are jointly or individually blamed for eroding the foundations of Ameri-can family life. The media fascination with AIDS, drugs, missing children, homelessness, the abortion and anti-abortion movements, third-wave feminist returns to domesticity, and yuppie child-rearing all can be, in part, connected back to the neoconservative designs of re-rationalizing capital to resurrect "traditional values" in postmodern family life. AIDS is portrayed as divine retribution or, at least, as the ironic result of tolerat-ing promiscuous heterosexual and homosexual practices, both allegedly anti-family in their inspiration. The Draconian designs of this cultural conservatism coldly suggest that if people only engaged in sex within marriage contracts (and perhaps then only for procreation), the AIDS pandemic would most likely disappear (once most of the Haitians are deported and all drug abusers live up to Nancy Reagan's "Great Refusal" and "Just Say No" slogan). Drug abuse is cast as a result of poor family life and normlessness induced by too much "secular humanism" in the mass media and in the welfare state's educational system. Reaffirming the virtues of traditional family living would soon contain the drug crisis. The missing-children crisis is alleged to be a result of the increase in divorce rates and the number of working mothers: if women stayed at home with their children and tended to their households, there would be no missing children and fewer divorces. The focus on homelessness also centers upon families failing to provide for their own nuclear members' care or their extended members' welfare.

The interest in postfeminist domesticity and yuppie childbearing provides new, Fondaist models for expressing individual initiative by system-affirming means. Women can choose, as rational moral agents, to embrace homemaking and motherhood as viable career options. Or they can choose to bridge a professional career with mothering—if they consume the right products and services. Yet, in the balance, they must spend more "quality time" with their offspring to keep the United States competitive with the Japanese. Fearing a "motherhood gap" with neo-Confucian cultures, collective capital also can deploy the diverse codes of Fondaism to reformat American family life as a demanding form of entrepreneurial/professional activity that all must excel at as relentlessly as they do at work in the marketplace: because American mothers and fathers fail their children, their parents, and their spouses, the United States falls behind in the world economy. Since the welfare state has dropped the ball and is leaving the field, it is now each individual's responsibility to police and provide for their own spheres of social reproduction. Driven professionalism, then, is to be taught to preschoolers and sustained as a critical personal ethic throughout their lifetimes. Collective capital wants disciplined, educated, self-sacrificing, motivated, but good-looking workers for its race in the global marketplace, and it is now every family's duty to produce them at lower social cost and with higher efficiencies.

Such cultural retrenchments are probably only temporary expedients (as in the "back to the family" counterrevolution against modern feminism in America during the depression of the 1930s and World War II) which, in turn, will energize fresh personal explorations into new and improved consummative developments once the crisis passes. Even if they fail and the United States remains permanently ensnared in its industrial decline, these same consummative programs will be needed to move imported Pacific Rim or European products in the U.S. market. Ultimately, the requirements of reproducing corporate capital set the basic tone and the outer limits of most individuals' activity, as either a progressive demand-side or a traditional supply-side function of capitalist productivity—under the social norms of permissive individualism encoded within the current modes of informationalization.

NOTES

1. See Christopher Lasch, *Haven in a Heartless World: The Family Beseiged* (New York: Basic Books, 1977).

2. See Stuart Ewen, *Captains of Consciousness: Advertising and the Social Roots of Consumer Culture* (New York: McGraw-Hill, 1976).

3. See Gillian Peele, *Religion and Reaction: The Right in Contemporary America* (Oxford: Oxford University Press, 1984), for more discussion.

4. See Paul Blumberg, *Inequality in an Age of Decline* (New York: Oxford University Press, 1980), 233, and the U.S. Department of Labor, Bureau of Labor Statistics, Special Labor Report 206, "Marital and Family Characteristics of the Labor Force in March 1976," *Monthly Labor Review,* June 1977.

5. Jean Baudrillard, *For a Critique of the Political Economy of the Sign* (St. Louis: Telos Press, 1981), 82–83.

6. For a discussion of intra-corporate planning and state-based macroeconomic management in advanced capitalist economies, see John Kenneth Galbraith, *The New Industrial State,* 3d ed. (New York: New American Library, 1978), 181–93, 202–12. Of course, business initially was opposed to Keynesian-style planning. Once World War II demonstrated that federal deficit spending could pull the economy out of economic depression, however, military and civilian deficit spending were used to manage America's macroeconomic performance after 1945. See Robert M. Collins, *The Business Response to Keynes, 1929–1964* (New York: Columbia University Press, 1981).

7. Eli Zaretsky, *Capitalism, the Family and Personal Life* (New York: Harper and Row, 1976), 29–32.

8. Galbraith, *New Industrial State,* 119–28.

9. See Timothy W. Luke, "The Origins of the Service State: On the Ironies of Intervention," in *Race, Politics, and Culture: Critical Essays on the Radicalism of the Sixties,* ed. Adolph Reed, Jr. (Westport, Conn.: Greenwood Press, 1985), 183–205.

10. See Immanuel Wallerstein, *The Modern World System* (New York: Academic Press, 1975).

11. Zaretsky, *Capitalism,* 114–15.

12. See Ralf Dahrendorf, *Class and Class Conflict in Industrial Society* (Stanford: Stanford University Press, 1958).

13. Zaretsky, *Capitalism*, 29.

14. Lasch, *Haven*, 6.

15. Zaretsky, *Capitalism*, 131.

16. Shulamith Firestone, *The Dialectic of Sex: The Case for Feminist Revolution* (New York: William Morrow and Company, 1970), 81–118.

17. Lasch, *Haven*, 41.

18. Ibid., 6–7.

19. See Juliet Mitchell, *Woman's Estate* (New York: Pantheon Books, 1971), 99–122; and Kate Millet, *Sexual Politics* (Garden City, N.Y.: Doubleday and Company, Inc., 1970), 61–108.

20. Sheila M. Rothman, *Woman's Proper Place: A History of Changing Ideals and Practices, 1870 to the Present* (New York: Basic Books, 1978), 18.

21. Quoted in Rothman, *Woman's Proper Place*, 22.

22. Ibid., 15.

23. Ibid., 21.

24. Ibid., 14.

25. See Daniel Bell, *The Cultural Contradictions of Capitalism* (New York: Basic Books, 1976).

26. Quoted in Rothman, *Woman's Proper Place*, 23.

27. Zaretsky, *Capitalism*, 65–77.

28. Ibid., 27.

29. See, for example, Harry Braverman, *Labor and Monopoly Capital: The Degradation of Work in the Twentieth Century* (New York: Monthly Review Press, 1974), and David Noble, *American by Design: Science, Technology and the Rise of Corporate Capitalism* (New York: Knopf, 1977).

30. Of course, a less "rational" path—namely, waging war on weaker colonial empires or semicapitalist economies on the capitalist periphery, like China, Ethiopia, Siam, or the Boer Republics—also presented itself as an alternative. Thus, Germany, Japan, Italy, and the United States pressed for continued colonial expansion despite their latecomer status as imperial powers. In turn, they sought concessions from weaker empires—Spain, Turkey, Russia, and China.

31. See Siegfried Gideon, *Mechanization Takes Command* (New York: Oxford University Press, 1948) and James Burnham, *The Managerial Revolution* (Bloomington: Indiana University Press, 1960).

32. Herbert Marcuse, *Counter-Revolution and Revolt* (Boston: Beacon Press, 1972), 11.

33. See Norman Furniss and Timothy Tilton, *The Case for the Welfare State: From Social Security to Social Equality* (Bloomington: Indiana University Press, 1977), 22–49.

34. See Morris Janowitz, *The Last Half-Century: Societal Change and Politics in America* (Chicago: University of Chicago Press, 1978), 320–63.

35. Lasch, *Haven*, 127–28.

36. Baudrillard, *Critique*, 72.

37. Ibid., 62.

38. Ibid., 58.

39. Ibid., 61.

40. Daniel Boorstin, *The Americans: The Democratic Experience* (New York: Vintage, 1973), 89–166.

41. Baudrillard, *Critique*, 93.

42. Ibid., 61.

43. Max Horkheimer and Theodor W. Adorno, *Dialectic of Enlightenment*, trans. John Cumming (New York: Seabury, 1972), 167, and Baudrillard, *Critique*, 62.

44. Ibid., 82.

45. Ibid., 85.

46. Hebert Marcuse, *One-Dimensional Man: Studies in the Ideology of Advanced Industrial Society* (Boston: Beacon Press, 1966), 10.

47. Ibid., 11–12.

48. Lasch, *Haven*, xvi.

49. Baudrillard, *Critique*, 136. On this point, Marcuse plainly identifies the dangers of reducing "liberty" to personal choice: "Under the rule of a repressive whole, liberty can be made into a powerful instrument of domination. The range of choice open to the individual is not the decisive factor in determining the degree of human freedom, but what can be chosen and what is chosen by the individual. The criterion for free choice can never be an absolute one, but neither is it entirely relative. Free election of masters does not abolish the masters or the slaves. Free choice among a wide variety of goods and services does not signify freedom if these goods and services sustain social controls over a life of toil and fear—that is, if they sustain alienation. And the spontaneous reproduction of superimposed needs by the individual does not establish autonomy; it only testifies to the efficacy of the controls" (*One-Dimensional Man*, 7–8).

50. Ibid., 133.

51. Ibid.

52. Ibid., 85.

53. Lasch, *Haven*, 167–89.

54. Ibid., 188.

55. Antonio Gramsci, *Selections from the Prison Notebooks*, ed. and trans. Quintin Hoare and Geoffrey Nowell Smith (New York: International Publishers, 1971), 293.

56. Ibid., 296.

57. Ibid., 296–97.

58. Baudrillard, *Critique*, 136.

59. Rothman, *Woman's Proper Place*, 177–218.

60. Quoted in Rothman, *Woman's Proper Place*, 180 (my italics).

61. For a fictional account of these sorts of expectations, see Marilyn French, *The Woman's Room* (New York: Summit Books, 1977).

62. Quoted in Rothman, *Woman's Proper Place*, 180.

63. See Erica Jong, *Fear of Flying, A Novel* (New York: Holt, Rinehart, and Winston, 1973), 14.

5

Discourses of Charisma and Televisual Electoral Politics

The 1980s are still a time of transition in American electoral politics. The republic continues to have one foot in the old party-based mode of electioneering as it steps with the other into a new media-based mode of electoral politics.[1] As a new cadre of professional political consultants sets about "wiring elections," the old ideals of a responsible two-party system of democracy are crumbling.[2] At the level of local municipal, county, and special district elections, along with races for the state legislature and even many House seats, the old machinery for party candidate selection and voter mobilization remains in place. Yet, for elections involving larger territorial units that encompass multiple-media markets, such as gubernatorial, U.S. Senate, and presidential elections, the new media-based mode of electioneering prevails. Increasingly it functions outside of the parties in new, paid-professional settings involving polling organizations, candidate political action commitees (PACs), and campaign consulting firms.[3]

This chapter, then, seeks to forge new generalizations about U.S. electoral politics, especially the new television-based modes of presidential campaigning. Even though traditional political ideology has been rapidly disappearing as a significant force in many voters' lives, the government, party, and media establishment act on television as if it still matters. Consequently, television simply cannot be portrayed as having merely an external impact or influence on political activity; instead, it must be interpreted *as* politics. Television has become the primary network through which scientifically rationalized communication techniques are used to exert influence over others. And it is the primary source of political information for many voters. The planned organization and management of televised spectacles accentuates the rational production and consumption of new variants of charismatic authority—usually called "image"—as part and parcel of marketing a winning candidate. Evidence drawn from recent U.S. presidential elections, especially the 1980 and 1984 campaigns, illustrates how these discourses of charisma dominate electioneering in modern democratic society.[4]

To expand on these arguments, this chapter first suggests that Weber's understanding of charismatic authority provides a useful model for analyzing televisual democratic electioneering. Second, it suggests how the emergence of informational production as a value-adding segment of economic life generates new techniques for rationally producing, distributing, consuming, and managing the products of charisma in political discourse through public opinion polling and televisual support building. Third, the analysis argues that electoral democracy at the national level is turning into a spectacular system, mediated almost exclusively through the electronic media rather than through face-to-face gatherings or bureaucratic mass institutions. Finally, it maintains that these new procedures of political practice are well suited to the informational regime of corporate capitalist society, but are ill-suited to the implementation of real democratic life on an equal popular basis.

A SOCIETY OF SPECTACLE?

The informationalization of America's advanced industrial society has greatly aided and abetted the operation of its national political institutions as a spectacular system. Partly accelerated by the internationalization of capital, by the state administration of science and technology as productive forces, and by the growing need to aesthetically and technologically intensify the process of production to remain competitive, informational modes of production, organization, and control are gradually displacing the old ones of industrial society. In particular, electronic media—and the complex codes of images they generate—have partially displaced large formal bureaucratic institutions as channels of personal identity, cultural communication, political administration, and social organization.

As Debord asserts, "In societies where modern conditions of production prevail, all of life presents itself as an immense accumulation of *spectacles*. Everything that was directly lived has moved away into a representation."[5] Life under informational conditions more and more is lived in the shadows of rationalized image rather than as the practice of prerational customs. In its concrete forms, as part of advertising, entertainment, the news media, propaganda, or consumer culture, these rationalized images of everyday life coalesce into complex cultural codes. These codes now broadly frame the "real time," "standards of living," or "quality time" of most consumers. Thus "the spectacle is the present model of socially dominant life. It is the omnipresent affirmation of the choice already made in production and its corollary consumption. The spectacle's form and content are identically the total justification of the existing system's conditions and goals."[6]

The information-intensive processes of this social regime cannot be dismissed as shadow play or mass deception. The spectacular society is a materialized, objectified lifeworld. "Lived reality," in the society of the spectacle, "is materially invaded by the contemplation of the spectacle while simultaneously absorbing the spectacular order, giving it positive cohesiveness. Objective reality is present on both sides. . . . Reality rises up within the spectacle, and the spectacle is real. This reciprocal alienation is the essence and the support of the existing society."[7] Accordingly, the spectacle grounds itself upon *image,* or the *"affirmation* of appearance and affirmation of all human, namely social life, as mere appearance."[8] As a result, corporate coded styles coexist with, and even at times prevail over, substantive communal meaning as the basic legitimation of human action.

The society of the spectacle has emerged during advanced industrialism as the logic of commodification has verged upon the complete occupation of everyday life; "not only is the relation to the commodity visible but it is all one sees: the world one sees is its world."[9] When virtually every aspect of existence is subject to rational calculation, efficient use criteria, and valorizing image intensification, spectacular image streams become the armature of social existence. When CNN promos assert "experience life on CNN," CBS ads declare "share the spirit," and NBC kickers claim "we are making tomorrow's memories today," these specific modes of spectacular production ironically reveal how the society of the spectacle *is* a social relation of people mediated by densely encoded images. In televisual America, the "real" world unfolds in the swarming dots of a twenty-five inch screen in trinitronic telereality.

The spectacular society thrives off the commodification of everything—images, ideas, values, history, policies, community, or power. "In the advanced regions," as Debord notes, "social space is invaded by a continuous superimposition of geological layers of commodities. At this point in the second industrial revolution, alienated consumption becomes for the masses a duty supplementary to alienated production."[10] Social science, in turn, plays a new role here in acting as the specialized producer of certain types of information to rationalize and guide this alienated consumption of codified culture. The scientific discourses of sociology, psychology, political science, macroeconomics, or the opinion survey all watch over the social and self-regulation of these processes. These sciences, closely if imperfectly, track the market shares, consumer satisfaction, and the velocity of circulation in relation to the political commodities produced and consumed in the spectacle.[11]

"When economic necessity," therefore, "is replaced by the necessity for boundless economic development, the satisfaction of primary human needs is defined by an uninterrupted fabrication of pseudo-needs which are reduced to the single pseudo-need of maintaining the reign of the autonomous economy."[12] Hence "the spectacle is a permanent opium war which aims to make people identify goods with commodities and satisfaction with survival that increases according to its own laws ... the real consumer becomes a consumer of illusions. The commodity is this factually real illusion, and the spectacle is its general manifestation."[13] It is a continual struggle to make this recognized in the larger culture. Many try to deny that such spectacles exert power in their lives. But however they might try to withdraw from identifying their needs and desires with these commodified realities, these forces increasingly underpin the range of practical possibilities in the larger culture. Working within these spectacular structures, then, average citizens/clients/consumers become a vital productive force as active consumers of images and products of both the economy and the state.

As its own product, a society based upon spectacle also continually elaborates its own new rules for self-presentation and self-understanding. The practices of democratic politics are no exception. Elections, in fact, are now the overarching icon of its commodified and packaged modes of democracy, the exclusive sign and signifier of democratic practice. Election forms and appearances, so closely monitored in all details by the news media, represent the spectacular sine qua non of democracy because they are all that is remembered from traditional democratic activity. Almost all the rest is rapidly disappearing in the wake of party de-alignment, declining participation, and citizen apathy. Formal scientific analyses of public opinion, electoral behavior, and political campaigning, therefore, have emerged in the past generation as specialized subsciences for the developing, if still imperfect, regulation of electorates. The voters' alienated consumption of prepackaged policies and opinions constitutes the target of electioneering. Yet such preformed political theater is not a deception; it is the essential organized reality of the political in its spectacular commodified forms. Democracy is no longer fully lived by the entire citizenry, but it is increasingly represented meticuloulsy in televised spectacles as if it were.

DISCOURSES OF CHARISMA AND THE SPECTACLE OF DEMOCRACY

Charismatic claims to authority become crucial in campaigns based upon spectacle. The interactive production and consumption by campaigners and voters of charismatic images during the state caucus and party primary process now substitute for an exclusively intraparty establishment nominating procedure.[14] In addition, the constantly shifting discourse of charisma also provides a justification for the voters' enthusiasm for candidates in the general election.

To fully understand the importance of charisma in contemporary electoral behavior, it is helpful to reexamine Weber's understanding of charismatic authority in modern society. He sensed the potential importance of charismatic appeals in American electoral politics before World War I. His thoughts about the charismatic leadership of bureaucratized political parties in Western representative democracies, in turn, provide useful points of departure for contemporary analysis. Weber uses the notion of charisma in the explicit sense of the word as a "gift of grace," which manifests itself as an extraordinary endowment of supernatural powers to an individual: "The term 'charisma' will be applied to a certain quality of an individual personality by virtue of which he is considered extraordinary and treated as endowed with supernatural, superhuman, or at least specifically exceptional powers or qualities. . . . What is alone important is how the individual is actually regarded by those subject to charismatic authority, by his 'followers' or 'disciples.'"[15] Charisma is not a personal trait or an attribute of personality. Rather, it is a collective recognition by the followers of the charismatic figure of his or her exceptional qualities, "which is decisive for the validity of charisma." As Weber contends, "Psychologically this recognition is a matter of complete personal devotion to the possessor of the quality, arising out of enthusiasm, or of despair and hope."[16] Therefore, charismatic authority tends to emerge only infrequently. It is a mode of *subjective legitimation* "born . . . of a belief in the mysterious gift of one man which that man shares with those who follow him."[17]

In modern settings, charisma has been reduced by many observers to a commonplace, like the personal allure frequently and mistakenly attributed in the popular press to unique personality traits of special individuals. While Weber admits that "charisma is fated to decline as permanent institutional structures develop," he also saw charisma as an integral if episodic element in modern forms of leadership, particularly in representative democracies.[18] "Not every modern method of choosing rulers, even in democratic societies, is free of all traces of charisma."[19] Weber regarded the West as somewhat unique inasmuch as the election of rulers in classical and medieval Europe had slowly evolved into many different representative popular democracies. In such regimes, the pre-modern traditions of rulers being popularly acclaimed by the ruled on some charismatic basis could develop into "a regular 'electoral procedure', with a 'right of suffrage' defined by rules, either direct or indirect, elections based on local constituencies or proportional representation, 'electoral classes' and 'electoral circles.'"[20]

These evolutionary tendencies in representative democracy have spread gradually throughout all of Western Europe, North America, Australia, and Japan. In his time, however, Weber considered the United States as having the most extensively developed "charismatic" electoral system because "even the formally supreme rulers are themselves elected, and there, of course, one of the most essential aspects of the business of an election is seen inside the 'nomination' campaigns of each of the two parties."[21] This mode of leadership selection accentuates the search for "real" signs of charismatic authority in American politics. The imperatives of influencing the masses on a nationwide scale and the costs of mounting a national campaign give both the primary campaigns and the general election a plebiscitary importance. In the United States's competitive two-party system, the various candidates are not only working for electoral victory, but they are also seeking the "recognition of a claimant as the personally qualified, charismatic ruler, either for the first time . . . or as a renewal."[22] Television has only accentuated these tendencies as the mediating institutions of storefront campaigns, volunteer canvassing, and local party organizations are eclipsed by electronic electioneering managed by media consultants and paid for with PAC money.

Historically, the availability of a well-regarded former governor, a war hero or popular patrician politician as a candidate—like Washington, Jackson, Grant, Roosevelt, or Eisenhower—could change the electoral equation. Weber notes, "If there is a 'hero' available, he seeks to break the domination of the party machine by imposing plebiscitary forms of designation, and in some cases by transforming the whole machinery of nomination. Whenever charisma gains the ascendancy in this way, it naturally runs up against the resistance of the normally dominant apparatus of the professional politicians, especially the bosses who organize leadership and finance and keep the party functioning and whose creatures the candidates usually are."[23] With television, however, candidates can work outside the traditional institutionalized parties, substituting their personal charisma for institutionalized bureaucratic resources. Similarly, the dynamics of televisually building a popular coalition or mass political following demand a new type of charismatic politics, even in advanced democratic societies. Television accentuates the plebiscitary mode. The initial models for this shift can be found in John F. Kennedy's 1960 campaign, and also Bobby Kennedy's or Eugene McCarthy's 1968 races for the Democratic nomination. However, Ronald Reagan's successful 1980 election campaign—beginning with the organization of his campaign PAC in December 1976 and based upon images from his years as General

Electric's corporate spokesman and Governor of California from 1966 to 1974—perhaps has finally set the mold for this style of democracy. Given the televisual network of communication, Weber's focus on charisma is even more crucial. Today, elections do not merely involve "a choice between candidates but a recognition of a pretender's claim to power." [24]

In this respect, American electoral campaigns now totally outclass all previous electoral processes that have gone before them. Weber observed in the early 1900s that presidential electioneering often "is purely emotional, on a level with party processions and festivals: the aim of all of these is to bring to the attention of the masses the idea of a party's power and certainty of victory and above all of the leader's charismatic qualification." [25] The medium of television has provided a perfect means for quantitatively expanding the element of spectacle, which compounds into a qualitative structural change. Televisual image production has institutionalized such forms of emotional influence over the electorate while structurally transcending bureaucratized party procedures. Rather than individuals proving their personal charisma in great crises, televisual sites of production continuously are generating a carefully coded aura of charismatic authority for potential nominees to public office. What Weber saw as glimmering episodic possibilities in the traditional American party structure, now have become a hegemonic fixture of contemporary electioneering in the United States.

As tokens of their charisma, the candidates' "look" or "feel" or "image" on television are displayed as cues to motivate or dissuade voters in the voting booths. As Diamond and Bates note, "what the voters want changes with time and events. Carter, inexperienced but decent, was right for the post-Watergate election of 1976. Reagan in 1980 was an idea whose time had come." [26] *Charisma* is the alienated objectification of the public's own aspirations returning to itself as image. Leaders self-select themselves for a plebiscitary affirmation in the polls, primaries, and party caucuses, which recognize not their formal claim on an office but rather the televisual legitimacy of their pretensions to power. Campaigners now try to capture fragments of the public's alienated aspirations to create their own aura of extraordinary powers, to whip up great popular excitement, and to command an emotional hero worship from the voters. No charismatic authority develops unless it is projected and recognized by the public in the spectacle's political theater. More flamboyant personalities, like Hubert Humphrey, John Connally, or Fred Harris, who could deliver barn-burner orations in packed lecture halls, did not gain telereal recognition of their gifts. Yet personally bland individuals, like Jimmy Carter, John Anderson, or Gary Hart, have drawn strong shares off of their telereal charisma, making them "charismatic." Even two almost completely colorless candidates—like George Bush and Michael Dukakis in 1988—could be given charismatic codings as "the most competent" or "experienced" managerial personalities with political talents "perfectly suited" for "the political challenges of the 1990s." After eight years of hyperreal prosperity under Reagan, the alienated aspirations of voters in the 1988 contest were reprojected back to them images of "experienced nonideological competence" in signs of their candidates' charisma. The informational means of production provide techniques to aesthetically intensify and symbolically enrich almost any individual candidate's apparent stand on the issues, personal character, or promise of electability as the markings of some charismatic difference.

TELEVISUAL DEMOCRATIC POLITICS IN AMERICA

Before further exploring political campaigning in the society of the spectacle, however, one must recognize that these televisual techniques have not entirely displaced or invalidated the traditional two-step communication process in mass political communications. Secondary reinforcement of mass media messages from friends, family, and local opinion leaders is still important. Face-to-face campaigning still predominates in the case of local or regional offices. The televisual electoral process is not a fully closed loop with guaranteed results arriving every time like clockwork; communication can be garbled. As the low ratings of recent national party conventions demonstrate, many voters simply "tune out" televised politics. Many voters simply choose to drop out, as the constantly falling rates of voter participation over the past generation illustrate. Old loyalties persist despite the new spectacular system of coalition building. There are still many "yellow-dog Democrats" and "dyed-in-the-wool" Republicans. Some voters still do try independently to judge the candidates' "effectiveness" apart from image. The telereal potential promised by former astronaut John Glenn in 1984 or TV evangelist Pat Robertson in 1988 also shows how early polling results can be wrong and how campaigning strategies often misfire. And as time has passed, voters have become more sophisticated about media imagery techniques and televisual discourse.

Nonetheless, the key linkage now in American democracy is the spectacular presentations of the electronic media, which are accessible to any viewer willing to participate by watching or listening. Most opinion leaders today play out their role as image critics or media commentators in everyday political discussions, highlighting or downplaying aspects of the spectacle's imagery. The reality of national politics is becoming the sound bites and film clips on the screen. Although this interpretation is imperfect, it leads into a more general model of this process that allows us to observe how and why electoral democracy is changing in the society of the spectacle.

Charismatic "Election" and the Electoral Process

The presentation of a charismatic aura today constitutes a separate new "election" process prior to the "electoral" process. As the institutionalized Democratic and Republican parties have taken a backseat to insurgent outsiders—who represent some nonbureaucratic, extra-party, mass movement–grounded effort to gain power—the production and consumption of charismatic authority as image seems increasingly significant in American politics as proof of one's "election" to wield power. Vague prefigurations of these trends are apparent in retrospect in Barry Goldwater's, Eugene McCarthy's, Robert Kennedy's, and George Wallace's campaigns as "new forces" outside of "party politics as usual" in 1964, 1968, and 1972. However, Jimmy Carter's and Ronald Reagan's successful "outsider" campaigns in 1976 and 1980 probably best exemplify the rational attempt to produce for mass consumption a charismatic image as part of the electoral cycle. Similarly, Reagan's 1984 re-election campaign continued this dynamic. Among the campaigns of the less successful contenders in both 1984 and 1988, Gary Hart's quest to be the candidate of "the baby boom" generation and Jesse Jackson's crusade to represent "the outsiders" of "a Rainbow Coalition" also might be seen as personal searches for popular "election."

In the post-Watergate environment of 1976 and 1980, Carter's struggle to show he was the best available instrument to create "a government as good as the American people" or Reagan's efforts to mount an anti–New Deal/Great Society "new beginning" were explicitly disconnected from the Vietnam- and Watergate-tainted political parties. Both candidates presented themselves directly to the voters as a personal package, challenging voters as consumers to attain collective greatness. "Why not the best?" was the subtext in both candidates' charismatic packaging. Both stressed their extra-party grasp of the "big issues" in American politics, and both underscored their unquestionable "electability" in the republic's hour of need. In addition, both stressed their "chosen" qualities in their individual personalities—their faith in born-again Christian values, their experience as important state governors, their unique knowledge as former engineers, farmers, veterans, labor leaders, and corporate spokesmen, and their untainted political records made outside of the mainstream parties and "Washington puzzle palaces." Here, televisual charisma comes into focus as the alienated spirit of the public embodied in a hero. In 1976 the public sought and chose an "outsider" hero to save itself from "Watergate/Vietnam." And in 1980 it chose another hero to save itself from "Iran/OPEC/inflation," who was renewed in 1984 for "four more years." The images of 1988's Democratic heroes were cast as a revival of 1960's "Boston-Austin axis" destined to save the public from "Central America/trade deficits/national debt," while the Republican ticket cast itself as a heroic defense against "tax-and-spend/Kennedy liberal/McGovern Democrats" in its near-landslide 1988 victory.

The intent of these charismatic discourses in the spectacle is plain. As Fiske and Hartley observe, "television discourse is not 'immutable' and 'impersonal' in nature, and its mode is the reverse of literate or formal logic: its mode is that of rhetoric. For instance, the television message is validated by its context, by the opposition of elements (often visual/verbal), and not the deductive requirements of the syllogism."[27] In the spectacle, saying and successfully showing oneself as charismatic "makes" one charismatic since verbal and visual cues reveal charisma in the act of claiming charisma. Carter's 1976 or Reagan's 1980 and 1984 acceptance in the polls, their primary victories, and their recognition in the news media served as signs to the public of their exceptional powers or qualities. Simultaneously, this popular recognition of their spectacularly mediated charisma constituted "proof" of their "elect" status, their gifts of grace, their "election" to stand for general election by the voting public. Without, and even despite, the mainstream Democratic and Republican parties' imprimatur, outsiders garnered widespread name recognition, high approval ratings, and firm support in the polls, which are the requirements for making genuine claims on having charismatic authority. Once the perpetual plebiscites of polling, or the state primaries, roll victories up in the outsiders' favor, the ensuing charismatic recognition can feed off its own production and consumption in the media.

Similarly, this sense of "election" can give voters a promised sign of greater gifts of grace in the general election. With an "elect" politician, the voters often can sum up their favorable views on the candidate in the "image," "feel," and "look" projected.[28] Hence, the symbolic struggle for charismatic authority increasingly emphasizes nuances in style, symbol management, and image cultivation, usually independent from any objective measure of effectiveness. In turn, hard or soft, strong or weak, warm or cold, open or closed, aloof or affable variations in styles are coded and decoded daily in the news media as being indicative of each candidates' leadership caliber, concern for the people, and approach to problems. Indeed, the range of voters' popular devotion and enthusiasm for candidates often rests on the politico's skillful or hapless effectiveness at simultaneously seeming warm, hard, strong, open, and affable in several different demographic markets. Given these dynamics, the candidates' body language, facial expressions, quirks of speech, and basic demeanor become much more important in the voters' calculations about whom to support. Changing them—as the defeat of the "old Nixon" in 1960 versus the victory of the "new Nixon" in 1968 suggests—to suit the coded expectations of the voters as media consumers is essential to even be a serious contender.

Arguably, electoral politics now is a popular docudrama in perpetual syndication. Even before the 1988 election really begins at the summer nominating conventions, the 1992 electoral cycle begins. Candidates and political leaders, then, are gradually transformed into celebrities or stars, who are "spectacular representations of a living human being . . . being a star means specializing in the *seemingly lived*," in the spectacular society.[29] The gaze of electronic media gives rise to pre-electoral scouting reports, tags potential charismatic recruits, and redshirts less promising walk-ons. In "working to stay informed," democratic citizens, as the *National Enquirer* records, "have enquiring minds"—and they want to know everything about their leaders as "stars." The ideological outlooks and policy stances of politicians pale in the shadow of the constant attention given to their cancer operations, peanut farms, golf-course goofs, crooked friends, cattle-ranch antics, or high-society wives. The "right stuff" is coming to mean "coping as stars" rather than excelling in rational political discourse. The gaze of television also continues after they leave office. Just as entertainment celebrities "exist to act out various styles of living and viewing society,"[30] politicos also act out the real political behaviors largely denied to the citizenry—participation, access, decision making, autonomous acting in the real arenas of power—along with their *People* magazine life-styles. Traditional democratic behaviors, then, for both the electorate and the elected, devolve into televisual systems. Candidates seek signs of their "elect" status in the new participatory behaviors of the silent majorities, who gain articulation by granting politicos their "election" to seek power and enact their alienated aspirations.

Polls as Perpetual Plebiscites

These participatory behaviors are particularly true of the perpetual plebiscite conducted in the polls on candidate popularity, image, and support. The two-party competition provides a constant "cola war" for the tastes of a "new generation" over how the parties' candidates constitute the ultimate "this is it" in politics. Getting more shelf space and keeping it longer means holding office more securely. Who leads, who trails; who dominates, who pales; who will be chosen, who will be rejected in the race to produce an electoral majority? Daily, weekly, and monthly, the polling process relentlessly scans many different demographic groups to answer these questions.

Polling segments the voters' consciousness into predefined categories and attributes, which provide useful handles for steering their preferences toward particular electoral outcomes desired by the campaigners. In turn, the modes of consciousness in these "focus groups" become independent variables in causal models of behavior management as pollsters probe the alienated aspirations of the public. Although the pollsters' techniques are inexact, probabilistic statements about different demographic groups can be made within given ranges of accuracy. Voters with x gender, racial, income, regional, ideological, or religious attributes will or will not vote yes or no for y candidate, issue, or image. Once these handles are fixed on the voters, pollsters can return periodically to turn them, monitoring how image presentations and symbol management have moved the populations with x, y, or z consciousness-attributes toward voting probabilities of a, b, or c levels on q, r, or s candidates and issues. Polls constantly seek to find the voters' "hot buttons" and tell campaigners how and when to push them.

Polling tracks how well or how poorly voters are experiencing their political lives on CNN, ABC, or PBS. Audience/market identification, definition, winning, and control is the goal of charismatic discourses in the media. Televisual politics must match the charismatic image. Otherwise, poor reception and disaffection may result if the televisual and actual realities are too contradictory.[31] Today's product must remain consistent with yesterday's and tomorrow's product. Retooling too rapidly a "new Mondale" or a "new Carter," as with "New Coke," is a dangerous gambit full of peril. Candidates must continue to look and sound like leaders, maintain their momentum, keep their support levels in the polls, and manage their images in accord with their behavior. If they do not, then their charismatic appeal can lose its shelf life. Televised reality is reality, and the voters respond to it that way. Recall McGovern's 100-percent support of Senator Eagleton and Eagleton's resignation from the ticket, President Ford's denial in the 1976 debates that Eastern Europe was under Soviet domination, Jimmy Carter's confused handling of the Iranian crisis, or Mondale's off-again/on-again switching of Democratic party chairmen during the 1984 party convention. All of these candidates were coded and decoded consistently in the media; namely, they were televised as looking ill-informed, indecisive, and ill-equipped as leaders. In societies based upon spectacle, televisual appearance constitutes political reality. Unless image managers can control this sort of damage—as they did with Reagan's comeback from his lackluster Louisville debate or with Mondale's claim of victory in the 1984 Super Tuesday primary marathon after taking only two states to Gary Hart's four—the negative imagery spoils the charismatic appearance of the candidate.

To an extent, polls can become circular systems feeding off their own findings. Ultimately, public opinion is a product with a very short shelf life; it must be perpetually remanufactured through ongoing surveys. Like the arms race, the energy crisis, the missing children problem, or the balance of payments deficit, it exists as a pseudo-event occurring at the artificially produced intersections of several statistical indices. From these mathematized montages, news commentators and campaign organizations make inferences about the meaning and importance of polls. The polls are treated as an imaginary mirror for the society of the spectacle to study its own features in. Yet in fact polls become another dimension in the self-constitution of the spectacle's features. Polls are produced to be consumed but are also consumed to be produced. One week, pollsters reveal to the polled their opinion distributions on certain key issues, and this action, in turn, partially redistributes the disposition of opinion the next week.

Polling introduces the voters as consultants en masse on the issues of the candidate's name recognition, command over loyalties, and types of demographic support. Having produced measurements of some blind spot in the spectacular packaging, the polling results serve as a targeting grid for new symbol-signing strategies and image intensification. New signs must suggest the right signified meanings in the opinions of the demographic universe under analysis. If Pat Caddell's theoretical 1984 "Candidate Smith" appeals to focus groups of baby-boomer yuppies in the Midwest, then some rhetoric reengineering and style shifts in Hart's campaign opened new fields of support for its candidate in Iowa.[32] If polls reveal Reagan's approval level slipping due to his bumbling 1984 debate performance in Louisville, then a snappy one-liner about Mondale's age in Kansas City puts the age and competence issue to bed for the rest of the campaign. On the next turn of the panel surveys, pollsters can find the fresh signing strategies suggesting the right signified outcomes in the voters' consciousness.

Polls therefore serve as a permanent electoral screen, asking voters continually to simulate their political choice as if they had to make it today. They can register any candidate's market shares for their image products, which are manufactured with careful advertising, sufficient funding, and well-timed media exposure. With this intervention into the montage of indices, a candidate can begin to gain recognition by being repeatedly recognized or can disappear as a discrete blip in other candidates' increasing series of approval and support. Every poll is simply a micro-election staged by professional analysts, and every election is ultimately the last macropoll affirming the data series of the previous multitude of micro-elections.

The News Media as a "Surrogate Electorate/Loyal Opposition"
The news media also serve as a surrogate electorate during much of any candidate's campaigning. The memory of the rational-activist citizen is kept imperfectly in circulation by the roving press corps. This relation is almost inescapable in spectacular societies inasmuch as the media construct and sustain the modern televisual mediascape. The media now, as the voters once did, attempt to pin down candidates' stands on the issues. News media personnel also constitute the core of opinion leadership in spectacular participation. They handicap the competing candidates in the electoral horse race, noting who leads, who lags, who is a sure bet, or who is a long shot. In seeking to make new "news," media personalities also work to extract pledges of policy direction, postelectoral responses to public problems, and assurances of state attention to pressing needs. Should the candidates backpedal on these promises or fail to deliver on their pledges, the news media also occasionally serve as electronic watchdogs, pointing out salient lapses in the candidates' memories. Periodically the news media even open direct lines of communication between the voters and the candidates on live talk shows or with phone-in formats in order to connect the voting public to the electoral competitors.

The news media now work face to face with politicos in the nation's videoplaces, and the viewing public must participate more remotely through the activities of this surrogate electronic electorate. Therefore, candidates recognize that media campaigning also presumes the critical subtext of "metacampaigning" aimed at the news media, which "is waged not so much to win public support as to convince the big contributors, party workers, reporters, and the other attentive political elites of the actual campaign's credibility."[33] Under these conditions, the political event or figure being covered is less important than the sort of coverage or presentation being obtained, which is actually the full event or actual figure being shown. The news media are not simply participant observers in the autonomous unfolding of political activity; they are instead observing participants. Their role as a surrogate electorate directly affects electoral campaigning and political action because the media's electronic images have become the definitive record of what is real.

The news media also portray themselves as a "loyal opposition." As electronic watchdogs with full-color, stereo, or videotape recall, the electronic news media can cast candidates as windbag politicos or struggling underdogs with a tone of voice, creative tape editing, or the arch of an eyebrow. The news media, then, to a very real extent, can help to create the data of public opinion surveys from focused coverage of candidates' finances, personal life, health, leadership, or political ties. For example, in 1984, President Reagan's apparent warlike cowboy image and Mondale's apparent inability to say no to special interests, as news-mediated political critique, grew from news organizations' documentary explorations of Reagan's off-the-cuff one-liners about the USSR and Mondale's response to party platform planks in San Francisco. In 1988 Gary Hart's "personal credibility" became the critical issue of his campaign when reporters documented his antics with Donna Rice. Pat Robertson's "competence" came into question as reporters confronted him with ridiculous utterances he made on videotape (about national defense and social policy, and on-the-air praying to turn hurricanes away from his tidewater Virginia home base) during his days as the host of "The 700 Club." Consequently, as party opposition to incumbent governments has waned with the bipartisan policies of postwar administrations, the viewing public in America accepts the news media as one surrogate for a loyal opposition. The substance of the news media and the stuff of the real are wholly intertwined. If an event occurs and it is not distributed widely in the media, then it basically does not occur. Correlatively, if a non-event occurs on the media, such as George Bush's offhand remark about "kicking ass" in the 1984 debate with Ferraro or Nancy Reagan's feeding answers about strategic weapons to the President, which were both inadvertently captured on undetected live mikes on otherwise slow news days, then it basically must become a significant happening in spectacular discourse, revealing "hidden dimensions" of the political race. The coverage, and not the story itself, becomes the story.

As a surrogate electorate, the news media therefore also have become a surrogate voice of the voters, articulating their concerns and interests in a standardized political code. In this regard, Noelle-Neumann notes, "The media provide people with the words and phrases they can use to defend a point of view. If people find no current, frequently repeated expressions for their point of view, they lapse into silence; they become effectively mute." [34] Without the media's codified political discourses on political issues and figures, which issue new tokens of discourse into circulation, the voters remain silent or at least are inarticulate in political discussion. For example, symbolic signatures—like Gary Hart's "New Ideas," Mondale's "Where's the Beef?," Glenn's "The Right Stuff," Jackson's "Rainbow Coalition," and Reagan's "New Beginning"—all were minted and circulated endlessly in the 1984 election coverage. Yet, only by adapting these tokens into their own outlooks can the voters forming the real electorate become "conversant" with the surrogate electorate's watchdogging, issue analysis, and pledge-extracting. In turn, voters can pass these tokens on to the pollsters, politicos, or reporters, when asked, which seals the cycle in the news media's role-playing as the real voters' surrogate voice. Once the president is shown on television to be "acting decisively" on Wednesday, when news media polling asks "Do you support the President?" on Friday, the polls anticipate and prefigure the response on Thursday and report that the level of popular support in the polls is climbing. The codification and commodification of opinions in the media markets through image-consuming reaffirms their spectacular valorization and returns them to the news media's ongoing production of new words and phrases in the spectacular public sphere. In turn, as Mark Alan Stamaty only half-jokingly maintains in his "Washingtoons," these stylized speech-acts circulate and affirm an entire lexicon of "rapid pacification fuzzwords."

The electronic media likewise package and present the mass rituals of democracy to everyone. Voters trek in real time to the actual polling places and then return to their screens and speakers to witness the democratic spectacular. They are its actors, who bring the electoral spectacle to its dramatic conclusion in telereal time in the stereophonic/trinitronic drama of the media. The final days and hours of the campaign are packaged as thrilling theater. State-by-state exit polls enable the making of accurate victory projections based on tiny segments of the electorate. Color graphics spin images of states end over end, dropping them on the side of the Democratic or Republican electoral vote roll call. The viewers accept new burdens of this kind of citizenship in democracy along with their roles as image consumers, symbol critics, and polling data points. Their only "exit" remains silence before pollsters and not voting on election day. "Loyalty" is shown by voting, watching, contributing money, listening, or volunteering time, while "voice" can be had in street corner encounters with pollsters or by wearing campaign buttons on one's lapel. Real democracy in face to face direct action at the local level or even in actual participation in significant national party affairs in a responsible two-party system are fading into history. Participatory democracy is sitting near the screen and speaker, cognizant of your part as a watcher. Spectacular democracy can fill the void with gavel-to-gavel coverage of televisual shows or a coast-to-coast pastiche of polling data translated into animated computer graphics. Television actually legitimates the elections's winners. Even though the electoral college will not convene for weeks in real time, American presidental elections can be called in telereal time before Hawaiian and Alaskan voting booths close election night in the society of the spectacle.

The memories of real democracy are played out in these television rituals. Citizenship is "being there," on and at the screen, as a player in the theater of polls, voting, and rallying. One acts and watches one's own actions in the final tallies—and thereby is a democratic participant. But, increasingly, political activity does not involve direct personal participation in rallies, marches, conventions, or caucuses; and in those instances when it does, direct participation occurs more and more as part of a scripted "studio audience" rather than as the expression of free participatory agents. Politics is lived as watching and listening to the electronic media. The "public sphere" is no longer the city square, an urban commons, city hall, or town meetings. It is instead a constantly shifting mediascape fused in the focal field of a remote Minicam broadcasting live to the viewers'/voters' television screens.

Political participation is "being a part" of political activity—but more vicariously and remotely. Signs and signing displace political discourse. Posting a partisan bumper sticker or being a dependable contributor on a direct mail list or wearing a political campaign button replaces engaging in political debate on city squares. Participation is like being a fan who votes favorably for media products by purchasing them, extolling their virtues, or wearing their iconic packaging. To be part of the movement, just buy its products, identify with its positive attributes, discount its negative qualities, and tout its appeal in one's personal sphere. Similarly, if a market researcher or political pollster asks for a voter's opinion, the political participant as fan can identify his or her name recognition or product knowledge on the "candidate as product" in a structured "taste test." In informationalizing democratic societies today, voting is consuming, and consistent voting is product or brand loyalty. Hence, watching and listening to the spectacle for new developments in product packaging and positioning in accordance with rationally organized imaging and symbol management constitutes a concrete form of political participation.

Campaign Imagery: Producing Charismatic Authority

Nonetheless, campaign imagery often is difficult to manage inasmuch as it passes through several different stages of production. Pollsters conduct surveys and visit with focus groups to assay the voters' particular concerns and current fascinations. With this information, campaign consultants produce a package of images that is then presented in paid media spots and cited in free news media coverage. The news media, in turn, produce a new stream of mediated images that are represented again to the campaigners and viewing public. Finally, audiences receive these multiple sets of symbolic presentations through paid and free media to interpret and absorb. Hence, campaign consultants must attempt rationally to manage what is presented to the media as free exposure and what is presented as paid presentations. They also must work to guide the news media's own presentations to its audiences and to steer the audiences' reception of these spectacular symbolic texts. And, last, they must gauge how the audiences represent their reception of these media messages to the news media, in opinion surveys, or in polls.

As the 1984 campaign revealed, the charismatic signs that candidates adopt in order to trigger the signified sense of leadership are usually tied to some mix of the big "issues," their personal "character," and their probable "electability." The gift of grace can be shown as belonging to one candidate instead of another because of that candidate's grasp on the "issues" facing the electorate. Gary Hart's "new ideas" theme or Walter Mondale's call to "the losers" in America mark this kind of charismatic construct. Another sign of charismatic authority is created through a presentation on the grounds of "character" traits that signify charismatic uniqueness. John Glenn's "astronaut/war hero/businessman/senator" imagery or Reagan's "leadership that works" approach illustrate this line of presentation. Signs of charismatic gifts also can be tied to a candidate's apparent probabilities of "electability." Being the probable choice of millions can give one "the grace" of the actual support of millions. Gary Hart's appeal to the rising generation of baby boomers, Mondale's exhortation of the long-gone New Deal coalition, Jesse Jackson's call for a "Rainbow Coalition," and Reagan's 1984 reenlistment of "everyone better off than they were four years ago" are incantations in the spectacular society for electable gifts of grace from the voting public. The campaign—as horse race—develops interactively as a spectacular confrontation between the competing charisma products all touting their special gifts of grace grounded in issue, character, and electability. The discourse of charisma in the media measures this rising charismatic appeal in opinion surveys and face-off polls.

In the 1984 campaign, for example, Ronald Reagan's media advisors, the "Tuesday team," manufactured a rich package of carefully chosen images to convey the president's charismatic authority. The televised reality of Reagan's spectacular texts were treated as reality by both the news media and the voting public. In turn, Reagan's campaign stood by its tele-realistic productions as the reality of 1984 in America. The voters chose to coproduce Reagan's products of prosperous hope in their imaginations rather than purchase Mondale's package of crisis-ridden gloom in the spectacular political market. Again, the voters (like consumers) functioned as a productive force, co-generating spectacularly intensified commodities in their imaginative desires. In this case, the commodity as a factually real illusion was very attractively packaged as "Springtime in

America, 1984," "Leadership That's Working," and "America is Back" to create the coalitions and voting blocs for a landslide. Those who validated these texts with their votes participated in Reagan's redefinition of the GOP's policies, electoral history and political agendas. Those who did not either remained outside the telereal coalition as Mondale backers or abstained.

Despite the worst recession since 1932, a total washout on foreign policy, substantially high unemployment, and growing federal budget deficits coupled with unprecedented balance-of-trade problems, the economic upturn of 1983–84 enabled the Tuesday team to package the realities of Reagan's first administration as a "telereal" American renaissance in the making. Consequently, Reagan's media presentations rarely referenced actual economic, political, or social events. Instead, they networked out of presidential "media events" or tapped into the telemythic self-understanding of the voting public, which has come to define itself over the past generation in new spectacular codes of comprehension. Correct political consciousness in 1984 was formated as the "feeling good" attitude of McDonald's commercials, "Mayberry, R.F.D." reruns, or Pepsi ads trumpeting the choice of a new generation. These forms also acknowledged that the successful product continuously must change. The crusading outsider coalition organized by the "man from Plains, Georgia," tapped into the populist attitudes in post-Watergate 1976 America. Reagan's 1980 presentation prefigured *Rambo* with images of a resurgent America that no tin-horn Third World dictator would dare push around. Likewise, a shadowy rerun of "new ideas," promising JFK-like vigor and Camelot II, filled both the Democratic and Republican 1988 programming schedules as Reagan's second term came to look more and more like Ike's second.

The eighteen-minute film, produced by the Tuesday team, which was broadcast simultaneously at the 1984 Dallas GOP convention and on the major television networks, typifies how the discourse of charisma affirms a candidate's "election" and builds electoral coalitions in the society of the spectacle.[35] In addition, clips from "The Film" were used repeatedly throughout the fall campaign. Reagan in these texts is connected with the conduct of everyday life, and the course of even ordinary daily events is made dependent upon retaining him as President. He is a central sign signifying the rebirth of America. Opening with images of sunrise over a farm, the film immediately moves into Reagan's 1981 inaugural oath of office, then into a stream of images: cowboys working in a corral, a worker at the bench, a paper boy, commuters, a flag-raising at a camp, the Capitol building at night with a flag, and, then, Reagan in the Oval Office remembering he is the custodian of a mighty institution as he recalls the meaning of America and the preceding images in its "new beginning." While he was "elected" by events and voters to rule, his charisma by itself was insufficient. The images humbly argue that he did not do it alone. He is merely the heroic human manifestation of America itself, which has annointed him along with his new team of staffers, Vice-President Bush, and a talented cabinet full of sacrificing men, who aid his extraordinary decisions and powers.

The narrative then turns again to an obviously "ordinary" man on the street. An actor, he looks totally staged yet completely "real" as he remarks that "the U.S.A. is back" with pride, newfound patriotism, and more jobs. This segment rehearses a line of reasoning for voters to rationalize their choice for president. Reagan, as the screen points out, is the moving force behind it all. The images imply that virtually all Americans are participating in this comeback, and all are invited to join again during 1984. More images of power and new growth follow: Niagara Falls, a child playfully running, a wedding party, people moving into a new house, welders at work, a farm in production, and the Statue of Liberty undergoing its face-lift while swathed in scaffolding. But this "new beginning" depends on the voters' continuing to purchase new products, like faith and patriotism, as the film returns to Reagan, who now is shown at a church service with the troops near the DMZ in Korea. Reagan intones that these are "wonderful young people in uniform" on "the frontiers of freedom" full of pride, esprit de corps, and a firm sense of duty. The image is clear: Reagan is a strong man, favoring a powerful defense and a growing economy to put America back on top. The film also reminds potential members of his coalition at their screens that inflation and the prime rate are down; home ownership, auto sales, and industrial production are rising. It then shows clips of Reagan talking on television, making his program clear and talking one-on-one nationwide with viewers in their living rooms. The narrative cements its coalition with more promises: The President will never cut social security; he cares for the ill and the old and for needy children. He keeps inflation down to protect older voters on fixed incomes and young families starting out. Again, the vital demographic subgroups and potential issue-group niches are assured and invited to participate in his coalition rather than Mondale's or Jackson's.

The text then cuts quickly to the March 1981 assassination attempt. Any great man could do what Reagan has done so far, the film hints, but only a truly extraordinary man with real gifts of God's favor could do all this after a nearly fatal shooting. Reagan directly comments that he did not know he had been shot, but jokes that as he was wheeled into the hospital, he had hoped his doctors were Republicans. And with melodramatic background music, he points out his own fortunate survival: God cared for and protected me. Stressing this gift of grace, he exclaims that from that fateful moment on, all of his time left belongs to the service of "someone else," or the Almighty himself. In turn, God's chosen agent, then, is shown on a sweep across the world. In quick cuts from points around the Pacific Rim, Reagan suggests he *is* "new ideas" in action, while Gary Hart is just talk. He knows the future of America lies in trade and peace with Japan, China, Korea, and our other Asian trading partners. Yet he also is mindful of America's historic ties to Europe, as the film shifts to Reagan at Pointe-du-Hoc in Normandy on June 6, 1984. Here, in the viewers' minds, he reaffirms that America has fought hard and sacrificed much—Reagan addressing veterans in a war cemetery in France— to create and protect the "freest society the world has ever known." Even so, as the image flow now returns Reagan to the Roosevelt Room in the White House with its military banners and sense of history, he assures everyone that he will work for peace and hopes no more battle streamers will hang from the battle flags framing him as commander in chief. Like the astounding cough-and-cold medicine ad in which an actor intones, "I am not a doctor, but I play one on TV," Reagan here implies "I am not the Emperor of the Western World, but I play one on TV." In turn, for continued relief, voters can prescribe for themselves "more Reagan" to remain secure.

Another cut assures the viewer that Reagan can "do it." Crossing billowing plains of grass and purple mountains in a rapid scan, the film shows Reagan back at his Santa Ynez mountain ranch. He rides, does ranch work, cuts wood—proving he is younger than his years and able to turn in another solid term of office. These images prove he is an activist president and vigorous man, rather than the napping pensioner his critics decry him as. Finally, as the background singing emphasizes an America of pride, in new fighting trim and committed to worthwhile values, Reagan is shown with his hands clasped in victory over his head, like Rocky in triumph, proclaiming "God Bless America." He asks with the humility of a God-gifted servant for the opportunity to continue the good works of the last three and a half years. At the convention, as the lights went up, the screen of "The Film" faded into "Reagan live," striding to the podium as if he materialized from the film.

The alienated desires of a new American coalition, seen as eighteen minutes of film, gained immediate objectification in this heroic individual. As political television's most consummate talking head, Reagan reiterated the key themes for his spectacular coalition, making these film images more telereal. Turning the verities of New Deal/Great Society electoral politics on their head, he asserted: The Democrats are now the party of fear, pessimism, and limits, while the Republicans are the rising movement of hope, confidence, and growth. While Mondale promises the old ideas of big government, tax and spend, and weak defenses, Reagan offered a vision of growth, individual freedom, and military might as the new ideas of the 1980s. Unlike the Democrats, the GOP remains pro-work, pro-growth, and pro-family; or, in other words, it is committed to America's "real values" and "true successes." The choice is clear: the Democrats or "America's Party." The image that President Reagan presented is the most potent one possible: the viewers' and voters' idealized image of themselves seen on the multiple screens that Reagan unrolls in their minds. The images may not be true, but the voters go for it because they *want* such artfully coded imagery to be true in their own decodings of its promise.[36]

Voter mobilization and coalition formation through self-suggestive imagery are the goals of this text. Reagan is presented indistinctly with many possible meanings in the Tuesday team's film. In turn, the film's many diverse audiences can construct their own satisfying gestalts from its symbolic narratives. The signifiers of power fuse freely with any signified in the voters' imaginations, masking the real referents of 1984 America with the telereal signs of charismatic Reaganism. Like an automobile commercial in which the buyers piece together images of the car with their own dreams of speed, freedom, and power to create personal utopias in the commodity form, "The Film" allows every voter to compose his or her own perfect image of the leader. Like the television pictures of Nancy Reagan at the Dallas Republican Convention waving to her husband on broadcast television, who is waving at her on closed-circuit television from an overhead screen, the viewers/voters use television images as campaign media managers do—to project the images that each wishes to see in self-affirming circularity.

Here is the power of the spectacle. The message of its political theater ultimately is made by and for the receiver. Each voter participates in producing, packaging, and consuming his or her own ideal candidate for president from the multiple icons of charismatic power that campaigners represent as images from the alienated aspirations of the electorate. Successful campaigners must retune their ideological programs to fit these menus of images if they are to capture the majority. Although their polling and marketing knowledge is not yet totally foolproof, the image-wrights also know, with increasingly high levels of certainty, *what* different groups of consumers receiving the images *want* to produce and *why* in their symbolic consumption. The correct entrées—power, vision, toughness, command, and compassion—are taped onto the media menu with the professional knowledge that the viewing public will "buy" them in their voting decisions. Hence, in the society of the spectacle, a multiplex, polyvalent political ideology is coproduced by the consuming public in a closely supervised setting at the television screen. With notions of freedom and popular choice inspired by corporate signatures like "7-Eleven, Freedom Waiting For You," "Oldsmobile, Can We Build One for You," or "Pepsi, the Choice of a New Generation," voters as consumers legitimate the electronic mode of democracy as they ratify or reject the packaged charisma of electoral candidates with their votes.

FROM PARTIES TO PACs, POLLS, AND PERSONALITIES

The advent of television, professional political consultants, and PACs during the period from the 1950s to the 1980s has completely transformed the rules of electoral politics in the United States. The ideals of a responsible party system for American democracy seem to be disappearing in a still ongoing party dealignment. A new inchoate electoral regime—predicated upon the extensive use of television as a mobilization, communication, and fund-raising structure—is rapidly taking its place. Whereas Weber saw the advent of charismatic authority in American electoral politics as the rare exception to the rule of bureaucratic party routines, televisual modes of electioneering coupled with the weakening of national party structures are turning charismatic challenges to party control into a new norm for electoral competition.

Under the old regime, war heroes or revolutionary figures had *real charisma.* Washington, Jefferson, Jackson, Lincoln, Grant, Teddy Roosevelt, and Eisenhower became candidates on the basis of their extraordinary political stature or military heroism. In the society of the spectacle, however, *telereal charisma* is rationally produced through marketing techniques by self-selected candidates to legitimate their pretensions to power. In fact, real military heroes, like John Glenn or Alexander Haig, have proven unable to translate their military achievements into charismatic authority. Instead, Ronald Reagan's charisma, fabricated during his stint with General Electric, Lee Iacocca's corporate-produced charisma, and Pat Robertson's "700 Club" charisma are now much better models for future candidates thinking about crossing over into the presidential markets in America's telereal democracy. Such charisma embodies promising, personal "American images" for viewers and voters to idealize themselves within. Beginning with JFK's dubious but aesthetically enhanced image as a war hero, serious author, and global statesman in 1960—and extending to Reagan's equally questionable symbolically intensified aura as a chosen redeemer for an America adrift on the dark seas of fear, pessimism, and limits in 1980 and 1984—this new mode of charismatic authority is gaining more leverage in America's democratic decision making.

The candidate rather than the party is crucial, because the alienated aspirations of the public are invested in televisual heroes. The party is still legally important in terms of getting on the ballot, and in some voters' minds remains an important attribute of the candidate. But with the post–1968 institutional reforms within both political parties, the candidates and their paid professional consultants are in command rather than the party bureaucracies. Ad hoc, single-purpose campaign organizations, frequently funded by a self-selected candidate's specialized political action committee, surface at the start of new electoral cycles to raise funds, hire professional consultants, conduct market-research polling, and engineer a charismatic image for the candidate. With the approach of the primaries or general election, the candidates' campaign organizations blitz the vital symbolic themes that their polling has uncovered as central in the voters' minds. Here, PACs are vital organizational adjuncts for campaigning in the society of the spectacle. PACs serve a vital mobilization function by attracting financial support and professional manpower in issue-group politics. Candidate-centered PACs can immediately provide the institutionalized visibility and monetary backing that political parties once afforded candidates. Only now, as the crowded field of seven Democratic and six Republican contenders in 1988 revealed, candidates can self-select themselves as potential leaders, while winning financial backing and political clout for their self-nomination from like-minded corporate, labor, and issue-group PACs.[37]

Media imaging and televisual symbol-massaging target the issue subgroups and demographic segments that precinct analysis, opinion surveys, or televised spots have identified or created as critical voting blocs. Volunteers, specifically mobilized to aid the campaign's candidate, move people to the balloting stations, take exit polls as voters leave, and canvass voters by telephone, urging them to vote. Whether paid professionals or unpaid volunteers, the campaigners ultimately are controlled by the candidate's campaign organization—for the benefit of the candidate rather than the party. The candidate's stand on the issues, media appeals, symbol usage, and voter identification gradually are both dealigned from party loyalties—as Ronald Reagan's use of traditionally Democratic party heroes, issues, and symbols illustrates. Instead, they increasingly are defined ad hoc by the results of professional experts' rational scientific analysis of polling data. Coalitions, issue positions, campaign themes, and electoral pledges emerge from opinion polls, symbol packaging, and PAC funding ties. By the 1990s, then, media managers are critical: "the addition of the right name expert to a campaign could give a certain credibility in the press's eyes, while movements of key people out of the candidate's organization were often read as signs of trouble or decay."[38] Public opinion and research on electoral behavior track the complex psychosocial needs shared by the voters, who accept the politicians' imagery and consume the theater of their own stylized activities. The discourse of political charisma is the outcome of these interacting discourses of the news media, the campaign organization, and the opinion survey. It enables the voters, electronic journalists, campaigners, professional pollsters, and the candidates to jointly manufacture the most timely and appropriate charismatic products of politics by refining the alienated spirit of the public into a loose package of images that voters eventually consume in the rituals of informational power: watching, volunteering, listening, polling, contributing, commenting, criticizing, and finally choosing.[39]

NOTES

1. See Walter Dean Burnham, *The Current Crisis in American Politics* (New York: Oxford University Press, 1982), 25–165. The media-driven political action committee (PAC) system of elite-controlled campaign financing simply expresses how the commodification of mobilizing public support and the targeting of new policy concerns works today. Candidate campaign organizations and parties (in part) function as entrepreneurial agents that sell policies and choices in the form of candidates to other organizations and to firms and individual voters. In exchange for receiving support for their policy agendas from candidates, elite groups invest cash, in the form of campaign contributions, in politicians. For a parallel formulation, see Thomas Ferguson, "Party Realignment and American Industrial Structure: The Investment Theory of Parties in Historical Perspective," in *Research in Political Economy* 6 (1983): 1–82.

2. See Thomas Ferguson and Joel Rogers, *Right Turn: The Decline of the Democrats and the Future of American Politics* (New York: Hill and Wang, 1985), and Thomas Ferguson and Joel Rogers, eds., *The Hidden Election* (New York: Pantheon, 1981).

3. See F. Christopher Atherton, *Media Politics* (Lexington, Mass.: Lexington Books, 1984); Kathleen Hall Jamieson, *Packaging the Presidency: A History and Criticism of Presidential Campaign Advertising* (New York: Oxford University Press, 1984); Harold Mendelsohn and Irving Crespi, *Polls, Television and the New Politics* (Scranton, Penn.: Chandler Publishing Co., 1970); Elisabeth Noelle-Neumann, *The Spiral of Silence: Public Opinion—Our Social Skin* (Chicago: University of Chicago Press, 1984); Thomas E. Patterson, *The New Media Election: How Americans Choose Their President* (New York: Praeger, 1980); Larry J. Sabato, *The Rise of Political Consultants: New Ways of Winning Elections*

(New York: Basic, 1981); and Austin Ranney, *Channels of Power: The Impact of Television on American Politics* (New York: Basic/American Enterprise Institute, 1983).

4. Such tendencies have emerged clearly since only the late 1950s, and they still apply most fully in the United States. Some dimensions of this analysis might also be useful for understanding senatorial, congressional, or gubernatorial campaigning in the larger states of the union or in major urban media markets. Similarly, the employment of rational techniques to develop a consumable discourse of charisma is spreading transnationally as well. Hence insights drawn from these American precedents increasingly seem applicable to televisual modes of politics in Canada, Europe, or the Third World. In Great Britain, for example, Labor's Neil Kinnock was packaged in a ten-minute film for the 1987 election entitled, "Kinnock," by Hugh Hudson and Colin Welland, who both worked on the movie *Chariots of Fire.* This American-style televisual tool apparently turned what might have been a Conservative landslide into a much closer race for control of the government. For additional discussion, see Sabato, *The Rise of Political Consultants;* Atherton, *Media Politics;* Harold Mendeljohn and Irving Crespi, *Polls, Television and the New Politics;* and John M. Russunello, "The Making of the President . . . In the Phillipines, Venezuela, France . . . ," *Public Opinion* 9, no. 1 (1986): 10–12.

5. Guy Debord, *Society of the Spectacle* (Detroit: Red & Black, 1982), no. 1.

6. Ibid., no. 6.

7. Ibid., no. 8.

8. Ibid., no. 10.

9. Ibid., no. 42.

10. Ibid.

11. In this regard, Baudrillard observes: "The political sphere also survives by a credibility hypothesis, namely that the masses are permeable to action and to discourse, that they hold an opinion, that they are present behind the surveys and statistics. It is at this price alone that the political class can still believe that it speaks and that it is politically heard. Even though the political has long been the agent of nothing but spectacle on the screen of private life. Digested as a form of entertainment, half-sports, half-games (see the winning ticket in American elections, or election evenings on radio or TV); like those old comedies of some time now, the electoral game has been akin to TV game shows in the consciousness of the people. The latter, who have always served as alibi and as supernumerary on the political stage, avenge themselves by treating as a theatrical performance the political scene and its actors. The people have become a public. It is the football match or film or cartoon which serve as models for their perception of the political sphere. The people even enjoy day to day, like a home movie, the fluctuations of their own opinions in the daily opinion polls. Nothing in all this engages any responsibility." See Jean Baudrillard, *In the Shadow of the Silent Majorities . . . or the End of the Social And Other Essays* (New York: Semiotext(e), 1983), 37–38.

12. Debord, *Society of the Spectacle,* no. 50.

13. Ibid., nos. 44 and 47.

14. See Edwin Diamond and Stephen Bates, *The Spot: The Rise of Political Advertising on Television* (Cambridge, Mass.: MIT Press, 1984), 373–85.

15. Max Weber, *Economy and Society,* vol. I, ed. Guenther Roth and Claus Wittich (Berkeley: University of California Press, 1978), 241–42.

16. Ibid., 242.

17. Reinhard Bendix, "Charismatic Leadership," in *Scholarship and Partisanship: Essays on Max Weber,* ed. Reinhard Bendix and Guenther Roth (Berkeley: University of California Press, 1971), 187.

18. Max Weber, "The Nature of Charismatic Domination," *Weber: Selections in Translation,* ed. W. G. Runciman (Cambridge: Cambridge University Press, 1978), 248.

19. Ibid., 241.

20. Ibid., 242.

21. Ibid.

22. Ibid., 241.

23. Ibid., 247.

24. Ibid., 244.

25. Ibid., 245.

26. Diamond and Bates, *The Spot,* 284.

27. John Fiske and John Hartley, *Reading Television* (London: Methuen, 1978), 117. These modes of argument have reduced the typical political ad from the 30-minute speech (in the 1952 presidential campaign) to the 30-second spot (in the 1980 and 1984 elections). See also Jamieson, *Packaging the Presidency,* 446–53.

28. This fusion of political consumption and nonpolitical consumption is clearly revealed in President Reagan's 1984 campaign advertising. In one text, entitled "America is Back," images of everyday life flow along with this voice-over: "In a town not too far from where you live, a young family has just moved into a new home. Three years ago, even the smallest house seemed completely out of reach. Right down the street, one of the neighbors has just bought himself a new car, with all the options. The factory down by the river is working again. Not long ago, people were saying it probably would be closed forever. Just about every place you look, things are looking up. Life is better. America is back. And people have a sense of pride they never felt they'd feel again. And so it's not surprising that just about everyone in town is thinking the same thing. Now that our country is turning around, why would we ever turn back?" (Germond and Witcover, *Wake Us,* 477). In another text, titled "It's Morning Again," the narration asserts: "It's morning again in America. Today, more men and women will go to work than ever before in our country's history. With interest rates at about half the record height of 1980, nearly two thousand families today will buy new homes, more than at any time in the past four years. This afternoon, sixty-five hundred men and women will be married, and with inflation at less than half of what it was just four years ago, they can look forward with confidence. It's morning again in America. And under the leadership of President Reagan our country

is stronger, and prouder, and better. Why would we ever want to return to where we were less than four short years ago?" (Germond and Witcover, 478). The political campaign symbols intermingle buying new cars (with all the options), moving into bigger houses, and starting new families with the product, "leadership that's working"—President Reagan. Here the political commodity and commercial commodity are indistinguishable in the spectacle, and the spectacle's survival is tied contingently to the consumer's/voter's acceptance of a political commodity that reputedly outshines its competitors. Just as consumers bought into GE's all-electric "House of the Future" with Reagan in the 1950s, they now could opt with Reagan in the 1980s for a promising "America of the Future."

29. Debord, *Society of the Spectacle,* no. 60.

30. Ibid.

31. Diamond and Bates, *The Spot,* 247.

32. Polling the voters in during 1983 and 1984, Caddell found a great deal of "unfocused interest" in the electorate for a "new ideas" program within the Democratic party. Creating a fictional "Candidate Smith," Caddell ran the concept of "new ideas in the Democratic leadership" in the polls with great success. In turn, political life imitated this political art. "Caddell's findings," Hart said later, "documented empirically what I had felt intuitively in 1982 and 1983. I didn't become Smith, I was Smith" (Germond and Witcover, *Wake Us,* 132). Yet Hart failed to see, as Caddell argued to him, that "this movie is not called *The Lone Ranger.* This movie should be called *The Return of the Magnificent Seven.* And you get to be Yul Brynner. . . . It is a generation coming back to get involved again," (Germond and Witcover, 134).

33. Diamond and Bates, *The Spot,* 6.

34. Noelle-Neumann, *The Spiral of Silence,* 173.

35. In this view, Richard Darman, Reagan's image manager in 1984, asserted that the president's charismatic authority must be videographically packaged as the iconic summation of America itself. Thus, "Reagan would seek reelection less on the detail of his performance or his platform than on the atmospherics of that second Era of Good Feeling he had helped bring to life. 'Paint Mondale as (a) weak, (b) a creature of special interests, (c) old-style, (d) unprincipled, (e) soft in his defense of freedom, patriotic values, American interests, (f) in short, Carter II,'" Darman had written in June. "Paint RR as the personification of all that is right with, or heroized by, America. Leave Mondale in a position where an attack on Reagan is tantamount to an attack on America's idealized image of itself— where a vote against Reagan is, in some subliminal sense, a vote against a mythic 'AMERICA'" (Peter Goldman and Tony Fuller, *The Quest for the Presidency 1984* New York: Bantam, 1985, 247).

This insight into the GOP's 1984 strategy clearly reveals how political consultants do approach charisma as an alienated objectification of national spirit returned to politics as the imaginary coding of political heroes or incumbent officeholders.

36. The aesthetic allure of the Reagan commodity clearly proved very compelling. As one convinced voter assured the press, "I think he's [Reagan] just

doggone honest. It's remarkable. He's been on television—what I have heard, about 26 times, talking to us about what he's doing? Now he's not doing that for any other reason than to make real clear. And, if anybody has any question about where he's headed, it's their fault. Maybe they don't have a television" (cited in Dudley Clendinen, "Actor as President: Half-Hour Commerical Wraps Him in Advertising's Best," *The New York Times,* Sept. 14, 1984, A18). Even the average voter "recognizes" that the television screen is today's "public sphere," flows along in the mediascape, and, ironically, perceives that access to a TV is a necessary requisite for political participation in this sort of mass politics.

Reagan's 1980 and 1984 victories provided lessons which the Democrats learned well. The copycat 1988 Democratic Convention in Atlanta shows that both parties have accepted these imperatives of televisual campaigning. Most major speakers in Atlanta were introduced by a video, and when they spoke into the camera, the television networks often would match the speaker's mentioning of "family" or "the downtrodden" with brief cutaways to a woman delegate with a baby, for example, or to a Native American, Hispanic, or black delegate.

The 1988 Republican Convention in New Orleans continued Reagan's televisual style of campaigning. A powerful video summation of the entire Reagan era served as the prologue to Reagan's farewell speech to the party, and a new campaign film introduced George Bush to the nation as a war hero, businessman, accomplished public servant, and loyal vice-president. Playing off of its images, Bush then delivered what most observers considered to be the best political speech of his entire career as he called for "a kinder, gentler America" in the 1990s. Still, given the completely staged quality of these video productions, many have called for putting an end to the traditional political conventions, arguing that they were becoming nothing but summer miniseries entirely staged for the television cameras. In fact, as the means of communicating their agendas to the nation, the parties might as well just substitute their candidates' videos for the broadcast of convention proceedings since the videos with the candidates' acceptance speeches are becoming the centerpieces of the entire show.

37. See Ferguson and Rogers, *Right Turn,* 114–222.

38. Diamond and Bates, *The Spot,* 258.

39. As Jamieson concludes, political ads play a critical system-affirming function: "Still, if political advertising did not exist we would have to invent it. Political advertising legitimizes our political institutions by affirming that change is possible within the political system, that the president can effect change, that votes can make a difference. As a result, advertising channels discontent into the avenues provided by the government and acts as a safety valve for pressures that might otherwise turn against the system to demand its substantial modification or overthrow. Political advertising does this, in part, by underscoring the power of the ballot. Your vote makes a difference, it says, at the same time as its carefully targeted messages imply that the votes that would go to the opponent are best left uncast. Political ads affirm that the country is great, has a future, is respected. The contest they reflect is over who should be elected, not over whether there should be an election. The very existence of the contest suggests that there is a

choice, that the voter's selection of one candidate over the other will make a difference. Ads also define the problems we face and assure us that there are solutions. If there are no solutions a candidate would speak that truth at great risk" (Jamieson, *Packaging the Presidency*, 452–53).

6

History as an Ideopolitical Commodity: The 1984 D-Day Spectacle

In the advanced capitalist societies of North America and Western Europe, as the preceding chapters have held, the conditions of modern informational production package ideology in everyday life "as an immense accumulation of spectacles," fabricated continuously from the mythologies of the mass media.[1] "The spectacle," as Debord affirms, "is not a collection of images, but a social relation among people, mediated by images."[2] As ideologies, these social relations are continuously coded and recoded in streams of images, creating a peculiar political discourse within and about the regime of transnational corporate society. Yet these spectacles are difficult to discuss inasmuch as their modes of presentation continuously revise or erase major segments of their configurations.

Pursuing the arguments of Chapters 2 and 3, this chapter will illustrate that nothing really is fixed permanently in the society of the spectacle except perhaps the image-intensification of social relations. The importance of particular constellations of signs is illustrated by the symbolic packaging of the D-Day ritual in 1984. Moreover, like classic rock concerts or great final sports matches, these images can be screened up for perpetual citation at future political anniversaries, international summits, or bilateral meetings that might need some heroic recall of transnational Western unity. To understand fully how these shifting ideologies can operate, one must take a case in point, like the 1984 D-Day spectacle, and dismantle its image clusters to reveal how social meaning, political purpose, and collective legitimacy are manufactured. This mode of critiquing ideology might allow one to judge who dominates whom and how that domination is created under the present regime of transnational corporate capitalism.

THE D-DAY SPECTACLE AS AN IDEOPOLITICAL COMMODITY

D-Day is History. It is "history," however, repackaged in the forms of the post–World War II transnational system prevailing within the EEC/NATO/ OECD nations. For the United States in 1984, Operation Overlord has not been simply "remembered" in *Time, Newsweek,* and *U.S. News,* or ABC, NBC, and CBS—it has been remanufactured and renovated for sale as an ideopolitical commodity in the psychosocial markets of the 1980s. In reexamining the texts of D-Day on the video screen, and reevaluating the codes of World War II in print layouts, one sees continuities being manufactured that otherwise would not exist. On one hand, there is June 6, 1944/The Normandy Invasion/D-Day: The Sixth of June, 1944/The Longest Day. These shards of time past are densely enscribed with hieroglyphs of origins and ends. They signal that D-Day then was *the* critical *event* in modern history, the spectacular drama of the Western Allies assailing Hitler's *Festung Europa* in pitched battle on an unprecedented scale. And on the other hand, there is June 6, 1984/The Normandy Beaches/D-Day: The Sixth of June + 40 years/Remembering The Longest Day. These tracks in the present are also complexly coded with images of origins and ends. They indicate that D-Day now is *the* ultimate *pseudo-event,* the dramatized spectacles of the Western Allies—discreetly, for this occasion, minus Prime Minister Nakasone, Chancellor Kohl, and Prime Minister Craxi—reaffirming the icons, illusions, and images of 1944 to answer the challenges of 1984.

Take as evidence, for example, how the covers of *Time* and *Newsweek* for their "D-Day + 40 years" editions interlock the imagery of the ongoing D-Day spectacles. As spectacle consumers, we look down the open bay of an LCI (Landing Craft Infantry) in 1944 on *Time's* May 29, 1984, cover. A gaggle of GIs jumps off this landing craft's ramp, wading into the battle on the beach, which is littered with debris, detonating shells, and dead American infantrymen. The photographer/viewer/consumer looks out of the empty LCI, which frames the birth pangs of the post–World War II world in the smoke of the Allies' Great Crusade and the Nazi defeat. Again, as spectacle consumers, we look up at a headstone cross in 1984 on *Newsweek's* June 11, 1984, cover. The dead and the survivors (divided on the ramp of *Time's* LCI) are reunited four decades later in *Newsweek's* Normandy cemetery between the signals of transatlantic security—an American veteran kneels between tiny American and French flags at an American grave in France. The photographer/viewer/consumer is looked in at from the headstone, which crosshairs simultaneously the signs of sacrifice in Ike's Great Crusade and the comfortable prosperity his victories made possible. As these signs indicate, "the spectacle presents itself simultaneously as all of society, as part of society, and as an *instrument of unification.*"[3]

The pseudo-events of June 6, 1984, as spectacular dramatizations of the real events of June 6, 1944, provide a unique opportunity to decipher the postwar transnational order's unending discourse with itself about itself. On one level, the social impact and political influence of these pseudo-events will be discrete, indefinite, and slow in coming. Yet, on another level, such pseudo-events are textual displays, overloaded with signs, illusions, and meanings, specially coded to reenergize the world-views of the millions who consumed them in the major transatlantic media markets in June 1984. As Barthes claims, "The emission and the reception of the message both lie within the field of sociology: it is a matter of studying human groups, of defining motives and attitudes, and of trying to link the behavior of these groups to the social totality of which they are a part."[4] The signs of these motives and attitudes, and the signifiers of their emission and reception in the contemporary society of the spectacle, are written all over the image clusters composing the daily output of the print and broadcast media. They need only be read in the following fashion.

WHO, WHOM?—MANUFACTURING EVENTS AND PSEUDO-EVENTS

As its own product, the spectacular society in America and Europe makes its own rules of self-presentation and self-understanding. D-Day/Normandy/June 6, 1944—these signs are mediagenic mythologies, or ideas-in-form-and-action, imposing their outline and substance on the consciousness of the consuming spectators. To respond to the crises of the 1980s, the society of the spectacle can rematerialize or reproject historical images of the 1940s as new social models, with their particular past social relations assigned to specific groups and persons today.

As Baudrillard argues, societies based upon such mythologies "can only produce and reproduce individuals as elements of the system. It cannot tolerate exceptions."[5] Therefore, in this century of world wars and the cold war, "man is not reproduced as man: he is simply regenerated as a survivor (a surviving productive force)."[6] In the years following Hiroshima, "we are all, in the framework of this system, survivors. Not even the instinct of self-preservation is fundamental: it is a social tolerance or a social imperative." And "when the system requires it," as at H-Hour: D-Day 1944 or comparable moments in Korea, Vietnam, and in the future, "it cancels this instinct and people get excited about dying (for a sublime cause, evidently)."[7] Coded scenarios, like the D-Day spectacle, construct the psychosocial means of, or take care of the emotional advance work for, delivering these cancellation notices despite individual resistance to militarization. The text of World War II, in part, reads with the glorious excitement of noble death for a sublime cause against an evil empire; its subtext also signals potential death for new docile generations today in an exciting cause against another "evil empire." Such patterns of mass docility and personal compliance, as Vaneigem observes, build in the spectacular society "from a mass of minor hypnoses: news, culture, city planning, advertising, mechanisms of conditioning and suggestion ready to serve any order, established or to come."[8]

In this transatlantic society of the spectacle, "everything, even artistic, intellectual, and scientific production, even innovations and transgression, is immediately produced as sign and exchange value."[9] World War II/D-Day/June 6, 1984—all are event-images, produced in advanced capitalist society, and then "reproduced, from the outset, immediately, as an element of the system, as an integrated variable."[10] As an average consumer or everyday spectator, "the subject is trapped in the factitious, differential, encoded, systematized aspect of the object. It is not the passion (whether of objects or subjects) for substances that speaks in fetishism, it is the passion for the code, which, by governing both objects and subjects, and by subordinating them to itself, delivers them up to abstract manipulation."[11] This regime has acquired its great powers inasmuch as it substitutes a manipulation of signs for a manipulation of forces.[12] D-Day and World War II since 1945 have been reconstituted as the ultimate objective signs of the postwar Atlantic order. They signify and dispense the benefits of a transnational code of "national security," "collective defense," and "regional unity." As Baudrillard claims, "in the 'fetishist' theory of consumption, in the view of marketing strategists as well as of consumers, objects are given and received everywhere as force dispensers (happiness, health, security, prestige, etc.). This magical substance having been spread about so liberally, one forgets that what we are dealing with first is signs: a generalized code of signs, a totally arbitrary code of differences...."[13] At this juncture, "D-day" in the mass media is the central subcode of this spectacular World War II code, dispensing its magical force to average consumers. Such myths are "depoliticized speech" in that they default permanently on the political project of speaking effectively about "the whole of human relations in their real, social structure, in their power of making the world."[14] That is, "myth acts economically," as Barthes claims. "It abolishes the complexity of human acts, it gives them the simplicity of essences, it does away with all dialectics, with any going back beyond what is immediately visible, it organizes a world without contradictions because it is without depth, a world wide open and wallowing in the evident, it establishes a blissful clarity: things appear to mean something by themselves."[15]

The D-Day commemorations, then, display the full powers of the mass media as mythic producers of teletraditional collective memory in America. For example, as corporate entities that existed and operated in the 1940s, CBS and NBC pulled old tapes and scripts from their files to be rebroadcast anew in nightly news segments. In addition to these daily miniseries on "World War II," both networks staged "D-Day Specials." CBS returned to 1944 from 1984 via 1964, rebroadcasting a one-on-one recall of "D-Day + 20 years" done by General Eisenhower and Walter Cronkite two decades ago. NBC intermixed "D-Day 1944" film footage with "D-Day 1984" video clips on a stylized set of signs, built from massive arrays of divisional patches, photo blowups, and battlefield maps. Anchorman Tom Brokaw closed the D-Day 1984 show with jaded musings over American unity found in 1944 and lost since 1964, backscored with a medley of nostalgic big band swing hits. In the corporate memories of Time, Inc.; CBS; Newsweek, Inc.; NBC; or The Washington Post Company, D-Day still is a rush of images that can be redirected to fill the mythic codes of the ever-changing present. As subtexts of Reagan's New Beginning, moreover, these images of June 6, 1984, unequivocally and uncritically affirmed what was in 1944, what should be in 1984, but what has not been since 1964 or perhaps even 1954: a united transatlantic alliance ready to contain and roll back the expansion of totalitarianism anywhere, anytime, at any price.

In late May and early June 1984, these densely coded streams of D-Day images formed into three distinct clusters. Image 1: old battle films replaying Allied and Nazi forces engaged in combat. Soundtracked with gunfire or big band swing, black-and-white clips of cruisers firing away at the beaches, troops crawling from foxholes, and fighters strafing enemy troop columns in "The Great Crusade" ran and reran on the nightly news. Image 2: veterans walking the Normandy fields. Wandering the acres of cemeteries brimful of their contemporaries, these worn, old people (ravaged now by time, pushing 59, 65, or 70) leave bouquets and tears of tribute at the graves of their generation (ravaged then in the instant of their death, remaining forever 19, 25, or 30). The newspapers and news magazines ran scores of their "eyewitness" stories. Image 3: Western leaders acting out rituals of commemoration. Before a multinational array of flags, warships, and honor guards, the assembled Western Allies' heads of state review new young NATO formations on Utah Beach beneath an airshow flyover of French jets during a transnational telecast on June 6, 1984. These three image-clusters coalign the past, present, and future in the codes of a complex, mediagenic D-Day text. Each sign-set sums up an era of history. Behind these signs and signifiers, however, what is signified?

IMAGE 3: A SPECTACULAR RITE OF TRANSATLANTIC UNITY

The sixth of June happens once every year and in some years past considerable time and energy went into memorializing D-Day in Normandy. In 1949, 1954, 1964, and 1969, many men of the allied nations of World War II returned to the beaches to mark these anniversaries with the local French inhabitants. Still, why was so much effort invested in 1984 for the fortieth anniversary? Why now, why in this form, and why with this particular content? Practical realities are part of the answer. Virtually all of the survivors of D-Day are now at least in their late fifties, while some are in their eighties. Fewer and fewer actual veterans will be around for the fiftieth or sixtieth celebrations. And, perhaps even more significantly, the current generation of Western leaders, who are now in their sixties and seventies, is the last to have actually lived through World War II.

A new generation of leaders, like Helmut Kohl, who was fifteen years old in 1945, is already rising to power. These leaders did not experience World War II as adults; this fact is critical. The symbolic categories, master codes, and sign systems of the 1944–84 Atlantic transnational zone-regime are totally grounded in World War II. Of the participants in World War II, President Mitterrand declared on Utah Beach that "we owe them what we are today." The Atlantic zone-regime, to a significant extent, has defined its purpose, goals, and meaning in terms of a collective triumph in World War II that became certain on D-Day in Normandy. Its ideo-political significance, summarized in the sign systems of the spectacular society, surfaces in this *Newsweek* passage:

> If blood was the price, the prize was the fall of Adolph Hitler and his thousand-year Reich. When 133,000 American, British and Canadian troops charged out of the English Channel and hit the beaches of northern France on June 6, 1944, they launched a final push that within 11 months crushed the German Army. It was the beginning of a new era. The largest military invasion in history laid the foundation for the Marshall plan, the recovery of Europe and the birth of the Atlantic alliance. It also confirmed America's rise from wary isolationism to a new role as the world's strongest power. Yet even as the Allies were pushing the Germans back across the farmlands of Normandy, the Soviet Union was advancing on the Polish frontier—dividing Europe almost as soon as it was liberated.[16]

The entire compass of the postwar era for the Allied powers—successes and failures, good and evil, origins and ends, purpose and meaning—

surfaces in this hieroglyphic of history. From a decisive battle, not in the East but in the West, the Nazis met their final defeat. A new era emerged that must be preserved—and defended against any new threats—with the same resolve that forged it. D-days, as spectacular dramatizations, serve as the penultimate transnational rite of unity for a generation of "veterans" that sees the world in these mythic terms and wishes its successors to share the same fantasies of power, solidarity, and destiny. As *Newsweek* maintained on D-Day 1984, "The latest generation of American, British, Canadian and French allies gathered with them [the veterans] to celebrate history's proof that an alliance can matter."[17]

The D-Day Rite and Disarray in NATO

In the mythologies of the NATO societies, World War II's codes of contradiction, opposition, and order remain valid from 1944 to 1984. The roles are the same, only the actors have changed. Today, NATO and the OECD, including the old Axis powers now, are "the Allies." The WTO and CMEA states, now numbering the old Allies of Poland and the USSR, are "the Axis." Aggressive troops from a totalitarian dictatorship, according to President Reagan, "are still there [in Central Europe], uninvited, unwanted, unyielding almost 40 years after the war,"[18] hiding not behind an Atlantic Wall, but behind the Iron Curtain. Europe, liberated in part from a "fascist madman," must now be defended to roll back the incursions of a "pathological" socialist ideology. The transatlantic society of the spectacle, as the self-defined source of moral "liberation," transposes the final conflicts with fascism into new codings for its "long twilight struggle" against communism, the spectacularly dramatized source of unjust "conquest."

The two "evil empires" are virtually identical threats to NATO's democratic peoples: the triumph over one must be the master code for relations with the other. Thus, from 1944 to 1984, and even more so today, the myths of World War II impose themselves on the cold war, pointing out "meanings" and "understandings" in the images of the present: the CPSU is the NSDAP, the General Secretary is the Reichskanzler, Moscow is Berlin, the KGB is the Gestapo, and the Red Army is the Wehrmacht; Afghanistan is Abyssinia, Angola is Spain, SALT I and II are Munich, and the Gulag is Auschwitz writ large. Thus *The Wall Street Journal* on June 4 and 5, 1984, as its "D-Day remembrance," runs a special front-page lead, a multicolumned analysis of NATO's military power, strategy, and capability in contrast to the WTO's military formations.[19] Again on Wall Street it is 1938, and Europe stands behind a new Maginot Line (tactical nuclear weapons) awaiting a new attack from totalitarian aggressors (the USSR) at its Achilles heel (Norway, the Fulda Gap, the North Atlantic, the

Persian Gulf, etc.). In this symbolic table of equivalence, the 1944 generation finds its familiar meanings in the ambiguities of 1984, and the 1984 generation, who never knew 1944, cannot completely find its own new meanings in the realities of the present.

Even though the USSR has displaced the Third Reich in the role of "Them" versus "Us" in the contemporary society of the spectacle, West Germany is still not entirely trusted in the West. As President Mitterrand suggested in 1984, "the enemy of the time was not Germany but the power, the system, the ideology that held Germany in its grip."[20] Of course, this mystification serves several purposes. It frees contemporary Germans, especially those too young or not yet born in 1945, from responsibility for the crimes of World War II. It also defines ideologies, systems, powers—totalitarianism—as the enemy of the past, and, by extension, of the present and future. And it directs transatlantic resolve and purpose against the new totalitarian systems of today (the USSR) that walk in the footsteps of Nazism (the occupation of Eastern Europe, the Gulag, military expansionism abroad, and ideological confrontation with the NATO partners). The Germans, however, have lost out in 1984 as they lost in 1944. As Helmut Kohl admitted regarding his attitude about the D-Day fest in Normandy, "The German Chancellor has no reason to celebrate a victory in a battle that cost 10,000 German soldiers their lives."[21] The ambivalence of the old Allies toward the *Bundesrepublik* still remains obvious four decades and three generations after World War II.

While Mitterrand "gallantly" saluted the "dead of Germany," no Western leader embraced West Germany, nor was Chancellor Kohl invited to the Utah Beach festivities. Indeed, in view of the "pacifism and neutralism" of the West Germans since 1981, it seems as if the entire D-Day spectacle was also a lecture to West Germany about its role and responsibility as a NATO nation. As Reagan told the NATO Alliance members, the bitter lessons of the two world wars are that it is best "to protect the peace," "not take blind shelter," and "respond only after freedom is lost." Clearly, these words of the Great Communicator were targeted, in part, at West Germany's pacificists, neutralists, and Greens. When Reagan addressed the audience of Western Allies at Pointe-du-Hoc, he claimed, "We are bound today by what bound us 40 years ago: the same loyalties, traditions and beliefs. . . . we were with you then; we are with you now."[22] Yet these words cannot pertain to the old Axis powers, and on June 6, 1984, no Germans or Italians or Japanese stood in the audience to listen. Indeed, forty years later, West Germany, Italy, and Japan are still only "candidate," and not full, members of the Western Alliance. Their leaders were welcome at the June 7, 1984, London economic summit, but all were snubbed at the June 6, 1984, Normandy rituals. The Germans, it would appear, even four decades after World War II, still cannot please their neighbors. In 1944, they clearly were too belligerent; in 1984, they are plainly too pacifistic. Still, to partially compensate Bonn for these snubs in 1984, Reagan, Thatcher, and Miterrand all bent over backward in May 1985 during the fortieth anniversary of V-E Day to reassure Kohl that "bygones were bygones." In an equally incredible political spectacle, Reagan even delivered a brief telecast address "honoring" Germany's war dead in a cemetery near Bitburg, even though it contained the graves of many Waffen SS troopers.[23]

Beyond the German question, however, rites of transatlantic solidarity, like the 1984 D-Day spectaculars, assume an even greater significance in view of the shifting centers of the capitalist world economy. The Pacific basin has eclipsed the North Atlantic region as a trading area; hence, the latter's economic decline must be masked by grand political spectacle. Japan, rather than a European country, is *the* major overseas trading partner of the United States in the mid–1980s. Seven of the United States' twenty major foreign trading partners are along the Asian rim of the Pacific Basin. Since the late 1970s, transpacific trade has exceeded transatlantic trade; and in 1983 U.S. trade with Asia surpassed American-European trade by $26 billion. Against the background of these new economic realities in the Pacific Basin, then, any opportunity to celebrate past victories and renew old alliances in Europe must be exploited to maintain the symbolic significance of the Atlantic region.

In contrast to the Normandy D-Day rituals, Pacific theater operations cannot receive spectacular treatments in the United States or Europe. The humiliating defeats by American forces in 1941 and 1942, as well as the actual conquest by Japan of U.S. Pacific territories, make the Pacific War difficult to celebrate. Unlike Hitler or Mussolini, Hirohito was rehabilitated politically in 1947, and he served as emperor until 1989. Even more troublesome, the U.S. economy by 1984 had become an integral and increasingly less prosperous part of contemporary Japan's "New Greater East Asian and Pacific Rim Co-Prosperity Sphere," which Washington had sought to crush militarily in 1945. The multiple D-Days from Guadalcanal to Okinawa, in turn, are too many and too bloody to memorialize at the symbolic expense of our main overseas trading partner and technological competitor. The ultimate D-Day-style invasion of Japan was made moot by American A-bombs. Hiroshima and Nagasaki are Japan's lasting stigmata of its failed imperialism. And to discuss their nuclear obliteration, everyone must confront the ugly realities of World War III yet to come. However, the great value of World War II and its D-Day myths lies in the carefully manufactured spectacles of preatomic "total war" in the European, African, and Pacific "theaters of operation," which are the finest mystifications of World War III's mechanically reproduced megadeaths in thermonuclear exchanges.

The D-Day Rite and Redemption from Vietnam

At one level, these media mythologies of 1944 are coded in tribute and celebration of "D-Day: the Normandy invasion + 40 years." Yet, on another level, these mythic codes of World War II are also intensely recorded and rerecorded over troubling images in the United States from the past twenty years. The year 1944 is important now in the United States, because 1964 and the nation's subsequent slide into Vietnam remain so ugly. The doubt induced by presidentially decreed air strikes in 1964 and 1965, the surprises at Tet 1968, the aimless invasion of Cambodia in 1970, the nation's internal divisions from 1973 to 1976—all are still on videotape, in news magazines, and on the spectators' minds, even now. For the Great Communicator in 1984, the Great Crusade of 1944 can mask and mystify the Vietnam Syndrome of 1974 (lingering still in the resistance of congressional subcommittees to the application of the Reagan Doctrine to Central America, Lebanon, and the Persian Gulf throughout his New Beginning). Every act of violent destruction, military power, and national resolve under President Reagan becomes, in part, a citation of D-Day: "The Great Crusade/Totalitarianism's Unconditional Surrender." To affirm the myth of origins and ends propounded on D-Day, the United States in the 1980s flames Libyan jets over the Gulf of Sidra, bankrolls guerrilla insurgencies in rural Nicaragua, pounds Lebanese towns to rubble with the *New Jersey*'s sixteen-inch guns, snuffs Marxist cadres in Grenada defending themselves from U.S. invaders, rolls new units of Euromissiles across West Germany to create "caution" in Moscow, and blows away Iranian ships, planes, and gunboats in the Persian Gulf to maintain the "freedom of navigation." In refutation of 1974, 1944 emerges again as the telling teletraditional reference of resolve.

Ironically, however, it was this *same* spectacular discourse of American hegemony that caused the failures of the Vietnam Era. At the level of the national decision-making elites, Washington in 1964 notified the spectators of America and Europe of their need to stand up to tyranny. At the level of the average citizen, many young soldiers disembarked in Vietnam with reruns of John Wayne and Audie Murphy World War II movies turning in their heads as their personal guides to military action. The mythic codes of D-Day—accept no Munichs, oppose dictators' salami tactics, hit the beaches for liberation—pointed Washington to Saigon. Saigon and Vietnam were key signs of a larger metacode in "the best and the brightest" worldview of the New Frontier/Great Society. Saigon in 1964 was an iconic summation of a global spectacle—it was Paris, Oslo, Brussels in 1940; it was Belgrade, Sofia, Budapest in 1945; it was Peking, Pyongyang, and Hanoi in the 1946–54 period.

In the shifting codes of superpower credibility, the metatexts of World War II thus imposed their agenda on the very different realities of 1964. But as a result, America's Vietnam "presence" quickly decayed into its "Vietnam Syndrome." Unlike 1944, massive U.S. involvement in Indochina was not a Great Crusade. It was a "brushfire war," a "counterinsurgency operation," a "police action," or a "sideshow" in the big contest with totalitarianism. Rather than "liberating" Indochina for democracy, U.S. and Allied Forces "pacified" the remnants of a French colony ruled by an indigenous military junta. Even allowing for vast differences in culture, time, and method, Americans in Vietnam (ordinary guys "just doing their jobs") all too frequently resembled Nazi Germans in Eastern Europe (typical citizens "just following orders"). The banality of this evil, in fighting Communist expansion in Southeast Asia, took the form of "free-fire zones," air cavalry "search and destroy" sweeps, and nightly telecast "body counts." Phoenix-program hit teams, like Waffen SS detachments before them, hunted down their Asiatic enemies, who were gripped by the scourge of Bolshevism, and executed them. One type of soldier swore to keep the Chi-coms off the beaches at Santa Barbara; the other pledged to force the Bolshevist hordes off its rightful *Lebensraum*. Even though "winning hearts and minds" displaced *Arbeit macht frei* as watchwords, both ironically wrapped their enterprise in the cloak of racial superiority, global destiny, and the defense of Western culture.

Fighting communism on the Eastern front or in the Mekong Delta justified atrocities; Babi Yar and Lidice were repeated on much smaller scales at My Lai and at free-fire zones across Indochina. As invincible supermen fighting subhumans, American troops consciously resurrected the jargon of the Native American genocide: Viet Cong territory was "Indian country," "the only good gook was a dead gook," "'slopes' placed no value on human life," and the "air cav" always dispersed "the hostiles" in the nick of time. Of course, for Americans the high intent behind their "democratic liberation" of VC villages allegedly made these distasteful brutalities of war morally necessary and right. It also differentiated their acts from those of the Third Reich, which after all were motivated by the evil intentions of a "final solution." Yet despite Berlin's and Washington's diversely motivated anti-communist projects, the corpses in the Ukrainian death pits and Indochinese rice paddies were still equally dead at the hands of great "anti-communist" crusades.

Once in "Nam," however, America's servicemen and evening news audiences soon recognized that the spectacular instructions from their

"World War II" codebooks did not fit Indochinese conditions. Despite John Wayne's best efforts in *The Green Berets,* the "Pearl Harbor to Tokyo Bay" collage of films starring Audie Murphy, Humphrey Bogart, Richard Widmark, and John Wayne—continously rerunning in the heads of the grunts before their rotations—soon snapped off the spool once they were "in country." Quite clearly, in view of these distorted codes, it is no surprise that a generation of Americans, weaned on such spectacular images of World War II, quickly developed a chronic lingering case of the Vietnam Syndrome. This alleged timidity to intervene militarily elsewhere, in turn, divided the nation as much as the war itself. Still, after years of continuing division and the mistreatment of Vietnam vets, the passing years of the 1970s and 1980s have brought amnesty to draft dodgers, a national Vietnam War Memorial in Washington, revisionist "Vietnam-era" movies, and even, in May 1984, the enshrinement of the only unknown Vietnam War soldier by President Reagan (on the eve of his departure to Europe for the 1984 D-Day celebration), during a nationwide telecast at the Tomb of the Unknown Soldier.

Movie plots and endings are also subtexts revealing the end of internal discord. In the course of a decade, "patriotic" rednecks and "dissident" longhairs went from murdering each other in *Easy Rider* to joining hands around a birthday cake and singing "God Bless America" in *The Deer Hunter.* With the D-Day spectacle of 1984, the bright hopes of World War II have virtually occluded the dark days of Vietnam, despite some recurrent flashbacks from Central America. In fact, Rambo and Chuck Norris have both been back "in country" during the 1980s to spectacularly redefine the undeniable power of the individual "American fighting man" against the red and yellow hordes, even when he is hamstrung with constant meddling by the Pentagon and Capitol Hill. While *Full Metal Jacket, Hamburger Hill,* and *Platoon* have sought to recreate some semblance of Vietnam *a la cinema verité,* Clint Eastwood has also pushed down Rambo's and Chuck Norris's cinegraphic trails of our warriors' redemption by taking them out of Vietnam and into Grenada with *Heartbreak Ridge.* The worst of these militaristic fantasies are played out now in high-tech death films, ranging from *Top Gun* to *Iron Eagle.* In these cinema spectacles, swaggering, xenophobic American youths use F-14s and F-16s to obliterate one-dimensional communist or Third World foes while riding along against a soundtrack of high-energy rock-and-roll. With such legitimizing images already spinning in their heads, the American public in the 1980s passively accepts, or even cheers, the news of Libyan jetfighters and Iranian airliners being splashed by the "brave boys" of the U.S. Navy, proving after all is said and done that "America is back." Today's approved coding of "patriotism" returns full circle in these modern equivalents of jingoistic World War II movies that featured John Wayne or Randolph Scott "battling 'the Nips' across the Pacific."

Indeed, Vietnam by 1984 attained its zenith of mainstream commodification under the aegis of Time-Life Books, Inc. At the hands of this firm, Vietnam has become a multicolor, multivolume historical encyclopedia completely repackaged in action layouts. Just like World War II, which Time-Life Books, Inc. sells by inviting the spectator "inside Hitler's dark empire" to "Explore the Twisted World of the NAZIS" for ten free days of important reading, the Vietnam War is rerun as "THE VIETNAM EXPERIENCE," telling in realistic detail "for the First Time—THE REAL STORY OF VIETNAM." In TV ads and direct-mail flyers, the consumer is enticed with tough copy: "It was a war like no other war. Dirtier. Meaner. More frightening than all the rest. Where at any moment death could scream down from the sky as an incoming 85 or reach up from the earth on the poisoned tip of a punji stake." The packaging of ideological collaboration here is highly sophisticated, promising that, "If you were there, this is your story. If you weren't, here's your chance to learn what it was really like . . . ," all for only $14.99 plus shipping and handling. When such "history" can be purchased on a monthly installment plan from a corporate image factory, it signals the final colonization of its ideopolitical significance by the society of the spectacle. Stacked along the aisles of collective choice in its bright attractive packaging, next to the comparably priced and packaged "World War II" product, "the Vietnam experience" thus acquires new shelf life as another over-the-counter nostrum for young Americans anxious to keep their world safe for democracy.

IMAGE 2: WORLD-WAR TOURISM AS SPECTACLE

The mythological discourse of the D-Day spectacle, for the most part, works only to the degree that the photographic images and historical consciousness of the entire post–1945 transatlantic community, as Barthes notes, have been "worked on" continuously for four decades.[24] By themselves, D-Day photographs and commemoration rituals are neutral, uncoded messages. Beyond these first-order images, however, which freeze "reality" for continual reproduction, several additional sign sets of united might are enscribed into these black-and-white or color videotape signs of history.[25]

Since 1939, when World War II began, the "World War II" product line has grown continuously as a prosperous sector of the American culture industry. Global combat against fascism, of course, was aestheticized to legitimize America's role as an "Arsenal of Democracy" even before Pearl Harbor. Following the Day of Infamy, however, the culture industry fully mobilized its workshops and plants to manufacture images of democratic peoples decisively defeating authoritarian regimes. No one was exempt from serving in these spectacles of struggle. Even Bugs Bunny, Daffy Duck, Elmer Fudd, and Donald Duck were drafted in the cartoons to sell war bonds, build war machines, and fight the fascists. After V-J Day, however, these images of the Allied Powers battling totalitarianism remained key parts of the permanent read-only-memory in the mass consciousness.

Fictional movies and factual newsreels—John Wayne on Wake Island or ordinary G.I. Joe at Bastogne—are fused into a seamless sign system of valor, sacrifice, courage, and duty. The black-and-white figures of U.S. Army units in newsreel signalectics "are" John Wayne, Dana Andrews, and Humphrey Bogart battling their way across Europe. Likewise, such mythic movie stars in dozens of World War II feature film signifiers "are" those ordinary Joes struggling with the Axis. In these sign systems, millions of "American boys from next door" simply wish to knock out Hitler, Mussolini, and Hirohito, and then get back stateside to their hometowns, jobs, and loved ones. Fictional films of World War II are docudramas imposing its conflicts, duties, and costs on everyone: documentary newsreels of World War II also are the sign sagas of the 1941–45 period in the modern society of spectacle, informing post–1945 spectators of their ultimate civic responsibilities. Fact and fiction, movies and news, myth and history compose a single text in the "World War II" codes. "World War II," as a media mythology of the society of the spectacle, is no longer simply a chronicle of world historical events. It has acquired *this* particular image, which is given in *these* particular significations. "Mythical speech," in Barthes's perspective, "is made of a material which has *already* been worked on so as to make it suitable for communication: it is because all the materials of myth (whether pictoral or written) presuppose a signifying consciousness, that one can reason about them while discounting their substance."[26]

World War II, like all modern wars, was a bloody, organized chaos on its battlefields where cold, hungry, tired men, blinded by smoke and deafened by noise, survived day by day through reptilian reactions of kill or be killed. But the culture industry's manufactured "World War II" spectacle has coded the mass consciousness of World War II quite differently—as "Modern History's Great Crusade Against Diabolical Evil"—in its grainy black-and-white Wirephotos, scratchy radio broadcasts, and Technicolor feature films. Through these packaged iconographs, most media consumers in the spectacular society are permanently "part of" the dramas of "World War II": Stukas diving down on Poland, the boats of Dunkirk, Afrika Korps tanks rolling over Tobruk, the battleship *Arizona* ablaze at anchor, frozen bodies in Stalingrad's snow-covered rubble, Ike chatting with D-Day paratroopers, a B–17 exploding over its target at Schweinfurt, death-camp victims bulldozed into mass graves, Red Army soldiers hoisting the hammer and sickle over burning Berlin at the Brandenburger Tor and the Reichstag, Hiroshima's vaporized citizens and industries billowing into a mushroom cloud behind the *Enola Gay*. These images are known in every American household. They are logos of the postwar era, manufactured and distributed widely in the transatlantic societies of the spectacle as special trademarks of the new transnational regime. The D-Day icons are also packaged in such images—empty LCI bays, Nazi pillboxes, GIs on the beaches, an armada at sea. Like Santa at Christmas, fireworks on the Fourth of July, or Pilgrims at Thanksgiving, these signs are signatures, advertising the real birthday—June 6, 1944— of American world hegemony. Since 1945, to create solidarity, discipline, or purpose, America's national leaders have had only to access these sign files in the mass consumers' memories—despite their less effective reception among the baby-boom "successor generation"—to elicit positive feelings of "national unity" or "collective security."

Similarly, on D-Day 1984, the Normandy cemeteries were cast as ciphers of final sacrifice and signs of ultimate purpose. Being a soldier ultimately means accepting this role as a nation's predesignated "human sacrifice" to the state's quest for power, which necessarily is marked by a nation's will to waste as many of its soldiers' lives and as much its citizens' wealth as is necessary to prevail in its quest. In the society of the spectacle, such images serve notice: average consumers and producers frequently will be called upon to serve as warriors, defending this regime of mass consumption. Most survive, but many do not come home. In exchange for their sacrifices, and to screen the real purposes of the state, the dead are assured a place of honor and a never-ending role as texts of national purpose and meaning. To defend the "freedom of choice," the spectacular society must mobilize its spectators. In Normandy on D-Day 1984, the visitors' stands and military cemeteries were not full of soldiers; on the contrary, they were full of truckdrivers, carpet salesmen, farmers, carpenters, shop foremen, students, miners, junior executives, steelworkers, plumbers, and schoolteachers. Rituals, like D-Day memorials, allow the spectacular society to colonize the social consciousnesses of new generations of consumers with these sacrificial sign images, created from photo displays of both their fallen fathers and the honored veterans, in preparation for their present-day defense of "the freedom to choose" for those yet unborn.

"The freedom of choice," of course, is confined to the prepackaged arrays of the corporate marketplace, namely, one's freedom to choose a

Chrysler or a Pontiac, steak or salad, Miami or Orlando. But—it *is* a choice. Just as the cemeteries signal some of the costs of choice, the roving bands of old vets are signs of its rewards. The spectacles of June 6, 1984, focused on numerous groups of old men and old women, touring in pilgrimage the bivouacs and battlegrounds of 1944. Clad now in windbreakers and bill caps, these spectacularly encoded tourists of 1984 are the same gangs of spectacularly encoded average consumers, who in olive drab and denim overalls drove the American war machine to victory during 1944. They are G.I. Joe and Rosie the Riveter + 40 years. Their presence is the sign of Everyman/Everywoman recognizing themselves in a call to defend the colors and enjoy the spoils of victory.[27]

IMAGE 1: A SPECTACLE OF PLAUSIBLE WARS

The D-Day spectacle also is encoded with subtexts on the acceptability of war. World War I (poison gas, mindless trench warfare, machine guns mowing down raw recruits in no-man's-land) and World War III (the terrifying unknowns of thermonuclear, bacteriological, and chemical exchanges) are threatening, dire sign systems, enciphered in the discourses of senseless mass death. World War II, even with its hours of carnage like D-Day, is the ultimate iconograph of plausible, survivable, purposeful war between advanced industrial societies. As a war of clear battle lines and common purpose, it was everything to Americans that World War I, Korea, and Vietnam were not. Virtually every casualty of World War II found an honorable grave, and practically all of its victorious survivors could console themselves with the necessity of defeating fascism despite the high human costs.

The images of World War II and D-Day 1944 present dual sides of war—war as destructive but survivable, horrible but necessary, wasteful but redemptive. Modern war, in the sign systems of D-Day, is *hell*; but it is also *life*, lived as adventures with foxhole buddies and fondly relived in good memories at forty-year reunions. These spectacular subtexts are vital codes of mystification in the society of spectacle, which has unfolded in the dark eclipse of thermonuclear firestorms since the mid–1950s: the reason why the battle myths of World War II are so central to the spectacular regime of mass consumption is because the war plans of World War III assure hemispheric mass destruction on twenty minutes' notice.

World War III will feature few if any Normandy-style invasions. Its battles are designed to be nothing but automated Auschwitzes, arriving in MIRVed warhead buses from subspace. Technocratic managers, operating nuclear command posts from deep inside mountains or from circling jumbo jets, will trade megadeaths for megadeaths, cities for cities, missiles for missiles for a few days until the smoke, debris, and dust envelope the planet in a "nuclear winter" of unknown duration. Neither the victors nor the vanquished will be able to console themselves with World War III's "noble purposes" in this destruction. Similarly, no monumental cemeteries for the fallen will enshrine World War III's victims. Their remains will instead be picked over in the dark along blast craters by any bacteria, worms, and roaches hardy enough to outlast nuclear war. World War III promises, at this juncture of superpower competition, to leave few survivors, little triumph, and no glory.

Consequently, World War II continues to signal the *correct* codes and *ideal* images of the "profession of arms" in the societies of spectacle. D-Day is a master text, enscribing the military enterprise of United States as superpower with nobility, purpose, and valor. During an era in which superpowers manufacture their security within the hardened silos of ICBM fields, the anachronistic myths of pre-nuclear personal combat must be affirmed to legitimize the "national defense" provided by Reagan's Strategic Air Command and Gorbachev's Strategic Rocket Forces.

Among the transatlantic allies, D-Day is the central spectacular text in this mystification of World War III's "final countdowns." However, the supreme myth of D-Day, as the 1984 spectacle illustrated, is the daring attack by 225 U.S. Rangers upon a large coastal artillery emplacement on the cliffs at Pointe-du-Hoc, between Utah and Omaha beaches. Although pre-attack reconnaissance did not disclose that the German guns had been moved before D-Day and the Rangers suffered 165 casualties while scaling the cliffs to destroy the German emplacements, this episode of combat is one of the master videodisks of all of America's D-Day images.

President Reagan chose this site as the setting of his transatlantic D-Day address because, in his words, it was *here* that Americans "began to seize back the continent of Europe." [28] This site of a heated skirmish, accomplished mountaineering, and military professionalism in 1944 symbolizes the "same loyalties, traditions, and beliefs" in 1984. [29] Reagan's cinemagraphic worldview recasts World War II as the spectacular society likes to see it. D-Day was not the anonymous annihilation of hundreds on Omaha Beach; it was instead, as the Pentagon's professionals now pretend World War III will be, the clean, quick strike of well-trained experts at Pointe-du-Hoc doing the job right at the first go and on time. In these images, World War II was not, and World War III will not be, war with the hard parts, the stupid waste of life, or the foolish reversals.

The icons of Pointe-du-Hoc spectacularly dramatize the "new look" for the U.S. military in the political codes of the 1980s. Images of Vietnam smack of World War I's and World War III's ugly death scenes: Khe Sanh,

Cambodia, Quan Tri, and Hue all encode war as a juggernaut of organized chaos, leaving nothing in its tracks but burnt earth, twisted metal, and dead meat. The subtexts of Pointe-du-Hoc 1944, in particular, and the metatext of D-Day 1984, in general, recast the Pentagon and its armed forces as intrepid fighting men, engaged in combat against fantastic odds and delivering superhuman successes (despite the handicaps of democratic civilian control). Pointe-du-Hoc and Normandy must remain mythic; they are the exemplary sign sagas for all U.S. fighting men in the 1980s and beyond.

When seen only at this level, these spectacular equivalences might seem farfetched. Still, it must be remembered that the Pentagon's technocratic managers have racked up an incredible list of military defeats, draws, and retreats over the generation between the Inchon landing in Korea and the airborne and amphibious walkover in Grenada. Lacking any real triumphs for over thirty years, troops from frontline U.S. units in 1984 were mobilized in "reenactments" of their precursors' victories in 1944. An illusory triumph borrowed from the 1940s is better for the regimental elan of today's young soldiers than the real memories of more recent losses in Beirut, the Iranian "rescue" operation, or the last flight from Saigon. Today's Ranger charge on the Pointe-du-Hoc gunsites was a spectacular citation of the real Ranger assault on D-Day and its surreal fictionalization with Robert Taylor in *D-Day: The Sixth of June.* Today's 82nd Airborne drop into Normandy is a spectacular citation of the actual assault by paratroopers on D-Day, and its docudramatic replay with Red Buttons in *The Longest Day.* Rebroadcast on the video screens in D-Day 1984 dramatizations, the successes of the old veterans transpose their anti-totalitarian purposes (in 1984's codes) to the young recruits reliving those decisive victories (in 1944's codes) as public-relations spectacles.

After twenty years of U.S. spectators' disdain for the profession of arms, the spectacles of D-Day 1984 should thus evoke new ideal images for spectators—images of the Rangers' and Airborne's new victories to come in Lebanon, Honduras, Iran, or Nicaragua. However, these media-mythic texts also construct other equivalences and efface vital differences. If the moment ever arises, a 1984 Ranger's reenactment of a 1944 Ranger's rubout of a German machine-gun nest with a burst of submachine-gun fire can be made equivalent in military spectacle to modern U.S. airmen snuffing out Minsk, Pinsk, and Omsk with their MIRVed Minuteman IIs. In each episode, the followers of an "evil empire," Hitler's or Gorbachev's, get "what's coming to them" from the armed might of U.S. democracy. World War III's SAC equals World War II's Sergeant Rock; Sergeant Rock's "budda-budda-budda" submachine-gun liquidation of

Nazis equals SAC's aerospace "Blast-off"/"Takeoff"/"Standoff" atomization of Commies. In the last analysis, spectacular sagas of World War II are useful inasmuch as they organize these codes of consent. D-Day's spectacular staging erases the question of difference and establishes a linkage of equivalence in the moral conscience of today's soldiers and citizens.

D-DAY: THE BIG CODES ON THE SMALL SCREEN

In the final analysis, the 1984 D-Day spectacle commemorates the everyday lifeworld of transnational corporate capitalism and the transatlantic zone-regime. Because of D-Day 1944, on D-Day 1984, as President Reagan claimed and the spectators implicitly inferred, "this land [the EEC/NATO/OECD nations] is secure [technologically advanced and thermonuclearly armed], we [the average consumers and producers in the society of the spectacle] are free [unaffected by evil empires' fascist/communist/totalitarian roads to serfdom and still retaining our freedom of choice], these things [namely, the land/security/family/freedom, as the World War II media myths teach] are worth fighting [Normandy, Korea, Vietnam, Cambodia, Lebanon, Grenada]—and dying [fields of honor with flag-draped coffins, rifle salutes and uniform white crosses]—for."[30] Here World War II is a screen of time past and time present, interlocked in the EEC/NATO/OECD region's codes of anti-totalitarian collective choice. D-Day 1944/1984, for the Great Communicator and his transnational audience, is "a nonreflecting surface, an immanent surface where operations unfold—the smooth operational surface of communication,"[31] filled with teletraditional spectacles of superpower.

The Allied invasion of Normandy, as the D-Day spectacle illustrates, aimed to "liberate" Europe rather than "conquer" it anew. Under the Nazis, Normandy bore the marks of military *conquest:* machine-gun nests, tank traps, coastal artillery sites, and other heavy fortifications. Years after the Allied invasion, it carries the signs of economic *liberation:* beach houses, tourist hotels, vacation lodges, and other places for fun in the sun and surf. D-Day, June 6, 1944, marks the birthday of U.S. hegemony within the postwar transatlantic regime. Looking back at the old photo-texts of GIs wading ashore from *Time*'s LCIs, one realizes these average consumers and producers are agents of liberation for the post–World War II consumerist society of the spectacle. There are no field marshals' batons in these soldiers' knapsacks. Such militaristic aspirations, in the media-mythic codes, were harbored instead by the Nazi conquerors. The fieldpacks of the United States' fighting men are instead bulging with the corporate order books of the top salesmen. Throughout postwar Europe, the U.S. liberators soon provided their corporate-produced fantasies for the real liberation of personal desires and needs. The liberation of Europe paid off in the coming of the Sears and Roebuck catalog, liberal democracy, big band bebop, and Cadillacs—in marked contrast to the Nazi conquest that brought only *Mein Kampf,* concentration camps, "Lili Marlene," and panzer columns of Tiger tanks.

As the D-Day spectacles of organized consent reaffirmed, the ultimate victory of U.S. hegemony in the transatlantic alliance derives from its "liberation" of individual choice in the corporate marketplace. As one U.S. tourist remarked about the enthusiasm of the French at seeing the returning U.S. veterans, "The French people here are probably even more patriotic than us because they want to be Americans.'"[32] Signs of this triumph were combined, for example, with the 1984 D-Day spectacle on "The CBS Evening News" of June 6, 1984. After rebroadcasting the World War II spectacles of Allied victory over the Axis and the Western heads of state paying tribute to Operation Overlord on Utah Beach, CBS offered a final segment that focused on the annual Fanfare music festival in Nashville, Tennessee. There on the screen at the close of the D-Day June 6, 1984, video spectacle, a West German country-western band of Willie Nelson clones belted out "Auf der Autobahn, Wieder Wesen"/"On the Road, Again." One sign again sums up an era. Forty years ago, the Nuremburg rallies threatened the U.S. with "Teutonization"; yet, due to the Allied and U.S. victory on D-Day, 1944, Nashville recording studios instead have successfully colonized West Germany with their transnational "Texanization" of the Teutons.

Thanks to D-Day in the videocodes of "World War II," Americans do not journey to Nuremburg rallies to sing "The Horst Wessel March," but Germans fly to Nashville country-western fests to sing "Auf der Autobahn, Wieder Wesen" for the special enjoyment of America's average consumers and producers. While it is, of course, idiosyncratic, such an image ironically affirms the power of American arms during the 1940s in the production of spectacles in the 1980s. Yet at the same time, these West German ersatz Willie Nelsons also illustrate some of the tremendous pull exerted by images in today's informational circuits of cultural collaboration. In 1984 it is the collaborative attractions of image, rather than 1944's "arsenal of democracy," that now so firmly anchors American power in the transnational zone-regime of "Western Democracies" in North America, Western Europe, and the Pacific Rim.

NOTES

1. Guy Debord, *Society of the Spectacle* (Detroit: Red & Black, 1983), no. 2.
2. Ibid.

3. Ibid.

4. Roland Barthes, *Image-Music-Text* (New York: Hill and Wang, 1978), 15.

5. Jean Baudrillard, *For A Critique of the Political Economy of the Sign* (St. Louis: Telos Press, 1981), 86.

6. Ibid.

7. Ibid.

8. Raoul Vaneigem, *The Revolution of Everyday Life* (London: Left Bank Books/Rebel Press, 1983), 12.

9. Ibid., 87.

10. Ibid.

11. Ibid., 92.

12. Ibid., 90–95.

13. Ibid.

14. Roland Barthes, "Myth Today," *A Barthes Reader,* ed. Susan Sontag (New York: Hill and Wang, 1982), 95.

15. Ibid., 132.

16. Mark Whitaker et al., "The Men Who Hit the Beach," *Newsweek,* June 11, 1984, 18–19, and Otto Friedrich, "'Every Man was a Hero,' Forty years later, a military gamble that shaped history is recalled," *Time,* May 28, 1984, 12–27.

17. Steven Strasser et al., "An Old Alliance Celebrates Itself," *Newsweek,* June 18, 1984, 22.

18. Ibid., 23.

19. F. Kempe, "Muscular Foe, Warsaw Pact Forces Always Take Offensive in Invasion Rehearsals," *The Wall Street Journal,* June 4, 1984, 1, 30, and G. Seib, "Getting Smart, NATO Hopes to Curb Nuclear Peril by Using 'High-Tech' Devices," *The Wall Street Journal,* June 5, 1984, 1, 38–39.

20. Pico Iyer, "Tributes and Tears," *Time,* June 18, 1984, 38.

21. Ibid., 40.

22. Strasser et al., *Newsweek,* June 18, 1984, 24.

23. See D. Hoffman, "Reagan Visits Death Camp, Cemetery," *The Washington Post,* May 6, 1985, A1, A19; "'From Ashes Has Come Hope and Reconciliation,'" *The Washington Post,* May 6, 1985, A20; and "Kohl: Bitburg as a Symbol," *The Washington Post,* May 6, 1985, A21. For a more extended critique of Bitburg, also see Geoffrey Hartman, ed., *Bitburg in Moral and Political Perspective* (Bloomington: Indiana University Press, 1986).

24. Barthes, "Myth Today," *A Barthes Reader,* 95. Also see Clayton R. Koppes and Gregory D. Black, *Hollywood Goes to War: How Politics, Profits and Propaganda Shaped World War II Movies* (New York: Free Press, 1987).

25. Roland Barthes, "Power and 'Cool,'" in *The Eiffel Tower and Other Mythologies* (New York: Hill and Wang, 1979), 43–45.

26. Barthes, "Myth Today," in *A Barthes Reader,* 131.

27. See G. J. Church, "Daisies from the Killing Ground, For Returning Vets, Normandy Brings Crosscurrent of Emotions," *Time,* May 28, 1984, 28–33; L. Morrow, "June 6, 1944," *Time,* May 28, 1984, 10–11; and "Special Report: Reliving a Day of Terror and Triumph," *Newsweek,* June 11, 1984, 23–30.

28. Strasser et al., *Newsweek,* June 18, 1984, 24.

29. Ibid.

30. Lou Cannon, "Reagan Hails D-Day Valor, Visits Graves," *The Washington Post,* June 7, 1984, A1–A30.

31. Jean Baudrillard, "The Ecstasy of Communication," in *The Anti-Aesthetic: Essays of Post-Modern Culture,* ed. Hal Foster (Port Townsend, Wash.: Bay Press, 1983), 127.

32. M. Dobbs, "World War II Buffs Relive Normandy Days of Glory," *The Washington Post,* June 8, 1984, A25 and A30.

7

"Packaging" Chernobyl:
The Manufacture of Meaning from
a Transnational Ecological Disaster

On Saturday April 26, 1986, an unprecedented event happened. A severe explosion tore apart a nuclear reactor at the Chernobyl atomic power station in the Ukraine, killing two people and releasing fissionable materials into the environment. The meanings attached to this event, however, remain complex, diverse, and contradictory. None of them exists as such—they have had to be manufactured in both the East and West. As they are produced, the broader reception of such meanings is rarely clean or complete. Consequently, one might consider this chapter as an exercise in "product semantics," unwrapping some of the thoughtlines manufactured into the packaging of Chernobyl as an ecological disaster.

Against the backdrop of first-order events in the reactor itself and their ongoing secondary implications for the economies and ecologies of Western and Eastern Europe, the meaning of Chernobyl has been continually reconstructed by Moscow, the news media, the nuclear power industry, and the OECD nations to convey many other third-order ideological meanings. In this regard, Chernobyl is an excellent example of how "spectacles" develop and are managed in advanced industrial societies. "The spectacle," as Debord affirms, "is not a collection of images, but a social relation among people, mediated by images." As it is produced, consumed, and reproduced as a social relation, "the spectacle presents itself simultaneously as all of society, as part of society, and as an *instrument of unification*."[1]

When the West German Greens claimed that "Chernobyl is Everywhere," they ironically identified how nuclear disaster, both as an image and as global fallout patterns, does unify everyone in new social, political, and economic relations mediated by images. Although Chernobyl is everywhere, it has acquired different meanings in different places to suit the expectations of many different groups. How the images are presented and received—or coded and decoded by corporate managers, technical experts, or state bureaucrats facing often resistant mass publics—renders spectacles like Chernobyl intrinsically political. In order to create consent, reaffirm legitimacy, underscore managerial prowess, or contain mass protests, Chernobyl had to be reprocessed and repackaged in more tamperproof containers lest the concrete tomb over reactor no. 4 become the entire nuclear power industry's headstone. In the USSR, the repackaging was done in the wrapping of glasnost. In the West, its reprocessing was organized to deflect criticism from each OECD nation's nuclear power industry as well as to reflect the conventional negative images of Soviet totalitarianism.

In the advanced industrial societies of North America, Japan, Western Europe, and Australasia, such ideologies are generated continuously "from a mass of minor hypotheses: news, culture, city planning, advertising, mechanisms of conditioning and suggestion ready to serve any order, established or to come," [2] in order to contain or channel mass resistance to managerial control. This ideology usually speaks through the mass media in new myths and mythologies that abolish "the complexity of human acts." And "it gives them the simplicity of essences, it does away with all dialectics, with any going back beyond what is immediately visible, it organizes a world without contradictions because it is without depth." [3] Yet a great deal of effort must constantly be expended by corporate capital, agencies of the state, or technocratic experts to guarantee this "blissful clarity" in such new myths and to revitalize the larger ideology of technological progress that these mythologies legitimate.

Thus far, the news of Chernobyl has fit well within the "mechanisms of conditioning and suggestion" in both the East and the West. State agencies and technocratic experts have redefined it in mythic terms, reducing this nuclear disaster to a tragic retelling of the myths of Faust or the sorcerer's apprentice. *Newsweek's* issue on Chernobyl, for example, stated, "So nuclear power turns out to be a bargain with the Devil," and "the Devil always sets his own fee." [4] According to these official fables, the post-Hiroshima world has made a fateful wager: in order to enjoy the immense but dark powers of the atom, nuclear society either has made a pact with Mephisto for its soul or it has created an ever-more-threatening servant that can easily evade human control. Even General Secretary Mikhail Gorbachev felt the need to repeat these myths when he claimed that at Chernobyl "for the first time ever, we have confronted in reality the sinister power of uncontrolled nuclear energy." [5] Therefore, "in this Faustian bargain," as Alvin Weinberg claims, "humans in opting for nuclear energy, must pay the price of extraordinary technical vigilance if they are to avoid serious trouble." [6]

Such mythologies are quite useful: they can simplistically summarize the intrinsic complexity of the Chernobyl events. When causation is assigned to the Chernobyl reactor operators' or designers' technical blunders, the disaster can be attributed to inept magicians, who rightly paid their price of "serious trouble" for lacking "technical vigilance." As a result, the nuclear magic basically remains sound. On April 30, 1986, for example, a *New York Times* editorial reaffirmed the myths: "The accident may reveal more about the Soviet Union than the hazards of nuclear power ... behind the Chernobyl setback may lie deeper faults of a weak technology and industrial base."[7] Furthermore, such media mythologies suggest that the immediately visible image of Chernobyl can be taken as meaning something in itself without contradictions by reassuringly linking it up with existing mythologies about the USSR as an industrial power.

All the correct myths shared by Western publics thereby are revalidated. The nuclear bargain is not flawed—the USSR is simply too weak for Mephisto; Chernobyl is only a setback, revealing nothing about the hazards of atomic energy; the deeper fault is in (Soviet) man, who lacks a firm industrial base and strong technology; or Soviet nuclear sorcerers lack adequate magic, so their atomic apprentice ran amok. Moreover, the sorcerer's apprentice was unleashed only in the USSR. Western nuclear sorcerers are much more crafty, just as a *Los Angeles Times* story on April 30, 1986, claimed: "Minimum safety standards ... clearly have not been met in the Soviet Union, where most nuclear reactors—apparently including the ill-fated plant at Chernobyl—do not have containment structures of the sort that are almost universal outside Russia."[8] However, to understand Chernobyl more fully these myths must be challenged and criticized. The real complexity of human actions and the inherent contradictions in the world must be restored. Things never mean something by themselves. Instead, their ideological and mythological packagings are revealed through attempts to rationalize the experience in question. Although this discussion cannot presume to disclose "what Chernobyl *really* means," it will instead discuss how it has been "packaged" to fit into larger political agendas.

THE CHERNOBYL ACCIDENT AND ITS AFTERMATH: THE EVENTS

In February 1986, *Soviet Life* featured an article on the growing nuclear power station at Chernobyl, where six massive Russian Graphite Moderated Channel Tube (RBMK) nuclear reactors ultimately would generate six megawatts (MW) of electricity. The Ukrainian Republic Power Minister, Vitali Sklyarov, said that of the four reactors already on line, "the odds of a meltdown are one in 10,000 years," and that despite these odds, plant engineering designs guaranteed that "the environment is also securely protected." [9] A month later, however, a local resident, Lyubov Kovalevska, wrote in *Literaturna Ukraina* that work on the Chernobyl power station suffered from a "low quality of design and costing documentation," "defective material," "lack of organization," "weakened discipline and responsibility," and "a large number of unresolved problems." [10]

The Soviet RBMK-type reactor employs graphite as its moderator and uses boiling water as a coolant by circulating it through the core to extract heat. At the close of 1985, the USSR had 27.8 gigawatts (GW) of operational nuclear capacity; 15.6 GW of this national capacity was generated by 28 RBMK-type reactors, while 7 units more with 8.1 GW of capacity were under construction and 8 more with 10.6 GW were in the planning stage. [11] Chernobyl no. 4 was one of fourteen operating RBMK–1000-class reactors. All RBMK reactors are direct derivations of the ones at the USSR's first nuclear station at Obninsk (commissioned in 1954) and the six plutonium-producing units (made operational from 1958 to 1964) in Troitsk. [12] For this reason, Moscow does not export its RBMK units because weapons-grade plutonium is one of their immediate by-products. [13] Even so, Soviet authorities considered the Chernobyl atomic power station on the Pripyat River one of their safest plants. They argued that the RBMK's graphite moderation, which enables refueling without shutting down and also disperses fissionable material into more than one thousand primary circuits, "increases the safety of the reactor system" and that "a serious loss of coolant accident is practically impossible." [14] Unfortunately, Lyubov Kovalevska's on-site warnings proved more prophetic than the official mythologies repeated by Vitali Sklyarov or Boris Semenov in touting the ultimate safety of the Chernobyl power station.

The world's worst nuclear accident, then, was the product of a poorly conducted reactor operations test staged on April 25–26, 1986, during the planned decommissioning of Chernobyl's reactor no. 4 for maintenance. A similar test was staged in 1984 but proved inconclusive because of inadequate electrical equipment. [15] According to the official Soviet report to the International Atomic Energy Agency in Vienna, this second experiment was to have tested how long the plant's steam turbines would generate electricity after being cut off from their steam supply. The test's goals were to show that the turbines could produce enough power to keep the station's safety systems operational. [16] Yet in conducting these experiments, the plant's technicians, as the official review of the accident found, "were not adequately prepared for the tests, and were not aware of the possible dangers." [17]

As a result, normal operating protocols were purposely ignored or overridden. In staging the test, Chernobyl's operators committed six major errors that collectively and progressively contributed to catastrophe. First, they needlessly switched off the reactor's emergency core cooling system, which did not cause the accident but aggravated its consequences. Second, in response to a grid control instruction, they incorrectly set a power regulator that then dropped the reactor's power output drastically. The output stabilized at a point too low for the test. Fearing bureaucratic reprimands for botching a test that could not be repeated for at least an entire year, the operators frantically tried to boost the reactor's output. In their attempt they violated operational rules for the reactor's control rod settings by pulling out all but six to eight rods from the core, even though plant norms dictated that thirty should be the norm and that fifteen was the minimum to maintain control. This third mistake boosted power but led to their fourth mistake: With the reactor's output increasing, the operators turned on two extra cooling water pumps as part of the test program. This action radically altered the equilibrium of water and steam in the circuit, destabilizing the reactor. Fifth, in response to these fluctuations in steam and water levels, they blocked the automatic shutdown system for the reactor. Now they started their experiment—and committed their sixth and last mistake. They turned off the last safety systems, which should have engaged when the turbines were shut down.[18]

After these actions were taken, the reactor essentially was running by itself without any outside control.[19] Recognizing the crisis, the operators dropped the scram rods into the core. The rods fell, but did not completely seat because of heat distortion. In the ensuing power surge, output rose from 7 percent to several hundred percent over normal levels in seconds as part of the core went "prompt critical." Two explosions blew off the reactor's one thousand–ton, steel-and-concrete containment lid, and tumbled a two hundred–ton refueling crane into the core, which destroyed many cooling circuits. With its containment barriers destroyed, the reactor's fuel rod cladding broke down, generating hydrogen in the steam that exploded into fire. Over thirty fires broke out all over the reactor complex, and the reactor's graphite core also caught fire. Within minutes, reactor no. 4's core cracked open, its coolant flow was interrupted, the reactor building's roof collapsed, and an intense graphite fire spewed deadly radioactive isotopes into the atmosphere.[20]

From April 26 to May 11, 1986, the Soviet regime struggled to douse the disastrous radioactive fires and protect the remaining three reactors at the Chernobyl complex. Within hours, the population of Pripyat and the immediately surrounding countryside within 2.5 kilometers (20,000 and 26,000 persons, respectively) was mobilized for evacuation. The authorities began evacuating a ten-kilometer zone around the plant on Sunday, April 27. On May 3, a much broader zone within 30 kilometers of the reactor was evacuated, including over 30,000 people from Chernobyl itself.[21] By May 6, more than 95,000 persons (and over 17,000 cattle) had been relocated.[22] A fleet of military helicopters and teams of scientists—both under the guidance of Yevgeny Velikov, vice-president of the Soviet Academy of Sciences—took charge of containing the dangerous graphite fire in reactor no. 4. From April 29 to May 13, 1986, over five thousand tons of boron, lead, sand, clay, and dolomite were dropped by helicopter to quench the fire.[23] To contain the damaged reactor permanently, cleanup teams tunneled underneath reactor no. 4 to lay a concrete foundation for an immense new enclosure structure, or "tomb," which was built around the entire reactor complex. This building will serve as a high-level radioactive waste dump for many centuries to come.

The ultimate costs of the Chernobyl accident are hard to quantify accurately. Beyond the 31 "prompt deaths" (2 immediately and 29 more slowly, through March 1987) and the hospitalization of nearly 300 people with radiation sickness, "estimates" and "projections" come into play. In direct cash terms, Chernobyl is believed to have cost the USSR over $3 billion.[24] By 1988, the cost of the cleanup had risen to $13 billion. Agricultural production has been disrupted and prime farm land contaminated across the western USSR. Vegetables in Kiev were tested after the accident and found to have thirteen times the level of radiation at which they should have been destroyed. In Byelorussia, checks in Gomelskaya showed that 40 percent of the meat, 30 percent of the milk, 15 percent of green vegetables, and 90 percent of all fish exceeded radiation standards. International conversion formulas suggest that 30,000 to 50,000 additional people in European Russia and 3,000 people in Western Europe will die of cancers due to Chernobyl radiation.[25] Similarly, 2,000 to 15,000 mutations and genetic diseases are forecast to develop per million live births over the next generation.[26] And around the world in the aftermath of Chernobyl, the whole nuclear power industry was called into question, if only for a few months. Yugoslavia dropped its plans to build a second nuclear power station at Prevlaka; Mexico delayed operations even longer at its troubled Laguna Verde plant; and the Philippines mothballed a nearly completed reactor in Bataan.[27] Global output from pressurized water (PWR) and boiling water (BWR) reactors dropped 15 percent in 1986 as nuclear utility managers sought to play it safe after the accident. Undoubtedly, current and future reactor costs will rise from new regulatory oversights prompted by Chernobyl.

At this juncture, however, one must move from the actual events at Chernobyl and their immediate aftermath into the ideological repackaging of Chernobyl in the USSR and abroad. This detailed technical account of the accident itself only came to light four months later in a voluminous official report made by Moscow to the International Atomic Energy Agency.[28] By that time, most media attention had shifted elsewhere. The official story only could wrap another layer of meaning around the many other ideological packages already set out for display in the global mediascape.

"PACKAGING" CHERNOBYL IN THE EAST AND WEST

Nuclear accidents have happened before, but always in bureaucratically enforced secrecy.[29] In October 1957, Great Britain's graphite-moderated Windscale no. 1 pile caught fire, spreading radiation but causing no explosion or immediate deaths. During the winter of 1957–58, a radioactive waste dump apparently overheated and exploded like a volcano outside the plutonium-producing Soviet city of Kyshtym in the Ural Mountains. A vast area was devastated, and many people were killed and injured. In January 1961, three technicians were killed in the SL-1 military reactor in Idaho after incorrectly manipulating its control rods. During October 1966, the experimental Fermi no. 1 breeder reactor in Detroit partially melted down, forcing it to be decommissioned. And in March 1979, Three Mile Island (TMI) unit 2 lost its coolant due to equipment malfunction and operator errors and experienced a partial meltdown with some radioactivity release.

Chernobyl no. 4, however, was the first reactor in a disaster to breach its containment structures and actually spew large amounts of radioactivity into the environment (up to 3 percent of its fissionable materials). As the reactor fire spread dangerous isotopes downwind, sensors in Sweden triggered the alert. Once detected, the global media all turned on Chernobyl in order to produce ideologically appropriate images and mythically correct information for popular reception worldwide. The TMI crisis of 1979 now guarantees that what could have been concealed in the 1950s and 1960s would now be put on mythically limited display in both the USSR and the world. The substantive meanings and spectacular forms of Chernobyl, therefore, were generated by Geiger counters, meteorological models, fallout dispersion tables, radioactivity sensors, expert opinions, half-life charts, television cameras, news organization special reports, ham radio intercepts, and LANDSAT, SPOT, or KH-11 satellite photos. From this mosaic, the USSR, the media, the international nuclear power industry, and the leadership of the OECD nations fabricated their ideological packagings of Chernobyl.

In the East

In the USSR, on one level Chernobyl enabled Moscow to reiterate the common Faustian myths of technical progress of "Humanity Tragically Trapped by Its Own Runaway Technology." General Secretary Gorbachev's May 14, 1986, address clearly was guided by such myths in explaining to the world and the USSR one meaning of Chernobyl. On another level, however, Chernobyl served Gorbachev by expressing his break with the cultural and political stagnation of the Brezhnev era. It is unclear whether Gorbachev chose this glasnost for himself or whether the crisis forced glasnost upon him. Still, Chernobyl was eventually packaged in Moscow: first, as a subtle sign of cleaning out the Brezhnev era bureaucracy, and second, as an indicator of Gorbachev's commitment to frankness, openness, and effective publicity.

Neither one of these packaging strategies has been easy to follow. The traditional prejudice favoring secrecy and the practice of misinforming higher organs still prevails throughout the Soviet state in the wake of Chernobyl. Deputy Chairman of the USSR Council of Ministers, B. Y. Shcherbina, reported on national Soviet television that the information received in Moscow "was not the same that we obtained when we were in the area" and that "local experts had not made a correct assessment of the accident."[30] *Novosti's* V. M. Falin told *Der Spiegel* interviewers that "the first reports from the Chernobyl nuclear power plant were incomplete and ultimately turned out to be incorrect" and that "the first objective, detailed information came in before the Monday meeting of the Politburo" two days later.[31] At that meeting Gorbachev apparently ran into considerable resistance from members of the Politburo. Roy Medvedev maintains, "Gorbachev tried to assert a policy of lucidity and correct information within the Politburo. . . . He was backed only by [V. I.] Vorotnikov, chairman of the Russian Republic Council of Ministers, and [KGB head, V. M.] Chebrikov, whereas the rest apparently wanted a containment of information."[32] Gorbachev prevailed only when the scale of the accident and Western inquiries about it made a cover-up essentially impossible.

Although Gorbachev did not directly criticize Chernobyl's management by local officials in his May 14 address, *Pravda* reported on June 15 that the party organization at the Chernobyl site was "sharply condemned" by the local territorial apparatus.[33] The plant director and chief engineer were discharged for irresponsibility, inefficiency, poor discipline, and inadequate leadership, while the shift supervisors and plant foremen were described as being on the run. This administrative purge continued up the line in the Ukrainian party apparatus throughout 1986. Therefore, Moscow shifted the blame for the accident, the delay in evacuations, inefficient relief reports, and tardiness in reporting the accident for three days onto the Brezhnevite old regime in the local and regional party apparatus.

This concern with cleaning house and punishing lax workers was affirmed the following spring, and the policy of glasnost has continued since the accident. In March 1987, the chairman of the State Committee for Atomic Energy of the USSR told a visiting Nuclear Regulatory Commission (NRC) delegation that the persons responsible for Chernobyl would be put on trial soon in Kiev.[34] Members of the delegation also visited the Chernobyl power station and were shown its operating units and the two under construction or development. But glasnost was not total: the team learned some minor details, but basically the NRC delegation was told "nothing really new since Vienna."[35] Nevertheless, as the *Economist* noted, Chernobyl gave Gorbachev a unique opportunity. Already one year in office by April 1986, he had not changed Soviet society very dramatically: "Yet if he wants a new stick with which to bully his more cautious colleagues into reforming faster, Chernobyl has given it to him. Using it will be risky. Not using it means courting greater failures in the future. That is the Chernobyl choice, and Mr. Gorbachev's chance."[36]

In seeking to package Chernobyl at home and abroad in the new look of glasnost, Gorbachev has been somewhat more successful. During his May 14 speech he stressed the "accuracy" of Soviet accident reports versus the "veritable pack of lies" in the Western press and official commentary. While he portrayed his regime's open press policies on the Chernobyl disaster as relatively more frank and truthful, Gorbachev noted how it was overshadowed by false Western reports of "thousands of casualties, mass graves of the dead, desolate Kiev, that the entire land of the Ukraine has been poisoned."[37] At the same time, he linked Chernobyl to the danger of nuclear arms, calling for a summit with President Reagan to negotiate a test moratorium and announcing a continuation of suspended Soviet nuclear testing.[38] By lashing back at overdrawn Western criticism, Gorbachev sought to cast the USSR in the most favorable light as an honest, open, great power wrestling with the unknown mysteries and sinister forces of nuclear energy. He recounted why the accident happened, admitting to 13 deaths and 299 hospitalized casualties. He also emphasized that Soviet scientists had contained the threat and were capable of meeting the formidable technical challenges ahead. To prove he was serious about glasnost, Gorbachev apparently approved greater access to Chernobyl for the Soviet press, permitting unprecedented on-site interviews, dramatic close-up TV footage of reactor no. 4, and critical reporting on the local authorities' response to the crisis.

In the process, glasnost has perhaps hidden as much as it has revealed.

Like Khrushchev, Gorbachev might be moving much too fast, alienating and threatening the Moscow bureaucracy, which can effectively throttle the practice of glasnost.[39] The basic premise of nuclearization is not being challenged, nor have reporters questioned the Politburo about the USSR's previous atomic accidents, like the disaster at Kyshtym. The whole truth about radiation and its effects has not been told. Instead, glasnost has developed as an amalgam of self-criticism and self-praise made from the traditional idioms of collective strength and Soviet nationalism. Glasnost was used here to expose the corruption of the few for the progress of the many, but reaffirm the heroic, self-sacrificing spirit of individual Soviet citizens when faced with danger.

In packaging Chernobyl, the USSR stressed its "progressiveness" as a nation, fearlessly facing new technological frontiers with a new international openness. Even though it failed miserably to warn or assist its Eastern European allies and Western European neighbors in coping with Chernobyl's nuclear and economic fallout, the USSR has gotten away with its negligence—perhaps because these inconsiderate behaviors were almost "expected" from Moscow. Gorbachev's packaging, to a degree, has pinned this aspect of Chernobyl on "the old regime," while he holds out the much more promising image of himself and Raisa spurring the Soviet Union toward a more open, image-driven future of prosperity, reform, and peace. Overall, it seems to be working. The Western press has been quite favorable toward Gorbachev's program. At times, the Western media have even suggested that the general secretary with his stylish new pizazz surpasses America's "Great Communicator." In the USSR, as Gorbachev's apparent successes at restructuring the party and state structures illustrate, glasnost also seems to be overcoming some of the intelligentsia's disaffection with the regime, giving them a reason to contribute to Gorbachev's badly needed new plans for playing technological catch-up with the West. Despite the negative aftershocks from the crisis, Chernobyl clearly has produced some positive fallout for the international image-makers in Moscow.

In the West

In the OECD nations, Chernobyl also acquired mythic dimensions. As *Newsweek* asserted, "The disaster has exposed glaring weaknesses in the Soviet system: its backward technology, its sloppy safety standards, its inability to admit failure."[40] Thus, the accident was used, first, to assign fresh sources of meaning to the commonly circulated images of the USSR as a barbaric slave state with little regard for human life and, second, as new evidence of the Soviet Union's continuing backwardness as an industrial power.

Moscow did little to forestall these interpretations. The first admission of an accident was not made until two days after the reactor explosion, and then the Radio Moscow report from TASS only stated: "Measures are being taken to eliminate consequences of the accident. Aid is being given to those affected. A government commission has been set up."[41] On April 29, the "Vremya" evening news program reported two deaths, a portion of the reactor building destroyed, and the evacuation of Pripyat. The following day TASS denied Western reports of massive casualties, and not until May 4 (when film clips shot from a helicopter indicated the limited extent of severe damages at Chernobyl) did Moscow broadcast convincing images on "Vremya."[42]

On May 6, *Pravda* published comprehensive coverage of the accident and its aftermath; however, the Soviet government also stated in a news conference, "In our opinion, there was no direct threat to the population either of our own areas which are far enough away . . . or foreign countries" despite an increase in background radiation levels.[43] The next day TASS reported "a negligible portion of small radioactive particles was also distributed together with airflows over large distances and fell on the territory of Poland, Romania, and of a number of Scandinavian countries. Here a slight increase in background radioactivity was observed, likewise not a danger to the population."[44]

In fact, Byalistock and Wegorzew in Poland recorded radiation levels 1,500 to 1,700 times greater than normal background levels. Special iodine solutions were distributed to the nomenklatura of the PUWP (Polish United Workers Party) on April 28–29, 1986,[45] to counteract the radioactive iodine 131 in the Chernobyl fallout. In Stockholm on April 28–29, the level of iodine 131 was measured at 10 becquerels per cubic meter of air, while on the Swedish coast they were monitored at 190 becquerels per cubic meter.[46] On Gotland Island, 40,000 becquerels per square meter of grass were monitored, and levels of 8,000 per square meter were found in Great Britain. Throughout Europe, large stocks of vegetables, fruit, and milk were destroyed for weeks to prevent more radiation from entering human food supplies.[47] Still, a Soviet overview of the crisis was not given until Gorbachev's address on May 14 during the "Vremya" broadcast. By that time, the United States and the OECD nations had already assigned the usual meanings to the USSR, using Chernobyl as additional proof.

Following a UPI report, for example, the American media claimed a death toll figure of at least two thousand. Similarly, Secretary of State George Shultz said that he bet ten dollars that the deaths were far in excess of the two initially reported by Moscow. Kenneth Adelman, head of the U.S. Arms Control and Disarmament Agency, also decried Soviet causualty reports, calling them "frankly preposterous."[48] In the seesaw of superpower arms negotiations, the accident was also portrayed as meaning that Washington could not trust Moscow to verify nuclear treaties because of the Soviets' inadequate disclosures about Chernobyl. A May 1 *New York Times* editorial argued: "Gorbachev cannot win confidence in his pledges to reduce nuclear weapons if he forfeits his neighbor's trust over the peaceful uses of nuclear energy."[49] President Reagan also used Chernobyl to cast doubt on Soviet credibility at the Tokyo economic summit, while *Time* reported one American offical to have said: "'Imagine what they do to national security items if they handle themselves like this with just a civilian power plant.'"[50] In a similar vein, the London *Sunday Times* asked editorially, "'Who would trust the Soviet Union to allow proper verification of its nuclear missile sites when it does not even tell its own citizens of a fatal accident in one of its own nuclear power stations?'" The image of the USSR as a totalitarian monolith with little regard for individual human life gained fresh momentum in the Chernobyl afterglow. Although Soviet government, military, and party leaders displayed great concern for the local citizens of Pripyat and Chernobyl, and despite the way individual firemen, technicians, and helicopter pilots displayed incredible bravery and selflessness in containing the reactor fire, the bureaucratic confusion between Kiev and Moscow practically verified the cynical Western packaging of Chernobyl.

The Soviet Union surely deserves no praise for its handling of Chernobyl. As Hoffman concludes, "Any government, socialist or capitalist, that withholds from its citizens information about the dangers of nuclear energy or fails to help citizens protect themselves before and after a nuclear accident at home or abroad diminishes its legitimacy and effectiveness."[51] Nevertheless, as Bernstein recounts, when it comes to U.S. nuclear information policies—from the Manhattan Project to TMI—Americans must recognize that "their own government, at various levels, has sometimes suppressed information and deceived its own citizens about the safety and purposes of the U.S. nuclear program."[52]

Chernobyl also was employed as a fresh citation to the Soviet Union's deepening technological backwardness. By Tuesday, April 29, Soviet government officials were asking Sweden and West Germany for advice on fighting graphite fires.[53] Two West German robots were dispatched to explore the reactor, and with Armand Hammer's aid, an American doctor named Robert Gale, a UCLA bone marrow transplant specialist, was dispatched to Moscow to help Chernobyl's victims.[54] Moreover, White House press spokesman Larry Speakes announced that poor Soviet design and engineering were at fault in the crisis. To forestall comparisons with U.S. reactors, he assured the world that "ours are quite different from the

Soviet system and have a number of redundant safety systems built in." [55] Even though such claims were somewhat false, numerous Western experts came forward to assure the public that the Soviet reactor was antiquated, poorly designed, and lacked a containment structure. In Donald Regan's assessment, Soviet industrial backwardness was to blame, and *not* atomic energy itself: "Nuclear power is a good thing for the future of many nations, including our own—we shouldn't throw out the baby with the bath water and condemn all nuclear power plants because of this." [56]

To reinforce this picture of Soviet industrial inefficiency and incompetence, the Nuclear Energy Agency (NEA) of the OECD met twelve days after Chernobyl to assess its meaning for the West. They concluded that the NEA should study how to improve cooperation in future nuclear accidents, but that the designs of Western reactor types were quite superior to Soviet designs (Soviet reactors could not even be licensed in the West). Therefore, no reconsideration of OECD nuclear energy programs was necessary. Since 30 percent of Western Europe's, 16 percent of the United States', and 20 percent of Japan's electricity is nuclear-generated, the Tokyo economic summit affirmed the OECD's joint support of "properly managed" Western nuclear power. [57] *Time* boldly concluded that the key difference between East and West on nuclear energy was political: "The U.S. industry operates in an open society, subject to laws that give the public considerable say over where nuclear plants are located and some input as to when and even if they will go into operation. The same cannot be said of the Soviet Union, where the government makes all such decisions without consulting the public." [58] This, of course, will be news to many American nuclear activists fighting the Diablo Canyon, Seabrook, or Palo Verde units.

The American media, in particular, actively participated in packaging Chernobyl in terms of Soviet callousness and backwardness. In its typical style, the *New York Post* ran headlines (lifted from a New Jersey Ukrainian-language weekly) that bellowed "MASS GRAVE—15,000 reported buried in Nuke Disposal Site." [59] More reputable news operations did not do much better. For days—on the basis of an unconfirmed report from Kiev—UPI, AP, NBC, ABC, CBS, *The New York Times*, and *The Washington Post* used the figure of 2,000 deaths, with varying degrees of qualification, in reporting on Chernobyl. When put in context with official Soviet reports of 2 to 31 deaths, these reports implicitly "exposed" the USSR as the lying, untrustworthy dictatorship it had always been. For most of the week following the accident, news reports consistently overestimated casualties, claimed two or even more reactors might be on fire, and suggested the rescue and cleanup were going very slowly. Reports of Western aid—like the West German robots, Swedish technical consultants, and the American bone marrow transplant team—were also highlighted to stress the Soviet Union's technical inabilities in coping with the disaster. Yet, beyond buying SPOT or LANDSAT photos for visual confirmation of their dire dispatches, most news organizations relied on Western spokesmen and official handouts for most of their copy rather than any on-the-spot reporting.

This tendency undoubtedly was accentuated by the unusual press access to official spokesmen afforded by President Reagan's Far East tour leading into the Tokyo summit. Overall, as Dorman and Hirsch observe, "the initial Soviet statements turned out to be largely correct on a number of significant concerns—for example, the number of casualties, the number of reactors on fire, and whether or not the fire had been contained—while those of the Reagan Administration, which were taken by journalists at face value, proved not to be." [60] The American press also was remarkably slow about correcting its earlier sensational and inaccurate packaging of Chernobyl. By May 19, 1986, *The New York Times* and *The Wall Street Journal* ran stories reporting that the USSR had built substantial containment structures in its reactors and that American complacency about its own reactor designs was unwarranted. Yet these insights were mainly drawn from an NRC briefing given nearly two weeks earlier on May 8 and from NRC Commissioner James Asseltine's testimony before the House on May 5. While titillating inaccuracies were given front-page, first-column spreads in late April, the sober realities were tabled for two or three weeks, only to end up later as minor sidebars or back-page, second-section fillers. In the end, both the Western press and Washington flatly claimed that if some media reports had been inaccurate, "this was the inevitable result of the extreme secrecy with which the Soviet authorities dealt with the accident in the days following it." [61]

Beyond the Western nation-states, the most highly motivated Western group working to redefine the meaning of Chernobyl was the U.S. nuclear power industry. *Time* reported that from 1980 to 1986, over 60,000 MW of planned nuclear power plant capacity had been canceled or indefinitely postponed. Chernobyl threatened the industry with an even larger exodus of customers. A White House official echoed the industry's concerns: "We don't want the hysteria building around the Soviet accident transferring over to the American power industry." [62] Given the industry's political problems at Indian Point, Seabrook, Shoreham, Browns Ferry, Zion, Diablo Canyon, Palo Verde, and Three Mile Island, as well as problems with the TVA and WHOOPs reactor programs, its concerns were quite significant.

The week before Chernobyl the U.S. Committee for Energy Awareness was running public service ads decrying, "Nuclear Energy—Is America Being Left Behind?," and showing Old Glory at the bottom of a nuclear-power bar graph under a heap of other OECD nations' flags.[63] The Soviet accident, of course, cast a long shadow over such lobbying efforts by the nuclear power industry. Therefore, Chernobyl's meaning in the packaging by the Western nuclear power industry was simple—it had "no meaning" because the RBMK reactor was radically different than all Western PWR or BWR reactors. The Atomic Industrial Forum sent out mailings claiming that Chernobyl had no containment structure and that all U.S. reactors had the extensive steel and concrete protective barriers most Soviet units lacked.[64] A public relations blitz mounted by the Electrical Power Research Institute similarly claimed that Chernobyl was poorly designed because it lacked steel and concrete containments common in the United States.[65] The Edison Electric Institute simply stated that "we have not and will not have a Chernobyl-type plant accident here."[66] With no orders for new plants since 1978, the U.S. nuclear companies were justifiably worried. Before the Chernobyl accident, some experts saw orders for new plants by 1991 or 1996; Chernobyl's aftermath threatens to pull the plug on the United States' dying nuclear technology industry.

Subsequent revelations about the Chernobyl reactors' design, as well as the design of U.S. reactors, underscored the importance of assigning a negative, irrelevant meaning to the Soviet accident when it was headline material in the United States. By May 1986, it was revealed that the United States was operating two graphite-moderated reactors, one water-cooled and one gas-cooled, in Washington and Colorado respectively.[67] Theoretically, and contrary to the Edison Electric Institute's claims, a Chernobyl-type, graphite-fire accident could occur in either trouble-plagued unit. Moreover, the graphite-moderated N-reactor at Hanford, Washington, and four other similar units at Savannah, Georgia, which produce plutonium and tritium for the Department of Energy's nuclear weapons program, all lack adequate containment structures.[68] If their safety systems failed, highly toxic plutonium could be widely dispersed in the resulting reactor accident. After the immediate Chernobyl crisis had passed, the Atomic Industrial Forum admitted to "a little simplification" in its initial claims. By then, the threat to nuclear power's public image was contained as the negative meaning of Chernobyl settled on Moscow and a measure of reassurance stuck with the U.S. nuclear power industry. With problems like the questionable containment designs in General Electric's boiling-water reactors or Westinghouse's inadequately tested pressure-suppression systems, U.S. nuclear power seriously needed positive comparisons with the negative example of Chernobyl.[69]

This need to reclaim legitimacy for the nuclear project continued into

1987. For example, Steve Delaney anchored an hour-long NBC News special report, "Nuclear Power: In France It Works," which was broadcast in the United States on March 12, 1987. After opening with a review of the passionate controversies raised in the United States and West Germany by TMI, WHOOPs, and Chernobyl, the documentary looked at France's extensive nuclearization program. Since France has no gas, no oil, and no coal, it is shown as having "no choice" other than nuclear energy. As our gas, oil, and coal dwindle, we implicitly also have no choice. As a result, the report claimed, objective journalistic examination of nuclear power in France might restore reasonable good sense to a United States energy policy now terribly divided by passionate anti-nuclear emotions.

NBC News painted quite a positive picture of Paris and the atom in its "objective examination." The images were ones of precise safety, aesthetic design, and sophisticated control: France's standardized reactor designs; the tough training of skilled operators at the École Polytechnique; 49 working reactors, with 15 under construction, providing 70 percent of the nation's electricity and lighting; Paris, the City of Light; French villagers welcoming reactors as clean, safe places of employment; Électricité de France managers assuring all that accidents in France are virtually impossible and that the nuclear waste problem has been solved; France pushing into new dominance internationally as a supplier of nuclear reactors, fuel, and technology; French nuclear power generating money in electricity and high-tech exports; and the French willingly accepting nuclearization, as a mark of national pride and technical accomplishment, with little serious protest. The report stressed that France has an advantage over the United States, namely, government intolerance of dissent (which was also presented as usually coming from misinformed or ignorant malcontents) and unshaken public faith in the technocratic acumen of France's nuclear establishment.

The report did not point out how France's small size and population densities make such centralized systems of power generation somewhat more feasible than in the United States, nor did it discuss the numerous accidents that the French have experienced but rarely report. NBC News also neglected Paris's lack of nuclear glasnost about Chernobyl. Fearing a backlash about the fallout from the Soviet *Atomstaat*, the French *Atomstaat* claimed the radioactive cloud by-passed France in May 1986. Later Paris admitted the fallout did indeed hit France but did not call for public precautions because the levels of radiation were too low. Yet radiation in food and on the ground in some regions was four hundred times greater than background levels.[70] In sum, NBC News essentially presented a perfectly pro-nuclear package; nuclear energy means, as it does in contemporary France, many "good" things: freedom from OPEC oil, more jobs, greater shares of foreign markets, national consensus for a high-tech energy policy, and the silencing of troublesome environmentalists. It must be noted that these curious "elective affinities" for nuclearization in NBC's journalistic stance might have some connection with General Electric's takeover of the Radio Corporation of America and its media division, the National Broadcasting Corporation, in 1986. While one should not necessarily reduce this NBC special report to a crude capitalist or public relations conspiracy, General Electric prides itself on "bringing good things to life," which includes serving as one of the United States' main nuclear reactor designers and a major supplier of advanced nuclear technology at home and abroad.[71]

CONCLUSIONS

In the last analysis, the packaging of Chernobyl in both the East and the West has proven fairly effective. Within days after the accident, it was clear that many of its threatening meanings had been contained. As more and more information was provided, it became clear that Chernobyl had not really called the future of nuclear power into question. The mythologies of advanced industrial ideology instead used Chernobyl to reaffirm the impossibility of future human progress without *more* nuclear power. For example, Gene Pokorny of Cambridge Reports, a public opinion firm that has tracked American attitudes about nuclear power for nearly fifteen years, maintains that "a massive shift in public opinion is just not there."[72] During the aftermath of Three Mile Island, hard-core opponents to nuclear power jumped up to 18 to 20 percent of the adult population from 10 percent in early 1979 and has stayed at that level. By February 1987, Chernobyl had failed to make a permanent impact on anti-nuclear public opinion. "By and large," Pokorny reports, "American public opinion is where it was before the accident."[73]

Such polls do not measure the delayed, long-term effects of Chernobyl on worldwide opposition to nuclear power. But in the short term it appears that the diverse but competing packaging teams of the East and West in state agencies, the private sector, and nuclear professional forums have achieved their goal of assigning appropriate meanings to Chernobyl and framing its political reception among various mass publics worldwide. The mass reception of Chernobyl's repackaging apparently was quite positive. In the United States, the Cambridge Reports' February 1987 poll also revealed that 79 percent of the respondents described nuclear power as an important future energy source, up from 73 percent in the 1984–85 period. That same percentage of the February poll also believed that the United States would increase its use of nuclear energy, and 67 percent agreed that it was a "very good" or "realistic" source of power for the United States' large-scale electrification needs.[74] These diverse discourses by those-in-power, then, are the active speech of apparent order continuously speaking to reduce those-not-in-power to passive silence about the real disorder undergirding nuclearized societies.

Still, such ideological campaigns are not easy, nor are they guaranteed to prove successful. Images of reassurance must be presented directly enough for mass publics to coproduce their own affirmations of nuclear energy after considering the various trade-offs and the allure of its high technology. Images are manufactured, but the terms of their consumption or the nature of their reception are often incomplete. Chernobyl is so shocking because it is the unlikely statistical improbability suddenly become an immediately real, transnational, ecological disaster. It starkly contradicts images of technical precision and positive cost-benefit comparisions with coal, oil, or gas consumption that the nuclear power industry usually packages into its image advertising. The catastrophic meltdown that had been predicted to happen only once in ten thousand years took place less than ten years after the first unit at the Chernobyl power station came on line. (In fact, the entire RBMK system probably had only 250 reactor years of operation.) In certain respects, the ideological reprocessings of Chernobyl by the USSR, the Western media, the leadership of the OECD nations, and the Western nuclear power industry were interconnected. Each of them, working in its own fashion, sought to reaffirm the legitimacy of high technology and the authority of technological competence from an episode of high-tech disaster and clear technological incompetence. Chernobyl flashed "transmission interruption," "technical difficulties," or "broadcast interference" across the screens of power. It had to be repackaged as a warning to everyone "not to adjust their sets." Those with access, competence, and control of the codes were stalling those without access, competence, or code command, reassuring them "to remain calm and await further instructions" rather than increase their resistance.

Despite their best efforts, the nature of the reception of these images is open to question, given the growing resistance to nuclear power and nuclear weaponry. For the ecological opposition, Chernobyl served well as the fulfillment of its dire prophecies of nuclear disaster in deadly fact.[75] As the explosion spread dangerous isotopes across the entire Northern Hemisphere, Chernobyl seemed to revitalize the anti-nuclear movement throughout North America, Western Europe, and Japan, but especially in West Germany.[76] By mid-May 1986, West German protesters were clashing violently with police at the Wackersdorf site of Bonn's new nuclear-waste reprocessing plant.[77] Their concerns are very real: in addition to being sandwiched between the heavily nuclearized Soviet Union and France, West Germany operates twenty reactors within its territory, and another eighteen are within one hundred kilometers of its borders.[78] When a Chernobyl-style thirty-kilometer evacuation zone is placed over West Germany's five major northern and southern nuclear plants, the major cities of Bremerhaven, Hamburg, Mainz, Darmstadt, Worms, Ludwigshafen, Mannheim, Karlsruhe, Stuttgart, Heidelberg, Heilbronn, Würzburg, and Schweinfurt fall directly into a high-risk zone.[79] It is not at all surprising, then, that West German Greens first recognized that Chernobyl is everywhere, nor that a *Der Spiegel* poll showed that only 29 percent of West Germans supported building new nuclear plants versus 69 percent against in mid-May 1986.[80] Similarly, one year after Chernobyl, the Worldwatch Institute claimed the accident was the final blow needed to "collapse in country after country" the existing "pro-nuclear consensus."[81]

For the advocates of nuclear power, Chernobyl is simply another (albeit quite serious) variety of industrial accident, which actually took less lives in one event than most coal mining accidents, hydroelectric dam failures, or ordinary pollution from fossil fuels. Many shrugged it off, pointing out that the Bhopal chemical plant disaster, for example, was "much worse" in terms of human deaths. This "naturalization" of nuclear disaster seems to be one of Chernobyl's worst legacies. After the accident, many tough-minded exponents of nuclear power flatly announced that "within 30 years an accident like Chernobyl or Three Mile Island might be happening every year, 'We will get used to them, and newspapers will report them on page 37.'"[82] A poll of American nuclear scientists in April 1987 revealed that 77 percent saw a Chernobyl-scale nuclear accident as improbable, 82 percent saw U.S. reactors as safer after Chernobyl, and 66 percent saw U.S. reactors as quite safe overall.[83] Apparently, the image advertising of Chernobyl, like most expensive advertising campaigns, simply reinforced already existing attitudes, providing new reasons for individuals to continue to hold onto their anti-nuclear or pro-nuclear stance.

These reactions among many nuclear scientists, however, even among those opposed to nuclear power, still run down mythological tracks. Nuclear power here is reduced to a "complex technological system" that is "inherently fallible" because of the complexity, scale, centralization, hierarchy, or inaccessibility of the control systems needed to manage them."[84] In mythic form, once again, as Mephisto or the sorcerer's apprentice, "Technology" looms over "Man and Society" as a sinister threat. In fact, these control systems' attributes are not facts of nature, nor should their failure be regarded as natural; instead, they are the result of the purposive creations of peculiar bureaucratic structures in the state sector or corporate sector of the superpowers. Abstract naturalized forces, like fallibility, complexity, hierarchy, centralization, inaccessibility, and scale are, in fact, very political and totally artificial traits. They express the specific social relations of production embodied in the USSR by the State Committee for Utilization of Atomic Power, the Ministry of Medium Machine Building, the Ministry of Power and Electrification, and the Ministry of Power Machine Building, and in the U.S. by the Department of Defense, the Department of Energy, the Nuclear Regulatory Commission and various private nuclear utilities. Nuclear power and its flaws are not naturally necessary: They have simply become political necessities as nuclear power has become a vital means of production for states with these bureaucratic relations of nuclear production.

This military/political connection to the superpower state is essential. It is what the packaging of peaceful nuclear power continually obscures. Although no one has solved the intrinsic dangers of the nuclear fuel cycle or the problems posed by nuclear waste, safe reactors are feasible. The West German modular high-temperature gas reactor (MHTGR) and the Swedish-designed process-inherent, ultimately safe reactor (PIUS) seem to overcome the instabilities of current PWR, BWR, or RBMK designs.[85] But their technology originated in civilian design bureaus in the smaller, non-nuclear nations of West Germany and Sweden. Most existing reactors are based upon much older U.S. or Soviet military designs. Nuclear power reactors using the PWR systems favored in the West are derived from naval technologies first developed to power nuclear submarines. Likewise, nuclear reactors employing the Soviet RBMK technology are based upon plutonium production units for atomic bomb manufacture.

Nuclear power advocates mystify and obscure the real sources of fallibility behind complex technologies by blaming it on the technology itself. To a very significant extent, nuclear power generation was initiated in the 1950s as a partial atonement by nuclear weaponry designers for first using the atom for war. To compensate for Hiroshima, they sought to legitimate their work by turning nuclear energy to peaceful purposes such as generating electricity for peacetime consumption. The technology, in turn, is simply a material product of the overly complex and inherently fallible military-scientific bureaucracies that initially produced and managed it. If the handmill creates societies with feudal lords and the steam mill leads to societies with industrial capitalists, then it would appear that the nuclear power stations at Chernobyl and TMI follow from societies with the Ministries for Medium Machine Building, Power Machine Building, and Defense, as well as the Departments of Defense and Energy. Given these power-producing technologies' original roots in weapons production and their less than meticulous management by large complex bureaucracies, the nuclear accidents at Chernobyl and TMI are not hard to understand. Nuclear energy, at the bottom line, is essential for these bureaucracies because it makes possible the nuclear powers of the superpower state. The tendency among nuclear power supporters, in turn, to naturalize tremendous nuclear disaster only reflects, in a distorted form, the disaster of superpower states naturalizing nuclear supports for their tremendous power. In the end, the mythologists of nuclear energy in both the East and the West have had to repackage Chernobyl mythically in such ideological terms as humankind's saga of "no price is too high" to have nuclear power. Yet the deeper realities of Chernobyl belie all of its packaging and call the ultimate myths of nuclear energy into open question—the safe, clean source of energy too cheap to meter is finally shown to be a dangerous, dirty kind of power with costs too immense to measure.

NOTES

1. Guy Debord, *Society of the Spectacle* (Detroit: Red & Black, 1983), no. 2.

2. Raoul Veneigem, *The Revolution of Everyday Life* (London: Left Bank Books/Rebel Press), 12.

3. Roland Barthes, "Myth Today," in *The Barthes Reader,* ed. Susan Sontag (New York: Hill and Wang, 1982), 132.

4. L. Martz et al., "There's a Price to be Paid for Atomic Energy, and It Could be a High One," *Newsweek,* May 12, 1986, 40–41, 44, 49.

5. J. Greenwald, J. O. Jackson, and N. Traver, "Gorbachev Goes on the Offensive," *Time,* May 26, 1986, 32–33.

6. Alvin Weinberg, "A Nuclear Power Advocate Reflects on Chernobyl," *Bulletin of the Atomic Scientists* 42, no. 7 (1986): 57.

7. "Chernobyl's Other Cloud," *The New York Times,* April 30, 1986, A17, A19.

8. Cited in William A. Dorman and Daniel Hirsch, "The U.S. Media's Slant," *Bulletin of the Atomic Scientists* 42, no. 7 (1986): 56.

9. See M. Ryslsky, "The Nuclear Power Industry in the Ukraine," *Soviet Life* (February, 1986): 8.

10. Lyubov Kovalevska, "The Decisions of the 27th Congress Being Put into Action—It Is No Private Matter," *Literaturna Ukraina,* March 27, 1986. Cited in *Daily Report: Soviet Union* 3, no. 87 (May 6, 1986): 51–53.

11. "Latest Five-Year Plan Confirms Soviet Ambitions," *Nuclear Engineering International* 31, no. 385 (1986): 25.

12. Gordon Thompson, "What Happened at Reactor Four," *Bulletin of Atomic Scientists* 42, no. 7 (1986): 26.

13. Nigel Hawkes et al., *Chernobyl: The End of the Nuclear Dream* (New York: Vintage, 1986), 90. Also see David R. Marples, *Chernobyl and Nuclear Power in the USSR* (New York: St. Martin's Press, 1986), 1–35.

14. Boris Semenov, "The Nuclear Power Industry in the Soviet Union," *International Atomic Energy Agency Bulletin* 25, no. 2 (1983): 47–59.

15. Walter C. Patterson, "Chernobyl: Worst But Not First," *Bulletin of the Atomic Scientists* 42, no. 7 (1986), 34.

16. Ibid.

17. Hawkes et al., 99.

18. Ibid., 99–102.

19. Thompson, "What Happened at Reactor Four," 27–29.

20. Walter C. Patterson, "Chernobyl—The Official Story," *Bulletin of the Atomic Scientists* 42, no. 9 (1986): 35.

21. Herbert Adams, "How Radiation Victims Suffer," *Bulletin of the Atomic Scientists* 42, no. 7 (1986): 13.

22. Hawkes et al., 13.

23. Ibid., 174–75.

24. Ibid., iii.

25. Ibid., 209–10. See also Thomas von Hippel and Thomas Cochran, "Estimating Long-Term Health Effects," *Bulletin of the Atomic Scientists* 42, no. 7 (1986): 23–24, and Marples, *Chernobyl and Nuclear Power in the USSR,* 25–35.

26. Hawkes et al., 210. See also David Albright, "Chernobyl and the U.S. Nuclear Industry," *Bulletin of the Atomic Scientists* 42, no. 7 (1986): 29–40.

27. Hawkes et al., 221. See also David Fisher, "The International Response," *Bulletin of the Atomic Scientists* 42, no. 7 (1986): 48.

28. Patterson, "Chernobyl—The Official Story," 34–36.

29. See J. Greenwald et al., "Deadly Meltdown," *Time,* May 12, 1986, 39–44, 49–50, 52; B. Levin et al., "The Fear of Nuclear Chaos," *MacLeans,* May 12, 1986, 26–34; and Patterson, "Chernobyl: Worst But Not First," 43–45.

30. *Daily Report: Soviet Union,* "More on Kovalevska, Shcherbina Comments," 3, no. 88, Supp. 89 (May 7, 1986), L6.

31. "*Spiegel*-Gespräch, 'Wir waren innerlich nicht vorbereitet,' Walentin Falin, Vorstandvorsitzender der Sowjetischen Nachrichtenagentur, 'Nowosti,' über Tschernobyl," *Der Spiegel,* May 12, 1986, 139–43.

32. *Daily Report: Soviet Union,* 3, no. 107 (June 4, 1986), R9.

33. Erik P. Hoffman, "Nuclear Deception: Soviet Information Policy," *Bulletin of the Atomic Scientists* 42, no. 7 (1986): 35.

34. C. Bohlen, "Chernobyl Personnel Go On Trial, U.S. Delegation Visits Plants, Finds Radiation Level, 'Very Low,'" *The Washington Post,* March 14, 1987, A17, A19.

35. Ibid.

36. "The Cloud Over Gorbachev: Chernobyl's Lesson for Russian Leader," *The Economist* (May 24, 1986): 13–14.

37. *Daily Report: Soviet Union*, "Text of 14 May Gorbachev Television Address," 3, no. 94 (May 15, 1986), L1-L4.

38. Greenwald, Jackson, and Traver, *Time*, May 26, 1986, 36.

39. See D. Oberdorfer, "Soviet Economy Breaks Slump, U.S. Intelligence Agencies Cite Gorbachev's Policies," *The Washington Post*, March 31, 1987, A1, A30–31; "Catastrophe at Chernobyl," *The Economist*, May 3, 1986, 11–12; M. D'Anastasio, " 'Glasnost' Is Also Victim of Chernobyl as Propaganda Move Rises from the Ashes," *The Wall Street Journal*, April 23, 1987, 28; and F. Kempe, "Gorbachev's Handling of the Disaster Undercuts His Rhetoric on Candor," *The Wall Street Journal*, May 1, 1986, 22.

40. R. B. Cullen, J. Barnathan, and M. Kasindorf, "Why the Secrecy? In a Crisis, Old Instincts Rule the Kremlin," *Newsweek*, May 12, 1986, 33.

41. Alexander Amerisov, "A Chronology of Soviet Media Coverage," *Bulletin of the Atomic Scientists* 42, no. 7 (1988): 38.

42. Ibid.

43. Hawkes et al., 135.

44. Ibid., 136.

45. Ibid., 140.

46. Von Hippel and Cochran, "Estimating Long-Term Health Effects," 22.

47. Hawkes et al., 140–60.

48. Dorman and Hirsch, "The U.S. Media's Slant," 54.

49. "Mayday! and May Day," *The New York Times*, May 1, 1986, A26.

50. J. Greenwald, D. Aikman, and N. Traver, "More Fallout From Chernobyl," *Time*, May 19, 1986, 44–46.

51. Hoffman, "Nuclear Deception," 36.

52. Bernstein, "Nuclear Deception: The U.S. Record," 40.

53. See Greenwald et al., *Time*, May 12, 1986, 41; R. B. Cullen, J. Barnathan, and M. Miller, "A Fearful Flight from Chernobyl, Soviet Candor Sparks New Health Concerns," *Newsweek*, May 19, 1986, 36–38; and J. Tagliabue, "Request for Technical Help Cut Short," *The New York Times*, May 1, 1986, A10.

54. Cullen, Barnathan, and Miller, *Newsweek*, May 19, 1986, 36–38, and Greenwald, Aikmann, and Traver, *Time*, 44–46.

55. Greenwald et al., *Time*, May 12, 1986, 43.

56. Hawkes et al., 161.

57. Fischer, "The International Response," 47–48.

58. Greenwald et al., *Time*, May 12, 1986, 59.

59. P. McGrath, "Did the Media Hype Chernobyl?," *Newsweek*, May 26, 1986, 31.

60. Dorman and Hirsch, "The U.S. Media's Slant," 55.

61. Greenwald, Jackson, and Traver, *Time*, May 26, 1986, 32; McGrath, *Newsweek*, May 26, 1986, 31; and S. Diamond, "Chernobyl Design Found to Include Safety Plans," *The New York Times*, May 19, 1986, A1, A6.

62. Greenwald et al., *Time*, May 12, 1986, 43.

63. "Nuclear Energy: Is America Being Left Behind?," *Newsweek*, April 28, 1986, 62.

64. Atomic Industrial Forum, Inc., "Multiple Barrier Containment: Significant Differences Between U.S.-Soviet Reactors," *AIF Background Info.* (May, 1986), 1–3.

65. Dorman and Hirsch, "The U.S. Media's Reaction," 55.

66. Hawkes et al., 16.

67. Greenwald et al., *Time,* May 12, 1986, 59.

68. Hawkes et al., 163–64.

69. Daniel Ford, *The Cult of the Atom: The Secret Papers of the Atomic Energy Commission,* rev. ed. (New York: Simon and Schuster, 1984), 193–208.

70. Greenwald, Jackson, and Traver, *Time,* May 26, 1986, 33.

71. Anne B. Fisher and Peter Petre, "Nuclear Power after Chernobyl," *Fortune,* 113, no. 11 (1986): 130–32; and Peter Petre, "What Welch Wrought at GE," *Fortune* 114, no. 1 (1986): 43–47.

72. R. Gilette, "'No Clear Cut' Link, Chernobyl Seen as Reminder to U.S. on Safety," *The Los Angeles Times,* April 27, 1987, 1, 9.

73. Ibid.

74. Ibid.

75. Richard Rudolph and Scott Ridley, "Chernobyl's Challenge to Anti-Nuclear Activism," *Radical America* 20, nos. 2, 3 (1986): 7–21.

76. Greenwald, Aikman, and Traver, *Time,* May 19, 1986, 44–46; von Hippel and Cochran, "Estimating Long-term Health Effects," 18–24.

77. "'Wie sie ihre Wut loswerden . . . ? Die 'Pfingstschlacht' von Wackersdorf: brutale Chaoten, kopflöse Polizisten," *Der Spiegel,* May 26, 1986, 105, 108–09.

78. "In Tschernobyl, 'Eine glühend aktive Zone,'" *Der Spiegel,* May 19, 1986, 128–29, 133–35; "'So wie die Hiroschima-Bombe,' Tschernobyl: Ein Katastrophe für die Sowjet-Union," *Der Spiegel,* May 5, 1986, 136–39.

79. "Die Sache hat uns kalt erwischt," *Der Spiegel,* May 12, 1986, 19–20.

80. "Neue Mehrheit für Aussteig: *Spiegel*-Umfrage über Tschernobyl und die Deutschen," *Der Spiegel,* May 12, 1986, 28, 30, 32.

81. Worldwatch Institute, "Reassessing Nuclear Power: The Fallout from Chernobyl," *Worldwatch Institute Report* (March, 1986), 1.

82. Hawkes et al., 213.

83. S. R. Lichter, "Was Chernobyl Portent or Anomaly?," *The Wall Street Journal,* April 29, 1987, 30.

84. "From the Editors," *Bulletin of the Atomic Scientists* 42, no. 7 (1986): 2.

85. Bernstein, "Nuclear Deception: The U.S. Record," 40–43; R. L. Hudson, "East, West Move toward Safer Reactors but Experts Warn More Must Be Done," *The Wall Street Journal,* April 23, 1987, 28; and M. D. Lemonick, "A Chernobyl-Proof Reactor," *Time,* July 21, 1986, 60. The Soviet Union also backed expanded research into "safe nuclear reactor" designs by the IAEA during the summer of 1986; see Marples, *Chernobyl and Nuclear Power in the USSR,* 179.

PART IV

*Oppositional Politics in
Informational Society*

8

Power and Resistance in Informationalizing Postindustrial Societies

Given the previous chapters' provisional interpretations of how ideology and power seem to operate on several levels in informationalizing societies, what effective forms might popular resistance to power and ideological domination take at this time? As domination has pervaded everyday life through culture, technology, and the media, many entirely "new" social movements also have organized to resist these "naturalized" and "ordinary" means of enforcing control over particular groups' identities and communities. From a Gramscian perspective, such new social movements could be seen as fighting important struggles in what is left of civil society against the domination of a new postindustrial state in a complex cultural "war of position." [1]

New social movements should be examined as an important form of organized opposition in informationalizing postindustrial capitalist societies. As advocates of a politics of identity, these movements have a "newness" that can be traced to the challenges they are posing to the operant cultural codes of the existing state and corporate order. They turn culture into a new field of contention, both by resisting the naturalized domination of ordinary life underpinning the colonization of the everyday lifeworld and by presenting alternative cultural codes of behavior. The groups at the heart of this resistance are mainly extra-parliamentary, noninstitutional, left-leaning (*and* right-leaning) direct-action groups involved, for example, in the feminist, sanctuary, civil rights, peace, ecology, anti-nuclear, anti-abortion, community power, Christian fundamentalist, and local autonomy movements. The larger significance of the new groups has sparked considerable disagreement among political and social scientific analysts. Despite the many different labels that have been hung on them, such groups are still very poorly defined.

Virtually no consensus exists on what criteria one might use to label groups as new, or social, or part of a movement. Most observers cannot define what a new social movement is, but they seem to know one when they see one. Once they have sighted one of these movements, however, most political analysts concur that they are signs of something shifting on the political landscape of advanced industrial societies. During the past twenty years, these shifts have been connected to many causes and given many names. "The silent revolution," "postindustrial society," "legitimation crisis," "the distemper of democracy," "artificial negativity," "anti-politics," "localism/populism," "the molecular revolution," and "postmodernity"—all can be cataloged, for example, as descriptions of or explanations for these transformations in Western Europe, North America, and Japan.[2] Although these large-scale social transformations also still are not clearly understood, the new social movements are seen to be tied in many ways to it.[3] The questions guiding the discussion in this chapter, then, are simple: What political relation do the new social movements have to the sweeping new changes in the advanced industrial societies of the West? In particular, what ideological shifts and structural tendencies in the organization of advanced industrial societies do the new social movements perhaps politically articulate?

CATEGORIES FOR UNDERSTANDING THE NEW SOCIAL MOVEMENTS

Since the mid–1960s, as Eder observes, the conventional wisdom of mainstream social science almost always has written off the new social movements as simply the latest expression of "a normal collective deviance, nothing more than neo-romantic and neo-populist protest."[4] In pigeonholing such movements as neo-romantic or neo-populist, mainstream intellectuals and social scientists then can allege that "these new movements are actually old ones," carrying all the unsavory baggage of traditional romantic-populist protest groups—anti-rationalism, subjectivism, anti-intellectualism, and anti-elitism.[5] Inasmuch as these conventional treatments do not show how the new social movements actually are romantic or populist, they remain essentially "cynical explanations" of the new social movements' protests against modernity.[6] As Eder advocates, a more effective analysis must move beyond such cynical interpretations to outline a "developmental explanation" of new social movements.

Putting together such a developmental explanation, however, demands new conceptual perspectives. What categories are the most appropriate for understanding the origins, processes, and goals of the direct political action now being mounted by new social movements? Any effort to apply a narrow construction of orthodox Marxist categories drawn from an analysis of old social movements to the politics of new social movements very soon comes to naught. New frameworks are needed to mark the crucial differences between "the new social movements" and the "old social movements" (namely, labor unions, workers' parties, and other "proletarian" organizations). As a critique of nineteenth-century industrializing capitalist societies, classical Marxism no longer completely fits conceptually on the intellectual terrain of late twentieth-century advanced corporate capitalism under the management of the contemporary "service state."[7] In keeping with what earlier chapters have suggested, under today's transnational zone-regime, the class system, market structures, rules of commodification, mode of industrial production, state power, global macroeconomic competition, and group conflict all seem to bear less and less relation to classical Marxism.

While "the specter of Marxian theory still haunts the Left," as Cohen observes, "it would be extremely irresponsible today to perpetuate this image of modern society and its alternative."[8] The univocal political economy of orthodox Marxism, while it can shed some light upon the workings of the global economy, breaks down in an era characterized by comprehensive state intervention into all spheres of social reproduction. As Boggs notes, the new social movements, "explode the myth of a single set of laws governing all historical development: the feminist, peace, ecology, and radical cultural movements, for example, are both too pluralistic and autonomous to be neatly subsumed under a unifying logic of capitalist production, even if their growth is powerfully influenced by it. Popular revolts express a wide diversity of interests, priorities, goals, and ideologies; theoretical efforts to force it into a single pattern will only obscure its essence and, hence obscure the very dynamics of change in advanced capitalism."[9] To make these claims more concrete, the diverse interests, priorities, and goals of the new social movements must be contrasted with those of older movements.

With the transition to a more state-managed economy in the 1930s, for example, many planks from the social-reform program of labor unions became national policy, and since World War II, workers' parties in several OECD nations have won many electoral victories. The old emancipatory movements of socialist parties, trade unions, and proletarian protest groups, which were inspired in part by Marxism, slowly integrated themselves after 1945 into "the central bureaucratic network of regulations, supervision, and control."[10] On the other hand, new opposition groups have been kept at arm's length by the established political parties since the 1960s. They have experienced welfare-state liberal/laborite/ Marxian thinking as an established intellectual and political orthodoxy. Many of the new social movements' concerns are *not* purely economic. Instead, they relate more to cultural or administrative issues, like how rationally and legitimately the service state and corporate capital can operate within the guidelines of liberal democratic, mass-consumption economies. Whereas most old social movements believed that most if not all social problems could be solved by their politics of redistribution, the new social movements often see these "solutions" as creating many new problems without actually satisfactorily addressing the issues of material prosperity or social security. The old politics of resource distribution, then, gives rise to the new politics of cultural identity. These new groups increasingly have had to resort to innovative, noninstitutionalized, extra-parliamentary modes of political activity. Rather than returning to Marx, as Gorz observes, in search of new "strategies for labor," these new social movements usually have departed from Marx, bidding "farewell to the working class."

In defining conceptual categories for the new social movements, one must avoid overspecifying them in strictly class terms. Cohen sees two paradigms emerging at this stage of studying new social movements: Empirically oriented social scientists, mainly in North America, have formulated a *resource-mobilization* approach, stressing strategic considerations of organization, collective action, and interest mobilization. In contrast, more politically grounded social analysts in both the United States and Europe have taken an *identity-orientation* approach, emphasizing issues like consciousness, ideology, and solidarity. Overall, Cohen argues, the former approach is much less useful and informative. Instead one must transcend the narrow perspectives of resource-mobilization theory and its basis in strategic-action calculations. It must be recognized that the new social movements actually do "consciously struggle over the power to socially construct new identities, to create democratic spaces for autonomous social action, and to reinterpret norms and reshape institutions. It thus becomes incumbent on the theorist (a) to look into the processes by which collective actors create the identities and solidarities they defend, (b) to assess the relations between adversaries and the stakes of their conflicts, and (c) to analyze the structural and cultural developments that contribute to such heightened reflexivity."[11] This theoretical prescription might be applied, in turn, to the analysis of left-leaning, radical ecologists, for example, as well as right-leaning, pro-life, religious fundamentalists. Since the identity-oriented paradigm promises to move the analysis of new social movements onto new ground, it should be useful to consider some examples.

Informationalization as Social Transformation
The growing tendency toward informationalization in many advanced capitalist and industrial societies has become a major source of systemic

change during the last three decades. Most important, in Gramscian terms, the state and civil society seem to be evolving with information-alization into new postindustrial formations embodied within the transnational capitalist economy: a weak transnational "state," in the form of a multinational zone-regime, and an informationally mediated transnational civil society. With the growth of informational capital, a transnational economy grounded on a new global division of labor has unfolded. Everything from parts to technical innovations, as well as capital borrowing, resources, labor pools, management applications, corporate finance, product assembly, consumer marketing, and macroeconomic administration now has multiple international sourcepoints. A weakly integrated but powerful multinational military force has become institutionalized over nearly four decades to protect a close alliance of the NATO/OECD states from East bloc and Third World nationalist threats. To a very real extent, then, in the West a new kind of confederal, multinational state, or zone-regime, organized on a hemispheric scale in NATO/OECD capitals around the Atlantic and Pacific basins, now presides over an equally new and complex transnational civil society constructed out of fragments provided by corporate product mass marketing, international popular culture, multinational tourism, global electronic media, transnational scientific/technical communities, electronic financial dealings, and international organizations, as well as a collective civic culture of material progress, anti-communism, mutual defense, and liberal democratic decision making.[12]

The new social movements organizationally express popular reactions to the diverse conflicts sparked by the new territorial, cultural, and functional cleavages that have also emerged with informationalization. Along these cleavages, some individuals in new classes—both in the sense of social conflict groups and skill/property groups in changing economic niches within the informational means of production—are discovering that their needs, interests, and goals are not being served. The OECD states' institutionalized bureaucratic, corporate, and party/parliamentary structures have not effectively accommodated the driving issues of identity and community behind many of the new social movements. Consequently, these movements are finding new extra-institutional, nonparliamentary paths for following their new politics. They are mobilizing in order to pressure the administrative regime of the service state, corporate capital, and technocratic production into considering qualitatively new forms of development. Thus far, they have not been tremendously successful; nonetheless, their mobilizing efforts parallel some basic lines of contradiction within transnational corporate capitalism.

To elaborate some of the contradictions of informationalizing society here, Lipset and Rokkan's grid model of social cleavages should be useful. Despite its Parsonian theoretical infrastructure, this model may reveal the key dimensions of social cleavage—on an opposing grid of territorial/cultural and functional forces—in informationalizing societies.[13] These categories seem to capture contradictions of societies experiencing the informational revolution as accurately as those once seen in states undergoing national and industrial revolutions. As they argue, citizens in the highly institutionalized Western democracies "are only rarely called upon to express their stands on single issues," like the new social movements now attempt to do. Instead, as Chapter 5 also indicated, citizens have their choices in ordinary electoral politics typically framed in terms of narrow "historically given 'packages' or programs, commitments, outlooks, and, sometimes, *Weltanschauungen,* and their current behavior cannot be understood without some knowledge of the sequences of events and the combinations of forces that produced these 'packages.'"[14] In most Western democracies, protest groups, mass movements, and political parties have been the agents of conflict and instruments of political integration that, first, have defined these policy "packages" and, second, occasionally mobilize effectively enough to manage their electoral implementation.

Historically, other social movements have arisen outside of the institutionalized political parties. In order to gain maximum political clout, such movements usually have also had to take over, or ally themselves with, political parties. While some within the new social movements have pursued this strategy—like the Ecology party in France, the Greens in West Germany, advocates of the nuclear freeze initiative and the ecology movement in the United States, and peace candidates in the United Kingdom—they have also stuck to direct-action strategies. Mass demonstrations, peace camps, the occupation of military bases, takeovers of neighborhoods, organizing skill centers, establishing communes, and squatting are all more unconventional tactics aimed at confounding the operations of the service state's bureaucratic business-as-usual or at persuading the ruling elites through the media to accept alternative policies. When possible, some of their members have also engaged in "issue group" politics—referenda, initiative drives, bureaucratic hearings, and legislative lobbying. To become full-fledged political powers as ruling or opposition parties, the new social movements will have to take over more conventional machinery in the electoral/parliamentary process. Still, the emergence of new social movements seems to be more a sign of an old electoral/parliamentary order in crisis rather than the beginnings of a new party/parliamentary system for the future. Even though they have not taken over, or allied strongly with, any existing political parties, they are restructuring expectations about political behavior and the institutional packaging of vital policies.

In eras of structural change or deeply seated conflict, as Lipset and Rokkan observe, institutionalized electoral/parliamentary behavior and the political packaging that define them can often change fundamentally. During the national revolutions of the early modern era, conflict arose on a territorial/cultural level between central political authorities and local and regional political notables and on a functional level between the central secular state power and diffuse church authority. And during the Industrial Revolution of the nineteenth and twentieth centuries, a territorial/cultural conflict broke out between urban-industrial entrepreneurs and rural landed interests, while a functional contradiction bitterly divided the owners/employers/bourgeoisie and the tenants/laborers/proletariat.[15]

These multiple conflicts delimited the interests and cleavages in the English, French, American, and Russian revolutions, as well as the general Industrial Revolution. Within Lipset's and Rokkan's grid framework, the social cleavages over territorial/cultural issues imply that "the decisive criterion of alignment is *commitment to the locality and its dominant culture:* You vote with your community irrespective of your economic position."[16] However, on conflicts over functional concerns, "the criterion is *commitment to a class and its collective interests:* You vote with others in the same position as yourself whatever their localities, and you are willing to do so even if this brings you into opposition with members of your community."[17] At this juncture, analogues to all four of these historical crises have surfaced simultaneously within the OECD nations. These tendencies are not completely clear-cut, but they can be provisionally discussed.

First, in contemporary informationalizing society, two central contradictions appear to result from transnationalization: (1) one contradiction follows territorial/cultural lines as the conflict between the centralizing culture of zone-building regimes and the decentralist, ethno-nationalist cultures of localism; (2) the other contradiction derives from functional conflicts within transnational corporate capital, because of internationalization and the new global division of labor within its international networks in the techno-economic core, semiperipheral, and peripheral niches in the global economy.

The other two key cleavages seem to be the result of informationalization: The first again underpins territorial/cultural lines of conflict as the contradiction between industrial interests (in the old tripartite political economy of factory labor, industrial management, and bureaucratic states) pursuing a national program of a quantitative growth and social redistribution in mass consumer markets and informational interests (with a new political economy tied to the new professional/technical, middle-class "workers," multinational managers, segmented markets of consumers, and transnational zone-regimes) seeking an alternative program of qualitative growth and social rationalization. The second anchors functional conflicts between alternative cultural grammars of living, or between a technocratic system of expert empowerment and a more polymathic system of personal or clientele empowerment in the conduct of all aspects of everyday life.

Needless to say, ordinary electoral/parliamentary politics in present-day Western regimes virtually ignores these new structural contradictions and social cleavages. The conventional political packaging of the existing electoral order simply will not fit around them. Rather the emergence of the new social movements with their alternative "programs, commitments, outlooks, and *Weltanschauungen*" signal that the conventional political packages are imploding from within their increasingly outmoded systems of definition and delivery.

New Theoretical Frameworks

In defining new conceptual categories for the new social movements, one again must avoid overspecifying them in strictly orthodox Marxian class terms. Touraine, for example, in seeking a universal definition for the new movements, conceptualizes a social movement as "the organized collective behavior of a class actor struggling against his class adversary for the social control of historicity in a concrete community." [18] With this complex theory of social action, Touraine avoids tagging class purely in terms of a groups' material relation to the means of production. Even though he derides this Marxian conception as an anachronistic approach drawn from "industrial society, born in Scotland in the eighteenth century and diffused throughout Europe in the nineteenth century," [19] Touraine treats class as a conflict group formed in the struggles over authority, position, and control within a specific community. While no group or individual is "determined by a single social situation," class forms in the "conflict which in every type of society sets one *class* against *another,* the rulers against the dominated." [20] New social movements are the expression of this class dynamic in the modern "programmed society," based upon techno-bureaucratic administration, of informationalizing postindustrial systems. [21] That is, with a bit of theoretical renovation, and despite his disclaimers about Marxism, Touraine redefines the new social movements as a new functional equivalent of the proletariat, waiting to discover its historical consciousness as a new class-in-itself becoming a class-for-itself.

Beyond Touraine, and his construction of new social movements as class forces struggling against other class forces, Habermas defines the new social movements as fragmentary pieces of existing civil society working to retain independent identities and autonomy on the periphery of institutionalized state/corporate structures. Ultimately they oppose "the 'productivist core of performance' in late capitalist societies." [22] Operating from within the already highly rationalized lifeworld of advanced capitalism, these activists "seek to *stem* or block the formal, organized spheres of action in favor of communicative structures; they do not seek to conquer new territory." [23] In contrast to Touraine, however, Habermas clearly describes what kind of groups enter into conflict and why the conflicts arise. The new social movements are "opposed to the profit-oriented instrumentalization of professional labor, the market-dependent mobilization of labor, and the extension of competitiveness and performance pressure" [24] into the spheres of everyday life. Rather than using a class conflict model, Habermas mobilizes conceptual contradictions arising between "civil society" and the "state." As "civil society," the new social movements function as resistance and liberation movements, fighting the "state" and its colonizing of the everyday lifeworld with its bureaucratic instrumental rationality. "In short," Habermas observes, "the new conflicts are not sparked by *problems of distribution,* but concern the *grammar of forms of life.*" [25]

Touraine defines all social movements as working under virtually the same organizational horizon, but struggling over different axes of value cleavage in a general field of action. Habermas, however, differentiates the struggle along metaphorical lines of core and periphery. The new social movements are popular mobilizations of peripheral forces (women, minorities, local autonomists, anti-nukes, peace activists) against the packaged lifeworld of the overinstitutionalized core (the state, major corporations, the media, political parties, unions, and the military). Two alternative conceptual sets, then, emerge at this juncture. Touraine connects social movements to the indigenous class struggle of conflict groups within postindustrial societies. Seeing postindustrial society as a given, the movements are class forces working within complex institutional and extra-institutional settings to steer and control the "historicity" of a programmed society. Habermas connects the new social movements to the struggle on "the periphery" by "outsider groups" and individuals against "core" institutions and "insider elites" over the advancing rationalization taking place in the social lifeworld. These two approaches to social movements—as mobilizations to move society from one path of change to another or as liberation movements to emancipate spheres of activity from formal rationalization—echo themes advanced by Eder and Hirsch.

Complementing Touraine's notion of social movements, Eder identifies social movements as "social protests that try to lead society from one level of development to another" in direct relation "to modernization from the 17th century on."[26] Thus only two popular protest waves in Western history were also social movements: the bourgeois opposition to aristocratic/autocratic domination in the national revolutions of the seventeenth century and the proletarian opposition to capitalist industrialists that began during the Industrial Revolution of the nineteenth century. As struggles over modernity, both movements "challenged cultural traditions and provided a normative direction to social development,"[27] even though they ultimately did not transform the state. However, the experience of modern societies under welfare-corporatist and socialist-bureaucratic states has destructively reordered popular "autonomy, self-determination, and discursive procedures of decision-making."[28] New social movements, as developmental waves of protest, are significant in that they challenge the ordinary premises of everyday life in civil society. Their tacit encodings express a state/corporate "paradigm of the life-world," aiming to control any new popular developments within "the predicaments of modernity."[29] Since "the development of industrial productive forces no longer generates antagonistic social relations,"[30] the new social movements' opposition is articulated "in a new type of social antagonism between technocratic modernizers and the clients of bureaucracies."[31]

Refining this general line of analysis further, Hirsch maintains that these "technocratic modernizers" in the "Fordist security state" of welfare-corporatist advanced capitalism have become "insensitive and unresponsive to social interests and problems. Thus, larger parts of the population no longer feel truly represented. Hence social conflicts and problems unfold outside the bureaucratic sphere of control and perception."[32] The advancing rationalization of the ordinary lifeworld splits corporate capitalist systems into two divergent societies that are based upon two interconnected but distinctive political economies: a *modern sector* (or the informational core), comprised of high-tech plants, segments of the new middle class, and the skilled workers, and a *marginal sector* (or the informational semiperipheries and peripheries) comprised of the less competitive, declining industries and unskilled workers and the masses of the unemployable.[33] As this division deepens, non-productivist interests—like those in a healthy environment or in natural ecology—are marginalized within and across individual people. An example would be the justification for the destruction of the cities and of the natural environment by pointing to secure employment (as is the case in the nuclear and automobile industries). Here lies the material basis for the recent discussion of the so-called "change of values." Because of this development, social conflicts still result from the content of capitalist exploitation, yet they do not manifest themselves along traditional class lines. Nor can such conflicts find expression within the system of political apparatuses, because they are structurally excluded.[34]

Along these lines of productivist and nonproductivist social cleavage, the extra-institutional protests of the new social movements rise in opposition. In the advanced capitalist nations this opposition is expressed in anti-bureaucratic, anti-technocratic, anti-corporate modes of mass mobilization politics. As Hirsch concludes, "The rigid and opaque structure of the political system promotes the rise of these movements, which try to articulate and accomplish neglected needs and interests. As they do not correspond to the established system's notion of functional logic, they necessarily (and frequently without intention) are in opposition to it. These 'new social movements' find expression in several citizens' initiatives, in the ecology movement, as well as in spontaneous strikes or the occupation of factories."[35] In being frozen out of the mainstream channels of the service state, with its essentially statalized labor constituencies with their socialist or social democratic parties, the new social movements present an alternative vision of modernity predicated upon developing social institutions that might preserve more autonomous spheres of personal identity and social action from state/corporate instrumentalization. They present an alternative grammar for the *forms of life,* which stresses nonproductivist interests, discursive decision-making procedures, and a new mode of modernizing change that would empower clients, consumers, and citizens rather than the Fordist designs of state/corporate technocratic modernizers.

A Provisional Picture of New Social Movements

In certain respects, the cleavages induced by informationalization have clouded the political conflicts within advanced industrial society for many years. The process of informationalization has divided many nation-states internally along territorial/cultural cleavages. New groups, attitudes, and regions—drawing on informationalizing growth, values, and goals—frequently butt up against entrenched industrial interests. The service state and its political economy of industrial interests are an-

chored to some powerful forces: labor unions, industrial cities, manufac-
turing-oriented banks, industrial workers, national capital in heavy industrial sectors like steel, autos, or construction, and a welfare bureaucracy devoted to serving the needs of an industrial "economy of
scale."[36] This economic bloc parallels the "marginal sector" described by
Hirsch. Entire classes, cities, regions, and industries today are inextricably committed to this heavy industrial "smoke and steel" identity of the
economic growth models belonging to the era spanning the 1880s to the
1950s—an era marked by the determinant sign of smokestacks belching
out progress. At the same time, a new array of classes, cities, regions, and
industries have hitched their fortunes to the new high-tech, light industrial, "silicon valley" identity of economic growth strategies from the
later era spanning the 1950s to the 1980s, which is an era distinctly
signified on the screens of computer consoles and flashing streams of
data. This bloc is very comparable to the "modern sector" discussed by
Hirsch. For these new economic interests, the measure of aggregate economic power is in bytes, not horsepower, in the new political economy
of qualitative growth, widespread computerization, highly skilled labor,
and thoroughly rationalized "economies of scope."[37]

Informationalization has the potential to make both the greater empowerment and closer control of lay people in everyday life possible for
the first time since the consolidation of the Industrial Revolution. The
current industrial regime, bureaucratic service states, corporate high
technology, and transnational consumer marketing have all presupposed
the increasing disempowerment of people, or their "one-dimensionaliza-
tion," by creating endless dependencies on technocratic experts among
citizens, consumers, and clients. With the progressive colonization of
more and more corners of daily life, a very restricted state/corporate
grammar of life has been generated. This grammar has stressed passivity,
dependency, supervision, and uniformity as technocratic experts have
packaged material goods and scripted social roles for the increasingly
uniform masses of the postindustrial-era consumers, clients, and citizens.
Informationalized grammars of living have the potential to revitalize personal activity, independence, autonomy, and diversity among complexly
segmented groups of individuals. As the preceding chapters have suggested, though, they might also, of course, simply be dedicated to managing an even closer domination of individuals in their everyday lives.
While one class of technocratic experts in the marginal sector has a
vested interest in maintaining these relations of domination, another
class of experts in the modern sector is being pushed by many clienteles
to provide new kinds of reempowerment and to abolish technocratic
domination.

The relation of new social movements to the modern welfare state and corporate capital, then, is not usually one of purely external opposition. The West German Green Party, for example, is split into two basic factions—the anti-organizational, more radical *fundamentalist* faction, or "Fundis," and the more pragmatic *realists,* or "Realos." These factions are divided over how to work within the existing regime. In fact many new social movements may be seen as being internally divided along these same political lines. On the one hand, a strictly fundamentalist program offers stronger alternatives (based on direct action) to the prevailing cultural grammar and forms of life in capitalist liberal democracies. On the other hand, a realist political strategy (based on more conventional electoral/parliamentary politics) provides greater leverage for implementing some of these alternative forms of living, working, and decision making as policy. Many new social movements are much more realist, contenting themselves with working as weak oppositional forces to humanize or rationalize the operations of the welfare state. They essentially function as artificially negative forces, checking some of the abuses of intra-regime politics and balancing its coalitions.

Such groups do not necessarily challenge the essential cultural logic of modernity; indeed, they often play into its hands. A whole new ersatz *Gemeinschaft* can actually form in some settings. From the interactions of state bureaucrats, foundation-funded social scientists, and "neighborhood citizen groups," these designer "social movements" often legitimize and facilitate the existing regime's agendas of "public" administration by coproducing certain public goods. As the environmental, anti-apartheid, or liberal feminist movements illustrate, new social movements can also function as issue-group organizers, "domesticating" radical ideas from more fundamentalist groups to legitimize them as mainstream policy options. The irrationalities in modern service states seem to stimulate the emergence of such limited oppositional movements as countervailing influences against strictly bureaucratic decision making. Still, a few of the more radical but less numerous fundamentalist elements are trying to push across these tracks of artificial negativity to create authentic forms of post-bureaucratic, post-statist, post-corporate life by seeking new cultural patterns for modernity in new forms of "parallel power" structures in new local institutions.

From this brief overview of several theoretical approaches to the new social movements, the approaches can be characterized tentatively by seven distinctive traits. First, as Touraine, Habermas, and Eder suggest, new social movements are a *new* political opposition, characteristic of the recently consolidated bureaucratic welfare state regime, which has absorbed the old opposition of laborite parties and trade unions into its administrative apparatus. Second, as Cohen, Boggs, and Touraine argue, new social movements are post-Marxist, post–classical socialist, post-proletarian, and, in some sense, postindustrial in their theoretical program, sociological make-up, and practical politics. Third, new social movements, as extra-laborite and extra-statist forms of opposition, have largely organized themselves into extra-institutional, nonparliamentary structures, such as loose personal networks, affinity groups, neighborhood associations, regional pressure groups, ascriptive-trait fronts (sex, race, age, locality, ethnicity), media-management groups, residential communes, skill centers, or mobilization committees. In these new modes of political organization, issue-group politics are at least as important, if not more salient, than traditional interest-group politics. Fourth, as Eder and Touraine claim, these movements are forming on new territorial/cultural and functional cleavages breaking out within today's postindustrial changes, which may be as significant as the national revolutions in the seventeenth century and the Industrial Revolution in the nineteenth century. Fifth, the lines of conflict for new social movements are between core and periphery, technocratically empowered planners/producers/providers and disempowered citizens/consumers/clients. Thus, the struggle is, in large part, between the "lifeworld colonizers" and the "lifeworld colonized" as they fight over questions of *access, voice,* and *control.* Sixth, the mobilization of new social movements represents a developmental attempt to guide modernization from one phase into a qualitatively new phase of organizing everyday life. And finally, new social movements mark a new crisis of development, or the "crisis of rationalization," posed by the administrative challenges of managing (a) a rapidly changing high-tech *transnational economy,* (b) the coordination of a growing global nuclear/conventional/unconventional military competition between two new weak *transnational states,* the NATO/OECD and WTO/CMEA *zone-regimes,* and (c) a *transnational civil society* based upon the global production and consumption of commodified experiences, privativistic consumer durables, and personal services.

THE NEW CRISIS: RATIONALIZATION WITHOUT REPRESENTATION

What ideological shifts and structural tendencies in the organization of advanced industrial society do the new social movements politically articulate? The deep-seated conflicts of most new social movements with the existing service state and corporate capital appear to be significant signs of a systemic "crisis of development" in informationalizing advanced industrial societies. Such crises in development have erupted at key turns in the globalization of capitalism, as with the "distribution crisis" of the 1920s–1960s era. Typically, a developmental crisis involves:

- a shift in the relationship between *environmental pressures* and level of *politicization* on the one hand, and *governmental output and institutionalization* on the other,
- such that the *institutionalization of a new level of government output* is required,
- if the pressures resulting from the environment and/or the shift in politicization are to be prevented from leading to *the overthrow of the elite structure of the society* or to the changing of the societal boundaries.[38]

In terms of this framework, at this point in the informationalization of advanced industrial societies, all of these pressures are building in the present "rationalization crisis."

The overall substantive ends of advanced capitalist industrialism have been tied to ensuring greater technical efficiencies in instrumental rationality to provide "public goods," including social welfare services, political stability, economic growth, and mass consumption. The instrumental rationality of advanced capitalist industrialism, as it has grown on a transnational scale, has intruded into more areas of everyday life and fused political administration with economic management, actually undercutting the attainment of its substantive ends. It has confounded its own means/ends efficiencies. The transaction costs of instrumentally rationalizing everyday life on a global scale increasingly decreases the benefits of making the transactions. And in turn, more and more "public bads"—pollution, rising prices, resource scarcities, national conflicts, great-power competition, domestic violence, unemployment, or service shortages—are created in this process of providing less and less "public goods." Up to this point, the existing forms of the service state, transnational capital, and party/parliamentary institutions have not discovered effective solutions for the "rationality crisis," especially since they remain preoccupied with answering the last challenges of the "distribution crisis."

In certain respects, the "distribution crisis" of the last century, which has underpinned mass electoral politics in the OECD nations for the last fifty years, has been "solved" in some ways for many key political blocs. Plainly, large and growing pockets of poverty remain in the OECD bloc, and material want is a bitter fact of life in both the Eastern Bloc and Third World. Poverty outside the OECD region is also inextricably linked to plenty within the powerful advanced industrial countries. Nonetheless, in the eyes of many political groups throughout the Western zone-regime, "the primary problem of advanced capital societies, after two centuries of economic growth, is no longer the adequacy of resources or their 'efficient' allocation for maximum output."[39] Instead of distribution, the ultimate problem today is seen as being connected with rationalization, or "the way that output is produced, the definition of what constitutes output, what is produced, and who decides development policy."[40]

After two centuries of economic growth, many of the techno-economic challenges of struggling against material necessity have been met: given "x" operational conditions, industry can produce and distribute virtually any "y" product. However, the leadership of advanced industrial societies is often unmindful of the tough questions coming before and after that distrubutional problem: Who decides what x or which y? Why produce y with x? What do the production and consumption of y mean? How should the costs of x conditions be measured? Who guarantees the "givens" and "operational conditions?" And for whose benefit is x produced and at what cost? Such questions about choosing ends and applying means arise from a crisis within the overall rationality of advanced corporate capitalism. The popular challenge focuses on, as Marcuse proposed, "the system of profitable domination" that underlies such productivity. The old logic of simple economic efficiency and distributional equity does not provide a completely satisfactory set of criteria. The existing lines of consensus on substantive ends and instrumental means of the transnational zone-regime, capitalist economy, and civil society no longer seem true or trustworthy.

The overall opposition of many new social movements—in different ways and on diverse levels—centers on the rationalization problem, and the movements' diverse programs are largely tied to a renewed politicization of these issues. The new social movements stand for new groups of people applying the query "Who, whom?" to all aspects of contemporary political economy. Nuclear power is a prime case in point. The rationalization problem here is multidimensional: Who says we need so much energy and for what purposes are they saying this? Why choose this way of producing energy? How will nuclear energy's output be defined—as kilowatt hours, radiation leaks, less hydrocarbon pollutants, more jobs, extra cancer deaths, more electrified conveniences, more tons of poisonous wastes that remain dangerous for centuries? What costs and benefits are produced and in terms of whose standards? And who decides what is rational, reasonable, fair, efficient, hazardous, or safe? Here, the new social movements, like the anti-nuclear movement, are correct in arguing that narrow, authoritarian, business-biased, faraway bureaucratic forces all too often have imposed bad decisions, arrived at through faulty means, upon millions of citizens/clients/consumers who had little democratic input into them or legal recourse to their unfair or harmful outcome. In other words, the few wrongly dominate the many within liberal democratic governments, which allegedly are "of the people, by the people, for the people." This kind of anonymous authoritarianism, and the largely illegitimate rationalization without representation that it implies, is now the target of the new social movements' mobilization campaigns. Specifically, many new social movements tend to draw some basic lines of defense against the key prevailing practices of advanced industrial society: Fordism, Sloanism, and Reaganism.

Anti-Fordism and the New Social Movements

Fordism stands for an entire social compact drawn up on the premise of Taylorist industrial productivity. Taylorism represents the theory and practice of the many diverse "scientific management" movements over the past century. Taylorism, in its many forms, from hard scientific management to soft human relations techniques, "is an attempt to apply the methods of science to the increasingly complex problems of the control of labor in rapidly growing capitalist enterprises. . . . it investigates not labor in general, but the adaptation of labor to the needs of capital."[41] It therefore must deny identity to labor, turning it (and management as well) into "human resources" for economic production. In pursuing these ends, corporate capital has subdivided the labor process, dehumanized technical implements, and reorganized factory plants to extract the maximum output from labor. Yet at the same time Taylorism also ensures that this output is secured with the minimum concession of technical voice, design access, and material control to the workers.

In exchange for relatively higher wages and marketplace access to consumer durables, housing, and regulated opportunities for getting higher education, professional advancement, and commercialized social status, the modern industrial worker is invited to agree to work hard, perform well, and not cause political trouble. For millions of docile workers, Fordist mass production, marketing, and distribution techniques generated (beginning with the Ford Highland Park automobile assembly plant in 1913) a form of social development based upon "the standardization of the product and the routinization of its production."[42] As Gramsci argued in his "Americanism and Fordism," Fordism is the grand design for modern industrial production. After World War II, Fordism evolved as the central component of the corporate Keynesianism underpinning today's routinized, standardized mass-production economy with its service state, transnational capitalist marketing, and institutionalized party/parliamentary electoral leadership.[43]

The differentiation of the global division of labor in accord with the needs of transnational capital leads into transnational Fordism. Yet, as

Hirsch asserts, Fordism today increasingly presumes greater inequalities and stratification as new informational sectors pull ahead of old industrial areas. As transnational capital has established its priorities of production in many national economies, it simultaneously has reorganized local, regional, national, and international economic activity to suit its peculiar division of labor. In keeping with the previous forms of international capitalist markets, the transnational division of labor increasingly subdivides the cycles of exchange into ever-more-discrete core, semiperipheral, and peripheral areas, linking status with the kind of value-adding labor performed in each niche.

Core regions are dominated by transnational corporate administrative centers with an emphasis on high technology and capital-intensive, information-oriented, high-value labor. Such centers specialize in producing information, technology, or decisions while consuming manufactures and raw materials. Semiperipheral regions are devoted to a mix of core and peripheral production, using intermediate technologies and materials-processing, goods-producing, medium-wage labor. These regions specialize in consuming information and raw materials to produce durable goods, industrial products, and processed foods. Peripheral regions utilize low technology and labor-intensive, materials-producing, low-wage labor and specialize in producing raw materials, foodstuffs, and cheap manufactures, while importing manufactures and technologies.[44] Under a transnationalized division of labor, these differentiations into core, semiperiphery, and periphery destructively intrude into all nation-states, scrambling their previous bases of economic power. Backward regions and old colonies—that once were peripheral economies—have rapidly built core industries. And sophisticated major powers—that once were core economies—have become peripheralized within this new international division of labor. In the process, new class contradictions are unfolding along these functional cleavages between core, semiperipheral, and peripheral production.

From the 1920s through the 1980s, the entire social consensus of the Western democracies as core economies has been tied to the ever-growing elaboration of standardized products for their mass markets based upon routinized high-wage production at home as well as medium-wage, semi-peripheral and low-wage, peripheral production abroad. However, the informationalization of society, and the rise of economies of scope from the saturated industrial economies of scale, calls much of Fordism into question. The industries which once guaranteed high wages, increasing status, and professional security to workers are contracting or declining in size as jobs are exported abroad to low-wage economies or rationalized out of existence. In addition, new informational production requires new kinds of skills from fewer workers to produce fewer products for the highly segmented markets of scope. Often the jobs involved are much lower in pay and benefits. The service-state bureaucracy and its electoral party/parliamentary regime have not yet grasped the realities of this change; consequently, as the following discussion of Reaganism maintains, they are trying to forestall their decline—and Fordism's collapse—through protectionism, deficit spending, industrial subsidies, consumer-spending supports, and various reindustrialization schemes. Fordism's rationality is one of greater, more extensive, unending growth in the production and consumption of commodities. Yet the logic of informationalization is undercutting the basic bargains underlying the entire Fordist regime.

In the anti-nuclear movement, for example, the Fordist logic of this transnational division of labor is called into question by new classes of citizens/consumers/clients that doubt the metaeconomic utility of nuclear power. Fission-driven nuclear power plants are the product of highly concentrated, technology-intensive, state-dependent industries that are based upon the capital reserves, technical labor, and growth priorities of core regions in the global division of labor. However, the power market for nuclear plants in core regions was saturated early during the development of nuclear power. Consequently, more and more plants were planned, sited, or completed in semiperipheral and peripheral areas in order to sustain the industry's productivity and to cope with stricter regulatory requirements in core areas. Whole classes of people—workers, engineers, utility employees, technicians, and even some utility ratepayers—welcomed nuclear power for the jobs, tax returns, and cheap electricity it was alleged to provide. Furthermore, the existing service state and its constituent parties, bureaucracies, parliaments, and unions also have supported nuclear power.

Another class of electricity consumers, utility clients, and local citizens have questioned the economic efficiency and metaeconomic productivity of nuclear power plants. The plants' Fordist technologies often represent a high-tech enclave economy from the core colonizing semiperipheral and peripheral areas for the advantage of the core-area firms, bureaucracies, and trade groups that profit from them. Rather than providing safe, cheap, reliable energy, many nuclear plants have had dangerous operating accidents, expensive cost overruns, and costly downtimes. In addition, they have provided a technology base for nuclear weapons proliferation. Given the fear of accidents, managers working in core regions have sited many plants in more peripheral exurban and rural areas. The core regions impose the costs of investment, radiation sickness, and environmental degradation on the periphery, while importing the profits, taxes, and electricity from nuclear power back into the core. Meanwhile, nuclear plants are absorbing local capital, raising power rates, causing ecological hazards, and providing unreliable service in the semiperipheral and peripheral regions. In the end, even if they are not linked into nuclear weaponry production, nuclear power plants will leave behind radioactive nuclear waste and decommissioned reactors. Yet these poisonous by-products of the industry are so unsafe or are such unknowns that no locality—core, semiperiphery, or periphery—is willing to accommodate them. The metaeconomics of building a plant that will only operate a few decades after being under construction for years in order to produce electricity and an industrial waste that will be unsafe for centuries, as well as a security threat during its reprocessing, simply do not add up.

Having called upon the institutionalized party/parliamentary forces to accommodate their anti-nuclear interests, anti-nuclear organizations have either been largely ignored by the existing service state or accommodated slightly with additional regulations that assured that new nuclear plants would only be built in peripheral regions. Ironically, the cost of these regulations and the massive funds of capital required to build most plants have proven more effective in stalling new construction in most countries. Anti-nuclear activists, nonetheless, continue to organize a broad-based, extra-parliamentary, noninstitutional movement to work for new forms of progressive economic growth that do not assume inputs of fission-generated energy. Their opposition is a class opposition of peripheral and semiperipheral groups opposing their further manipulation by core regions, industries, or elites. Except for providing a few short-lived construction jobs, nuclear power only serves the interests of core regions that generate and manage the technology involved. With their greater pull in the existing national service states, core regions have imposed their corporate priorities for capital accumulation, technical development, energy utilization, and labor deployment to the detriment of semiperipheral and core regions.

Most industrial interests, and the prevailing service state order, have little or no concern for environmental problems except for those that bear directly on the efficiency of Fordist production. David Stockman's opinions, for example, illustrate such cost-accounting views: why should anyone seek to prevent water pollution in a river system if it costs thousands of dollars per individual fish saved when there is no promise of greater profit afterward? Because of such attitudes, the biospheric balance of nature in both industrial and informational regions is endangered by an unchecked pursuit of industrial growth. During an era of declining profitability, in particular, the weak existing environmental regulations on industrial pollutants and by-products are often ignored or loosened, with labor's consent, in order to sustain profit margins, protect jobs, and keep Fordist industries in production. Consequently, ecological degredation spreads further and further, lowering the general quality of life.

The environmental movement, however, represents a popular mobilization to guide future economic modernization down more ecologically reasonable paths of growth. By supporting environmental regulation, backing pollution taxes, accepting pollutant control fees, and pushing environmental protection, ecologists oppose the political agenda of Fordist industrial interests. In advocating the practice of voluntary simplicity, alternative technologies, bioregional communities, and qualitative growth, ecology activists present an alternative territorial/cultural agenda—tied to clean, light, informational production—to the traditional identities of declining industrial communities. Although these kinds of goals are derided regularly by the mainstream party/parliamentary institutions of the service state, the environmentalist new social movements do represent a broad mobilized public favoring an environmental transformation in advanced industrial sciences.

New social movements, like the ecology, anti-nuclear, environmental, Green, and local autonomy movements, then, are opposing Fordist industrial and social policies. The functioning of the Fordist order has depended on substituting docile workers for active craftsmen, capital-intensive plants for labor-intensive shops, energy-wasting output for energy-frugal production, resource-squandering industries for resource-stewarding manufacture, mass-managed tastes for individual choice, authoritarian paternalism for autonomous self-reliance, and routinized urban order for self-determined exurban autonomy. The new social movements do not wish to return to the preindustrial rustic rural life of pre-Fordist society; but, at the same time, they realize the ecosphere cannot sustain Fordism on a regional or global scale any longer. Fordism, in the last analysis, presumes that a minority of the world's population in North America, Western Europe, and Japan will use a vast majority of the world's resources to maintain the social contract between labor and capital. This industrial system is, and always has been, irrational in terms of substantive fairness and in light of instrumental efficiency criteria. The ecological and bioregional movements are struggling to decolonize the everyday life of informationalizing society of its Fordist assumptions. Finding equally satisfying modes of living while using less energy, capital, resources, corporate technology, and military force to guarantee Fordist growth is the new agenda of these movements. They ask the tough questions of Fordism: Why produce these products? What really is material progress? Who actually decides what to do? And who suffers the consequences or gets the benefits?

Anti-Sloanism and New Social Movements

Sloanism—named after Alfred P. Sloan, the organizer of General Motors' divisional structure and marketing program—represents corporate capital's efforts to "manufacture" markets and consumers for the products it demographically assigns to them through advertising and differential pricing of particular goods for various income niches. That is, corporate capital, in its "effort to reduce the *autonomous character* of the demand for its products and to increase its *induced character*," matches its corporate product cycles to the market-defined life cycle of the consumer. Thus firms use styling, designing, and packaging "to gear consumer needs to the needs of production instead of the other way around."[45]

The best example of these colonizing intrusions into consumers' preferences through advertising, styling, and packaging is still the array of General Motors' automobiles. Essentially similar masses of physical matter (automobiles) which all serve the same function (transportation) are differentiated symbolically as a ladder of status, cost, and success for consumers to climb during their lifetimes. Automobiles become signs of greater status with increasing prices and decreasing model runs as the product range extends from the bottom to the top, enabling additional status to be drawn from "invidious distinctions" as the consumer acquires particular cars out of these runs. Begin in youth with a "basic transportation" Chevrolet, rise with age to a Pontiac, a Buick, then an Oldsmobile, and end in late middle-age at the peak of success with a Cadillac. Sloanism represents this sort of wasteful imposition of superfluous marketing demands upon engineering processes as well as the advertising-based colonization of consumer consciousness. These practices submit the psychosocial identities of corporate customers to the marketing agendas of corporate styling committees and growth planners. In the end, Sloanism is the Taylorized production of consumers/citizens/clients for the Fordist output of industrial goods.

This struggle against Sloanism is at the core of many new social movements. The state/corporate colonization of the everyday lifeworld is the driving force behind advanced industrial life under transnational capital. Capital is revalorized and accumulated today largely via the Sloanist invention of new needs, demands, and wants for diverse income groups among modern consumers. In response, bioregional and local autonomy movements fight the Sloanist colonization of their communities and the acceptance of the mass-consumption, energy-intensive, suburban-styled kit of commodities imposed everywhere in transnational marketing. Feminist groups fight corporate capital's gratuitous sexist styling of "female" roles, products, identities, and needs. Ecology activists oppose the definition of personal status or success in terms of environmentally destructive automobiles, housing, and consumer goods. Vegetarians and animal liberationists oppose agribusinesses' stylization of a "good diet" in terms of dead animal flesh, while pro-family groups lobby against corporate advertising's portrayal of successful adult living as the swinging singles' never-ending quest for sexual adventure. Peace activists protest Sloanist defense-firm promotions pitched to the Pentagon and to Third World military juntas for jet fighters, nuclear subs, and new battle tanks, touted as exciting new products for maintaining "peace." Public-interest citizen's movements protest the stylized, issueless, content-free ad wars waged between professional electoral campaigns, which sell political candidates as if they were competing kinds of colas, peanut butter, or toilet paper while ignoring vital issues confronting the public.

The anti-Sloanist struggle of the new social movements, in many important respects, is the key battle for controlling socialization, cultural integration, and social reproduction. Sloanism is transnational capital's most basic tool for shaping the grammars of everyday life on the screens of power. The syntax for assembling personal identity, cultural ends, economic activity, and social organization in advanced capitalist mediascapes is generated from Sloanist premises in the culture fabricated by electronic mass media. The fight to defend alternatives—namely, personally defined life-styles in the family, church, and community with their own cultural grammars—constantly must resist Sloanism if it is ever to recover a more contextual rationality in the cultural reproduction of society.

Anti-Reaganism and the New Social Movements

Reaganism (identified as such because its best recent expressions probably have been many of the words and deeds of Ronald Reagan) delimits the new reactionary "progressivism" in the NATO/OECD nations that first emerged in their joint reaction to OPEC during the energy crises of the 1970s and 1980s. The rise of a transnational zone-regime on the backs of the NATO, OECD, IMF, EEC, GATT, and UN international coordinating bodies and numerous transnational subgovernments in the Western nation-states is a rather new fact of everyday world politics.[46] For nearly forty years, however, the advanced industrial capitalist societies around the Atlantic and Pacific Basins have maintained a common defense, a shared weapons base, an integrated financial system, a relatively open commercial market, a multinational industrial base, a free exchange of capital, technology, people, and ideas, a common program of containing totalitarianism, and an interdependent consumer culture of mass production. And although the various political parties and national parliaments of the diverse NATO/OECD states have little access, voice, or control when it comes to the other member states' affairs, there is a central transnational state, or zone-regime, that presides over the NATO/OECD zone's political economy and public life. The very density and scope of transnational commerce have virtually necessitated its gradual organization, but the central zone-regime also derives considerable purpose from opposing a similar but less well-developed WTO/CMEA zone-regime based on the USSR's imperium in Eurasia.

This state is not wholly the creature of transnational corporate capital's owning factions or salaried technostructure, but its leadership and management draw heavily from these personnel. The zone-regime also is not purely the product of the NATO/OECD states' professional civil, financial, or military technocrats, although they, too, clearly have a hand in its organization and operation. At the convergence of these interests there is an evolving apparatus for exercising the legitimate use of force, the definitive control over money and commerce, the ultimate determination of politico-moral values, and the hegemonic guidance of economic growth. Working within and above the nation-states of the NATO/OECD, this zone-regime controls the means for its own collective defense, commerce, decision making, and growth. As Chapter 6 argued, it purposely creates legitimacy for itself; and it is accepted popularly as being legitimate on an intranational, as well as on a supranational, level. Its financial ministries and monetary bureaus coordinate capital accumulation and investment among the economies of the seven major Western powers: the United States, Britain, Canada, France, Germany, Italy, and Japan. Even though this weak transnational state is the management center for dealing with global crises—witness, for example, its confused and inadequate supranational response to the Third World debt crisis, the energy crisis, the inflation problem, multinational macroeconomic growth, the nuclear arms race, international terrorism, or common defense issues— it largely has been insulated from public pressure because the individual member states' national electoral/parliamentary institutions and mass electorates have no immediate or direct points of entry into its collective workings.

Reaganism would sustain the powers of the privileged in traditional advanced industrial societies by brute force, social harassment, and a mean-spirited, neo-laissez-faire ideology as fewer public goods are produced to enable those with the means to consume their own private goods without restriction.[47] As the material standards of living for the many have declined during the past two decades, the prosperity of the few remains certain and secure. These ideas and policies have been unfolding for nearly two decades, but the Reagan administration in Washington has been the first ruling group to make them work successfully within the transnational zone-regime by touting an ideology of free-enterprise/supply-side economics. Reaganism, then, stands for the tough bureaucratic, military, and police protection of the traditional forms of Sloanism, Fordism, and Taylorism—the "American" or "Western" or "Democratic" way of life—now under attack in the world.

In protecting the old verities of advanced industrialism, Reaganism has combined cuts from state services with rampant Keynesian borrowing to free new investment funds for industrial growth.[48] However, private investment under Reagan was actually less than under the Carter administration. Under the Reagan program of giving more services to the rich and fewer benefits to the poor, "private investment has been concentrated, more generally, in the low-productivity, low-export service economy."[49] The focus of public spending in Reaganism, then, has shifted to new priorities: "the money has gone to private consumption, to defense research and procurement, to building hotels and shopping centers, and to financial, trade, and service industries."[50] By throwing millions out of work, reducing growth in nonmilitary state spending, and manipulating monetary policy, Reaganism has allegedly brought inflation under control, put aggregate productivity on the increase, and led to a growing GNP. Nonetheless, the United States' success on most of these economic fronts is not much better than that of the other OECD countries during the same time period, and it has come with high costs. In particular, America's economic and technological hegemony is being effectively challenged on almost all fronts by Japan.

This re-rationalization strategy is closely connected to a vast military build-up and a renewed willingness to cultivate an image of toughness through a show of military power. To protect the economic privileges of the middle classes and upper classes in the capitalist core, Reaganism stands for maintaining their share of subsidized public services as it lessens or eliminates the social services provided to the lower working classes and the "truly needy." To guarantee the declining industrial sectors' access to markets, resources, and capital, Reaganism also accepts protectionism, bail-outs, discriminatory tariffs, less environmental regulation, and trade barriers. Finally, to retrench the old industrial core's share of world markets and access to resources, as well as redynamicize

U.S. high-tech industries in the modern core, Reaganism has championed a major conventional and nuclear arms-building program to oppose East bloc and Third World threats.

Much of the centralist zone-regime system in the NATO/OECD states, particularly in Europe, Japan, and North America, focuses on military preparedness, nuclear weapons modernization, and aggressive posturing vis-à-vis the WTO/CMEA zone-regime. While it may be in the interests of all to attain a kind of "peace" by constantly preparing for nuclear war, the peace movement articulates localist values of opposing war machines that are imposed upon the ethno-nationalist cultures of the zone-regime's subject populations. The institutionalized political parties, labor unions, and parliaments of the various OECD nation-states usually must support any military build-up: it provides jobs, it proves their patriotism, and it enables them to stay inside the system and use it to reward their political constituents. New social movements, like the peace movement, represent an alternative popular mobilization that protests this militaristic vision of modernity.

Each nation-state's institutions provide for its country's security and for the zone-regime's defense by paying for the zone-regime's military deterrent forces. However, these supranational defense decisions and security goals are often not accepted by many of the people at large on the local level (unless, of course, they tend to work in defense plants or on military bases). For example, at the ethno-national, localist level, most Welshmen, Walloons, or Württemburgers have no quarrel with the Moravians, Mongolians, or Moldavians. However, the central military and political decision-makers of the NATO/OECD zone-regime have decided that their conflicts with the WTO/CMEA bloc necessitate the storage, deployment, or use of modern nuclear and conventional weapons in the United Kingdom, Belgium, and West Germany. As a result, the local communities of Welshmen, Belgians, and West Germans must surrender their land, energy, money, and freedom to the zone-regime's deterrence system and risk first-strike obliteration.

The electoral/democratic regimes in London, Brussels, and Bonn have already have signed away such local interests, turning many localties into current-day military bases and potential future targets. The localist, decentralized, ethno-national agenda of ordinary citizens for effective access, voice, and control in relation to distant transnational decision-making centers is the new political agenda being articulated by the peace movement. Lacking any other access points, local peace activists in the OECD states have used mass-mobilization demonstrations, pressure-group lobbying, initiative efforts, street theater, and media appeals to try to influence the zone-regime and its respective constituent national militaries. Refusing to pay taxes, picketing military bases, declaring towns nuclear-free zones, and voting for freeze legislation are all additional techniques being employed at a local, ethno-national level. Many peace activists will admit that the USSR is an expansionist, brutal regime, yet they also question the military rationality of the transnational zone-regime in the NATO/OECD bloc inasmuch as distant disputes between Washington and Moscow—over the Koreas, for example—can lead to a military confrontation that uses one set of bloc states to launch and absorb nuclear strikes on opposing bloc states. More frequently, these military instruments are used "conventionally" in Third World adventures in places such as Vietnam, Algeria, Angola, Grenada, Nicaragua, Lebanon, Libya, and the Persian Gulf. Despite what each zone-regime's elites argue in transnational security terms, local activists point out the real "who/whom" trade-off in the global military competition. The cleavage is between the centralist agenda of a transnational zone-regime and the decentralizing, ethno-national purposes of diverse localities. The political weight of existing nation-state institutions often falls between this supranational and subnational contradiction because they are expected to serve both territorial/cultural masters: the supranational zone-regime and the subnational local citizenry.

Many new social movements therefore take an anti-Reaganist stance, particularly with regard to issues related to peace, the ecology, and economic growth. On the one hand, a major strand in mainstream social analysis has connected the "decline" of Western power to an "increase" in East bloc and Third World military power. On the other hand, millions of people are questioning the passive grammar of living which rests upon claims such as "our thermonuclear bombs, missiles, and bombers are bigger and better than theirs." Gorbachev's twin programs of perestroika and glasnost in the late 1980s, of course, have only added fuel to the fire of mass discontent with the Western zone-regime's military policies. The peace movement sees the Reaganist mode of "producing" security and making defense decisions as bankrupt. The "new patriotism" of the post-Falklands/post-Grenada period, in particular, is also questioned by the new social movements as the chauvinist costume of superpower bullying, wrongheaded cultural values, and dangerous foreign policies.

Along comparable lines, the ecology and environmental movements are resisting the resurrection of anti-environmentalist/pro-growth attitudes under Reaganism. After nearly fifteen years of activism that achieved limited success against air, water, and chemical pollution, the backlash of Reaganism's definition of activist goals as costly luxuries threatens almost everyone with new socially irrational pollution problems in order to gain limited increases in industrial growth. Reaganism's mean-spirited characterization of advocates of quality growth, ecology, and peace as proponents of "fear, pessimism, and limits" hints at a neo-Fordist/neo-Sloanist program to provide the declining industrial regions of the OECD nations with one "last hurrah," regardless of its ecological, economic, and global costs elsewhere. The Reagan administration's tactics toward Canada regarding the acid rain issue plainly illustrate this stance. Despite clear serious evidence of global danger, ozone layer depletion, forest death, and soil erosion, for solutions Reaganism puts its trust in the same market capitalism that causes the crisis. Again, new social movements seem to question attaining "prosperity at any price" as they ask who decides/who does not, who pays/who benefits, and who survives/who dies under a Reaganist model of advanced industrial political economy?

In the protests of the new social movements, the central political tendencies of advanced capitalist economies and states are revealed. The strategies and values of Taylorism, Fordism, Sloanism, and Reaganism are all of one piece. Each assumes the other; hence, none of them function very well without the other components. Yet it is also clear that their continuing practice has much to do with the rationalization crisis. Their coaligned continuation presents one alternative future for the further modernization of the NATO/OECD zone-regime. New cultural grammars of everyday life, vaguely outlined in the politics of new social movements, project another set of alternative futures for the informationalizing advanced industrial societies. While none of these alternatives has any obvious political advantage at this point, it is apparent that some new social movements do have fresh approaches to the challenge of the rationality crisis. Despite their often artificially negative impact, some of the groups are trying to substantively justify—in terms of procedural democratic norms and immediate economic impact—who should decide what is produced, how output is measured, and why production should be undertaken from the vantage of increased voice, access, and control for the groups of people who will actually suffer or benefit after corrective policy steps are taken.

THE LINES OF RESISTANCE

This chapter has presented a developmental and identity-oriented interpretation for the wars of position being fought by the new social movements, illustrating how and why these new mobilizations of popular protest are much more than merely neo-romantic/neo-populist reactions to secular social changes. Actually the new social movements can be better understood as the initial expression of the incipient class conflicts and periphery-versus-core cleavages in the emergent postindustrial states and informational societies of Western Europe, North America, and Japan. By challenging transnationalization and informationalization in the OECD nation-states, the new social movements place the culture and politics of identity at the core of their resistance. Yet, at the same time, they are often first mobilized and loosely organized by crises and conflicts their members see and hear in the media.

With the advance of informationalization, the misapplication of old modes of industrial instrumental rationality to the challenge of informational changes has evoked a general "crisis of rationalization" in the ongoing modernization of these rich OECD countries. New social movements can provide fresh forms of resistance to the Fordist, Sloanist, and Reaganist policies of the older industrial elites, trying to administer their way out of industrial decline. The "old wave" working-class movements often support these strategies as much as the ruling elites. The struggle against scarcity and the problems of distribution are not completely settled, but today's "new wave" opposition is oriented toward new issues: the local defense of peripheral cultures, life-styles, and values against their corporate colonization by core and zone-regime cultures. In other words, most new social movements' opposition transcends labor-versus-capital conflicts—it usually is post-proletarian, postindustrial, post-socialist, post-Marxist, and post-distributional.

The ideologies and class interests that the new social movements articulate can perhaps be summarized as those of a new complex social bloc: informational "new middle-class" workers, anti-industrial resistance groups, high-tech local entrepreneurs, anti-lifeworld-colonization groups, and peripheral culture defense groups. Despite their various immediate agendas, most of these class and regional groups are following programs broadly inspired by anti-Fordism, anti-Sloanism, or anti-Reaganism. Their ideological goals and group interests aim at a common end: empowering clients/consumers/citizens in lifeworld decolonization struggles while disempowering technocratic experts in everyday life and undercutting their enclaves of expertise.

While supporting many of the benefits of material affluence to the transnational community, the new social movements also articulate a systematic critique of everyday life within advanced industrial society and represent an alternative strategy for guiding systemic change into qualitatively different phases of modernization. They are excellent examples of how new, popular oppositions might wage culturally driven struggles against modern nation-states and transnational regimes. The changes these groups advocate are not necessarily neo-romantic or neo-populist in an industrial sense. Rather they often are grounded upon an informational transformation, tied to the "modern" instead of the "marginal" sectors of the OECD economy, and directed at politically, technically, economically, and culturally enabling more individuals and households to enjoy more autonomy in informational economies of scope with localist administrative structures. Beyond this general description, however, the alternatives of many of the new movements are more utopian and ill defined on both the left and the right sides of the political spectrum. Likewise, there are not as yet any articulate normative discourses about the specific moral identity and uniqueness of most new social movements' ethical and political programs. In this respect, a great deal more thinking must be done. Although late-breaking neoconservative and neo-Marxist critiques will try to shoehorn the programs of the new social movements into their increasingly questionable industrial categories, this preliminary overview might provide another map to follow into some other, more fruitful paths of investigation.

NOTES

1. For another variant of this approach, see Carl Boggs, *Social Movements and Political Power: Emerging Forms of Radicalism in the West* (Philadelphia: Temple University Press, 1986), and Antonio Gramsci, *Selections From the Prison Notebooks,* ed. and trans. Quintin Hoare and Geoffrey Nowell Smith (New York: International Publishers, 1971), 228–39.

2. Ronald Inglehart, *The Silent Revolution* (Princeton: Princeton University Press, 1977); Alain Touraine, *The Post-Industrial Society* (New York: Random House, 1971); Daniel Bell, *The Coming of Post-Industrial Society* (New York: Basic, 1973); Jürgen Habermas, *Legitimation Crisis* (Boston: Beacon, 1975); Michael Crozier, Samuel Huntington, and Joji Watanuki, *The Crisis of Democracy: Report on the Governability of Democracies to the Trilateral Commission* (New York: New York University Press, 1975); Paul Piccone, "The Crisis of One-Dimensionality," *Telos* 35 (Spring 1978): 43–54; Timothy W. Luke, "Culture and Politics in the Age of Artificial Negativity," *Telos* 35 (Spring 1978): 55–72; George Konrad, *Antipolitics: An Essay* (San Diego: Harcourt, Brace, Jovanovich, 1984); James O'Connor, *Accumulation Crisis* (New York: Blackwell, 1984); Felix Guattari, *Molecular Revolution* (London: Penguin, 1984); and Hal Foster, ed., *The Anti-Aesthetic: Essays on Post-Modern Culture* (Port Townsend, Wash.: Bay Press, 1983).

3. See Carl Boggs, "The Intellectual and Social Movements: Some Reflections on Academic Marxism," *Humanities in Society* 2, nos. 2 and 3 (1983): 223–39, and Jean Cohen, "Between Crisis Management and Social Movements: The Place of Institutional Reforms," *Telos* 52 (Summer 1982): 21–40.

4. Klaus Eder, "A New Social Movement," *Telos* 52 (Summer 1982): 18.

5. Ibid., 6.

6. Ibid.

7. Timothy W. Luke, "The Origins of the Service State: On the Ironies of Intervention," *The Journal of Sociology and Social Welfare* 11, no. 2 (1984): 432–62, and Claus Offe, "New Social Movements: Challenging the Boundaries of Institutional Politics," *Social Research* 52, no. 4 (1985): 817–68.

8. Cohen, "Crisis Management," 21.

9. Boggs, "The Intellectual and Social Movements," 228–29. This attitude is not shared universally. O'Connor, for example, connects the "localism/populism" of the new social movements to working-class resistance against corporate capitalism. See his *Accumulation Crisis,* 179–249. Similarly, Klaus Eder sees lower middle-class radicalism at work in the new social movements' activism. See "The 'New Social Movements': Moral Crusades, Political Pressure Groups, or Social Movements," *Social Research* 52, no. 4 (1985): 868–90.

10. Joachim Hirsch, "The Fordist Security State and New Social Movements," *Kapitalistate* 10/11 (Spring 1984): 79.

11. Jean Cohen, "Strategy or Identity: New Theoretical Paradigms and Contemporary Social Movements," *Social Research* 52, no. 4 (1985): 690.

12. See Timothy W. Luke, "Informationalism and Ecology," *Telos* 56 (Summer 1983): 59–73. For further discussion, see Kees van der Pijl, *The Making of an Atlantic Ruling Class* (Verso: London, 1984); Richard J. Barnet and Ronald E. Mueller, *Global Reach* (New York: Simon and Schuster, 1974); David P. Calleo, *The Imperious Economy* (Cambridge, Mass.: Harvard University Press, 1982); Michael Hudson, *Global Fracture: The New International Economic Order* (New York: Harper and Row, 1977); Robert O. Keohane and Joseph S. Nye, *Power and Interdependence: World Politics in Transition* (Boston: Little, Brown, 1977); Robert L. Rothstein, *Global Bargaining: UNCTAD and the Quest for a New International Economic Order* (Princeton: Princeton University Press, 1979); and Daniel Yergin, Martin Hillenbrand, eds. *Global Insecurity: A Strategy for Energy and Economic Renewal* (Boston: Houghton Mifflin Co., 1982). Regarding transnational civil society, see Jürgen Habermas, *Legitimation Crisis;* Ronald Inglehart, *The Silent Revolution;* Herbert Schiller, *Who Knows: Information in the Age of the Fortune 500* (Norwood, N.J.: Ablex Press, 1981); Jean Baudrillard, *In the Shadow of the Silent Majorities* (New York: Semiotext(e), 1983); and Marshall McLuhan, *Understanding Media: The Extensions of Man* (New York: McGraw-Hill, 1964).

13. Seymour M. Lipset and Stein Rokkan, "Cleavage Structures, Party Systems, and Voter Alignments: An Introduction," in *Party Systems and Voter Alignments: Cross-National Perspectives,* ed. Seymour M. Lipset and Stein Rokkan (New York: Free Press, 1967), 1–64.

14. Ibid., 2–3.

15. Ibid., 13–15.

16. Ibid., 13.

17. Ibid.

18. Alain Touraine, *The Voice and the Eye* (New York: Cambridge University Press, 1981), 77.

19. Ibid., 66.

20. Ibid., 67–68.

21. Ibid., 10–24.

22. Jürgen Habermas, "New Social Movements," *Telos* 49 (Fall 1981): 34.

23. Ibid.

24. Ibid., 36.

25. Ibid., 33.

26. Eder, "A New Social Movement," 10.

27. Ibid.

28. Ibid., 11.

29. Ibid.

30. Ibid.

31. Ibid., 17–18.

32. Hirsch, "The Fordist Security State," 84.

33. Ibid., 85.

34. Ibid.

35. Ibid.

36. See Ralf Dahrendorf, *Class and Class Conflict in Industrial Society* (Stanford: Stanford University Press, 1959), 36–71.

37. See J. D. Goldhar and Mariann Jelinek, "Plan for Economies of Scope," *Harvard Business Review* 83, no. 6 (1983): 141–48.

38. Stein Rokkan, *Citizens, Elections, Parties: Approaches to the Comparative Study of the Processes of Development* (New York: David McKay Co., 1970), 64–65.

39. Martin Carnoy, *The State and Political Theory* (Princeton: Princeton University Press, 1984), 3. On this point, Marcuse notes that "in the contemporary era, the conquest of scarcity is still confined to small areas of advanced industrial society. Their prosperity covers up the Inferno inside and outside their borders; it also spreads a repressive productivity and 'false needs.' It is repressive precisely to the degree to which it promotes the satisfaction of needs which require continuing the rat race of catching up with one's peers and with planned obsolescence, enjoying freedom from using the brain, working with and for the means of destruction. The obvious comforts generated by this sort of productivity, and even more, the support which it gives to a system of profitable domination, facilitate its importation in less advanced areas of the world where the introduction of such a system still means tremendous progress in technical and human terms" (*One-Dimensional Man* [Boston: Beacon Press, 1964], 241).

40. Ibid.

41. Harry Braverman, *Labor and Monopoly Capital* (New York: Monthly Review Press, 1974), 86.

42. Charles F. Sabel, *Work and Politics: The Division of Labor in Industry* (Cambridge: Cambridge University Press, 1982), 33.

43. Antonio Gramsci, "Americanism and Fordism," *Selections From The Prison Notebooks,* 277–320.

44. See Immanuel L. Wallerstein, *The Modern World System: Capitalist Agriculture and the Origins of the European World Economy in the Sixteenth Century* (New York: Academic Press, 1976), and Giovanni Arrighi, Terence R. Hop-

kins, and Wallerstein, "Dilemmas of Antisystemic Movements," *Social Research* 53, no. 1 (1986): 189–206.

45. Braverman, *Labor and Monopoly Capital,* 265.

46. For a discussion of international regimes, see Oran Young, "International Regimes: Problems of Concept Formation," *World Politics* 32, no. 3 (1980): 331–56; Robert Jervis, "Security Regimes," *International Organization* 36, no. 2 (1982): 357–77; and Donald J. Puchala and Raymond F. Hopkins, "International Regimes: Lessons from Inductive Analysis," *International Organization* 36, no. 2 (1982): 245–75.

47. For a systematic analysis of the revival of inequality under Reagan, see Thomas Bryne Edsall, "The Return of Inequality," *The Atlantic Monthly* 261, no. 6 (1988): 86–94; Emma Rothschild, "The Real Reagan Economy," *The New York Review of Books* 35, no. 11 (1988): 46–53; Rothschild, "Reagan's Economic Legacy," *The New York Review of Books* 35, no. 12 (1988): 33–41; and Theresa Amott and Joel Krieger, "Thatcher and Reagan: State Theory and the 'Hyper-Capitalist' Regime," *New Political Science* 8 (Spring 1982): 9–36.

48. See Timothy W. Luke, "Rationalization Redux: From the New Deal to the New Beginning," *New Political Science* 8 (Spring 1982): 63–72.

49. Rothschild, "Reagan's Economic Legacy," 37.

50. Ibid.

9

The New Left, Critical Intellectuals, and Social Revolution: The Role of the New Media in the Politics of Image

Advanced corporate capitalism in the informationalizing economies of America, Japan, and Western Europe conducts an endless discourse with itself, about itself, and for itself to elaborate its reified market culture on the screens of power. In this discourse, as the previous chapters have maintained, continual streams of densely encoded images can integrate virtually anything and everything on the mediascape (at least partially) into the logic of commodification. The cultural complexities of family life, ecological disaster, electoral democracy, international conflict, popular political protests, or historical time itself are not immune. Each of the preceding chapters has examined in some detail how the market economy of industrial societies becomes more generalized as a market culture of nearly complete commodification under informational conditions of production. In the bright, familiar packaging of "the sixties," for example, the happenings of a revolutionary decade now serve as the marketable containers of 1990s consumer goods, while the political upheavals, cultural innovations, and social struggles of that era in America, Japan, and Western Europe are almost completely eclipsed in hyperreal image. In the codes of the mass media, the sixties' political significance simply is marked in the era's differences with and sharp separations from other similarly packaged historical commodities, like the "fifties," "thirties," or "seventies," with their less revolutionary attributes.

THE NEW LEFT AND THE MEDIA

In order to illustrate how the resistance of New Left forces grew out of, and then became ensnared within, the codes of the mainstream mass media, even now one must pick through the incomplete pieces, last signs, and remaining fragments of an era jumbled into the "sixties" container. The New Left's coverage by the mass media of the 1960s illustrates the central importance today of using "new media" alternatives as channels of information. Tentative steps toward such alternatives began in the 1960s and 1970s with the hundreds of "underground" or "alternative" newspapers, books, magazines, and comic books. Even though these alternative channels of information spawned their own national "Liberation News Service," most either were short-lived or turned into yuppie entertainment guides by the late 1970s.

While the material technologies of community cable television, citizen's band radio, home videotape, audiocassettes, low-power/local-broadcast radio or television, photocopying, mainframe computer networks, and microcomputers are still produced in the existing corporate economy, not all of their potential applications have been integrated completely into the conventional product cycles of the mass market. Their full aesthetic, commercial, and political potentials, then, are still being explored. Such new media could provide crucial sites for a strategy of contestation: organizing progressive personal and social change by defining new cultural categories of media reception, generating alternative codes of interpretation, or subverting the present modes of communication from within. By working from the margins of society, and by challenging the regulation of social discourse and practice in the larger culture, resistance groups might deconstruct the contingent, discontinuous, and elective nature of domination in informationalizing societies. Effective use of the alternative media could help create new sites and spaces, relatively free from the mass media's marketing imperatives, with which emancipatory alternatives to the more commodified cultural forms prevailing in everyday life could be openly discussed.

Alternative media, once effectively structured around these ends, could foster critical styles of expression, construct alternative modes of social identity, or concretize new critical communities of action, practice, and analysis. The corporate sector has already recognized their potential for "in-house" communications "off-loaded" from common-carrier phone, data, and broadcast networks. Just as some of the new media have afforded corporate capital the means of creating its own closed, cheaper, secure, and more accessible systems of communication, other new media also offer activists practical opportunities to create more open, free fields of communication for resistance. Further, if the means and ends of cultural production were put in the hands of local, communal networks of media users and producers, more people could develop fresh counter-codes of media reception and cultural consumption in their own thinking. Yet there is no need for an elite intellectual vanguard: nearly all people already are thinking critically about their lives at least some of the time. Once partially disengaged from the collaborative imperatives of mass media market building and maintenance, they might recognize the validity of new media-borne critiques of ideology, critical discourses, and counter–image production that could turn the codes against themselves. As user-based and use value–oriented mediations, new media structures could then be used by resistance movements to mount attacks more directly on the owner-based and exchange value–oriented coding systems of the mass media. This chapter will explore some of the new media's potential for perhaps encouraging some progressive cultural transformations in the present. Many New Left activists in the 1960s failed to recognize and adapt the revolutionary potentials in many of the new media to their purposes of transformation. As a result, their efforts often were reinterpreted and adapted as more conventionally coded images in the mainstream media to further the purposes of corporate media managers and the logic of permissive individualism.[1]

To an extent, the opening passages of Marx's *Eighteenth Brumaire* accurately capture much of the spirit and substance of sixties radicalism, trapped as it was in the spectacles of the mass media. Maturing in an era that embraced the "end of ideology" thesis of the 1950s, many activists in the United States, Europe, and Japan clearly had to borrow the names, battle cries, and costumes of their revolutions from others. And, ironically, they chose the illusions and icons of radical change, packaged in film, voice, and videotape, from revolutionary movements in Moscow, Peking, Algiers, Havana, Cairo, New Delhi, Accra, Hanoi, Djakarta, and Conakry, which were incessantly broadcast and rebroadcast in the global mass media in spectacles of decolonization, nation-building, and peasant revolution.

From these readily available and prepackaged texts of radical transformation, 1960s radicals—black, white, brown, male, female, young, and old—ironically borrowed the packaging and scripts of Third World revolutions to contest the collaborative powers of consumer culture. Yet in presenting these time-honored disguises and borrowed languages as their own, the New Left and counterculture movements fell far short of revolutionizing themselves anew or creating a new order that had never yet existed. Lacking secure access to a larger audience, like the diverse audiences potentially afforded by the new media of today, these activists instead concentrated upon winning attention in the corporate mass media by subverting their coding conventions. Although they initially succeeded, the coding conventions on these screens quickly adapted to, and then blunted, the thrust of the New Left's critical projects. The New Left intended to create revolution, but, in the process, it unintentionally revolutionized the workings of corporate America. The central tragedy of sixties radicalism, then, was its inability to transcend these ironies of mass culture. In spectacular images of rebellion from the mass media, 1960s radicals found the illusions needed to conceal from themselves the corporate limitations on the content of their struggles while keeping their enthusiasm on the high plane of great historical tragedy. The various American countercultures, which had produced rebels without a cause in the 1950s, generated revolutionaries without a base in the 1960s and 1970s.

A tough-minded review of the 1960s, then, may miss the real thrust of this era's events. The revolutionary break of the New Left with "bourgeois" culture, society, and politics actually was defined (almost entirely, albeit quite ironically) by consumerist codes of mass marketing. The counterculture's principles were simple: individuals find their self-actualization through accepting (but also countercoding) the conventions of ordinary commodity consumption. By refunctioning certain material goods and redefining particular wish-fulfilling images, the counterculture accepted most of the ends of consumerism, even as it repudiated many of its existing means. The revolt of the repressed in the 1960s was denominated in the "product revolutionization" coding of corporate capitalist product demography. The revolutions of the sixties, it now would appear, have turned out to be episodes of weak, negative, but corrective, popular feedback rather than as events of destructive, system-transforming, violent change. "America," like everything in media spectacle, was and is an evolving "product" which can use more expansive and elaborate countercultural codings for its continued economic and political growth.

In the 1960s the American dream machine was not "performing" as its civics-book operating manuals and formal constitutional warranties had guaranteed to the dream buyers. Urban squalor, black inequality, rural backwardness, spreading pollution, denials of civil rights, suburban anomie, and mass poverty—which were and are virtual constants in twentieth-century America—gained new urgency in the codes of transformation posed by Third World revolution. Added to the explosive issue of using military conscription to fight an unpopular and undeclared war, these problems all were seen by the social movements of the 1960s as obvious signs of a poorly performing product or an increasingly faltering service. A weak consensus favoring complete changes in its methods, conditions, or models of operation—a product revolutionization—gathered momentum in the 1960s, strongly aided and abetted by the black and white countercultures. Old, rundown, unimproved America was "broken with" in this "revolutionization" of 1960s radicals; but, as with most products of corporate change, this revolutionary breakthrough only led down the aisles of collective choice to a redesigned model: new, improved America.

The communitarian revolutions of the New Left, black power, and other counterculture movements in the 1960s ironically assisted the existing projects of corporate growth and economic liberalism, accelerating the collapse of arbitrary limits imposed upon the individual pursuit of life, liberty, and happiness. The post–1945 promise of permissive individualism in the 1960s was still an unfulfilled project for entire categories of "individuals"—blacks, the young, women, ethnics, Latinos, gays, old people, ghetto dwellers, the rural poor. Many social taboos, political rules, and cultural attitudes in traditional Fordist American society constituted a restrictive culture of petty apartheid, preventing goods and services from circulating much beyond the secure sphere of middle-class, middle-aged, male-dominated, straight, WASP communities.

News clips of the Watts, Detroit, or Washington, D.C. riots encapsulate the revolutionary situation of the 1960s. Within a society of spectacle—which defines identity, purpose, and meaning in terms of commodities—marginalized, underemployed consumers leap out of shattered store windows, carrying away the best icons of American consumerist identity (TV sets, vacuum cleaners, air conditioners, reclining chairs, stereo systems). Denied the educational and economic opportunities and legal equality necessary to acquire these totems of consumption more conventionally, the outsiders rioted. In the revolt of the repressed, these riots became "the shopping spree" denied to them by the petty apartheid of the traditional marketplace. In the name of revolution, women's liberation, black power, gay rights, or flower power, the New Leftists—in their theories—fought for authenticity, personal fulfillment, and self-actualization, which meant, in practice, increasing access for these outsiders to corporate capitalist goods and services. Although the limited-access outlets in the underground and alternative press allowed activists to make their critiques, the New Left's revolutionary project could often only sign off and sign on the consciousness of the mainstream mass audiences under communicative conditions set by the corporate-run and state-regulated mass media. As a result they only could attack the basic conditions of mass collaboration while at the same time reinforcing the hold of collaborative forms of power over even more people than before. Despite its best radical intentions, the counterculture unexpectedly served as the shock troops of mass culture and its corporate producers, helping to tear down many of the last cultural constraints on circulating all commodities to anyone, anytime, anywhere. Without more independent free spaces based on local community-controlled and user-regulated new media, the more radical New Left critiques of commodity production and consumption per se simply remained lost or impossible transmissions in this era of corporate-designed social change.

Admittedly, with its street demonstrations, sit-ins, and revolutionary communiques, the counterculture broke with many of the traditions prevailing in Fordist America, and some victories were realized. The peace movement, civil rights activists, environmentalist organizers, and the feminist movement all gained important new benefits for many hitherto excluded groups in society, although many today remain deprived. Nonetheless, the conservative case against Jane Fonda and the New Left simply misses the key outcome of the sixties. Similarly, the televangelists' rage against "secular humanism," which Chapter 3 pointed out, confuses the real effects that their own gospel of wealth promotes in capitalist culture with the incoherent and ineffective fashions of sixties radicalism. In fact, as Chapter 4 argues, Fondaism, and the logic of permissive individualism it is based upon, are increasingly important to the ongoing reproduction of American capitalism today. As Western Europe and Japan reindustrialized in the 1950s, seeking to market high-quality goods worldwide, traditional industrial America and its Fordist culture already were in the grip of a severe crisis, even before Vietnam. Fondaist-style codes of individual self-management were an effective response to the crisis, calculated to recharge economic growth in the United States through a service-based, information-driven, transnational economy. In the last analysis, the 1960s counterculture and New Left cannot transcend the ironies of mass culture, because they themselves are some of mass culture's ultimate ironies. The spectacle systems continuously being manufactured by mass media have not only survived the commodification of New Left revolution, they actually have been made stronger through occasional doses of this sort of self-administered "artificial negativity."

THE NEW MEDIA IN THE STRUGGLE OF IMAGES

The videos, soundtrack, and texts of the "revolutionary sixties" continue to grow as a minor culture industry unto itself. The sixties' images have been repackaged, rerun, and rereleased for expanded distribution in the mass media during the 1980s and 1990s. In broadcast, cassette, and cable media packaging, these stylized images have served as spectacular baseline models for social movements during the 1980s in the United States, Japan, and Western Europe for the anti-apartheid, disarmament, and anti–nuclear power struggles. Alternative uses for these new media might have a vital role to play: with their potential for more local control, popular access, community programming, user-generated content, more critical styles of discourse, narrowcast image codes, and immediate use value in their operations, the alternative new media today present some real possibilities for developing even more sophisticated, critical countercultures.

These possibilities, however, should not be read simplemindedly as a plea for every revolutionary to own his or her own VCR and Minicam. They also do not constitute a writ of authority for some clique of self-deputized "public intellectuals" to seize the "means of information" in order to beam emancipatory programming on the major networks into every living room. No one probably would tune in anyway, because many already believe they are liberating themselves as they mimic the moves on Fondaist workout tapes. Workable agendas for real change must also be fused, first, with new critiques of the coding systems behind commodity production and consumption in informational societies and, second, with a widespread willingness of many people to act differently based on these radical critiques of what they ordinarily accept as the basis of their cultural identity. The limited protests being mounted by some new social movements suggest that this is happening, but at a fairly slow pace. Still, recontextualizing uses for the new media might provide some new tactics for a popular resistance and the critique of ideology. If the existing cultural codings of transnational corporate consumerism are to be overcome, then more progressive popular cultures must be created by everyone favoring more authentic localist modes of living beyond the dictates of market culture.

The alternative new media are significant because they might provide fresh sites for media users to more effectively criticize, resist, or countercode the corporate codes of media-borne ideology, as well as to more rapidly mobilize popular resistance by becoming producers of new codes of understanding. Many people recognize how the codes are worked by those behind the screens of power when others encode the media. But, these new media can put ordinary people behind the camera, microphone, or keypad to unravel these codes and produce the cultural foundations for their own enlightenment and emancipation. The electronic media—as the electron cannons that have been used to demolish the walls of personal autonomy and contextual rationality in everyday life—might also be turned against the established interests hiding behind the screens of power. Styles, conventions, and images of ideological integration can be directly attacked in audio or videocassette presentations of popular countercritiques. Sexist or racist images in movies, ads, music, television, or news, for example, can be rerecorded, recontextualized, and remixed in an audiovisual critical analysis to reveal how cultural production serves as ideology. Oppressive working conditions or job rules can be documented on audiotape or videotape for critical presentation to broader audiences that otherwise might be skeptical about workers' claims. By the same token, air, water, noise, architectural, or chemical pollution can be documented by local victims in order to prove its existence and persuade others to resist it.[2] New media allow almost anyone to subvert the codes of ideological acceptance, integration, and legitimation with the counterimages and texts of critical political analysis. The unconscious tracks of domination, the normal fit of ideological assumptions, and also the naturalized presentation of repressive practices might all be isolated and critically analyzed in new emancipatory discourse open to everyone and conducted within new media presentations.

Alternative uses of the new media should also attempt to make the technologies involved a community technology, in opposition to corporate efforts to control the commodification of information and communication in all modern media. Working outside of market imperatives and corporate profit targets, the alternative new media could project a more educative, critical space that would be accessible, immediate, broadgauged, and multipurposed. In critical exchanges on "real" public access radio and television or by circulating audio and videocassette presentations, people could construct a more critical, open, pedagogical community network of new media users and producers as part of the new oppositional forces in contemporary informational society.

At the same time, such productions could gain additional exposure on low-power/local-broadcast radio and television or on community-access channels on cable television. Media users, using their own video and audio recorders, could produce their own discourse and images for local criticism and consumption. Here the new media can create power for their users by presenting anyone conversant in the shifting codes of media production with the possibilities of reaching and persuading broader audiences hoping for something more than the superficialities of market culture. In the United States, Europe, and Japan, these potentialities are being recognized by minority groups, women's organizations, student circles, and critical intellectuals as they establish underground radio stations, obtain low-power/local-broadcast TV licenses, work to open community-access cable channels, and produce homemade video documentaries on issues of local political import for public hearings.[3]

Alternative new media, then, are already being put to such countersystemic uses, some very progressive and some quite reactionary, in many different contexts. In the United States, an entire subcultural community in many areas is centered on avocational citizen's band (CB) radio use, from emergency relief teams and citizen neighborhood watch units to ham radio operators' intercommunity and international communications. Similarly, CB radios are used daily by millions of drivers with radar detectors in a systematic subversion of local and regional traffic control by city, county, and state police units. Photocopying machinery is used locally to generate political literature, signs, and symbols by independent groups too small and poor to establish their own press. New computer hardware and software has made electronic on-line publishing and true desktop publishing a promising reality. Thousands of personal computer users are establishing local, regional, and national networks for penetrating and exploiting some of the information stored in major computer banks, data sources, and information utilities in new ways.[4] These resources are available to both the radical right and the radical left. Computer bulletin boards already connect computer networks of diverse groups, including libertarians, right-wing fundamentalists, followers of the neo-Nazi Aryan Nation, environmentalists, and anti-nuclear power activists. By linking their supporters together, these electronic networks of diverse groups of computer users are building communications channels and information connections that can turn computing power to popular, communal uses outside of, and counter to, the prevailing informational regime.

In the same vein, audiocassette recorders allow communities and individuals to produce and distribute political messages directly. For example, the radical currents of the Islamic Revolution throughout the Mideast have exploited this technology to rapidly spread their revolutionary appeal underground without relying only on the conventional print or broadcast media. Reactionary white supremacists and fundamentalist Christian activists in the U.S. also have packaged their anti-systemic appeals against mainstream consumer society in audiocassette form to quickly distribute their message to individuals and small groups of believers. Videocassette recorders can be put to the same use, achieving added impact. Pat Robertson, for example, used direct-mail audio and videocassette appeals to gain supporters during the 1988 presidential caucuses and primaries. Although this approach did not win him the Republican nomination, it did demonstrate new media possibilities. With a little education, VCR owners can learn that their units will do more than play *Debbie Does Dallas* or record daytime soap operas for nighttime viewing. As personal videocassette recorders and camera systems become more accessible to households, an entire new sphere of critical discourse could be generated among individuals and small groups by putting them to these new unexpected uses, as new forms of video critiques, media analyses, or political documentaries are produced for immediate popular access and communal use. Local groups could conduct critiques on their own terms of community environmental policies, urban service delivery systems, housing conditions, work situations, or mainstream media analyses by producing video documents framed in critical, noncommercial, local vernaculars of analysis. Of course, serious limitations exist: these technologies are not cheap; people possess varying levels of coding competence; and not everyone is equally motivated to participate in such critical activity, despite having a similar critical frame of mind. And—as Chapter 3 illustrated in its review of televangelism—the quest for funding can often replace the quest for change in media-based discourses. Plainly, campaigns of resistance against the commodification of everyday life should not assume the form of a packaged kit of Fondaist discipline and training (on VHS, Beta, records, or cassettes) for only $39.95. New media productions made by popular resistance groups could turn out to be as mean-spirited, ineffectual, or just plain stupid as those of mainstream media, but for now this possibility is an open question.

These alternative uses of the new communications technologies represent the opportunity for making a new beginning despite many pitfalls. They might provide an initial beachhead to reclaim everyday cultural reproduction from market-based dictates. The logic of commodification would not necessarily be contained immediately, and it might simply co-opt these efforts to serve some of its own unfulfilled purposes. Still, firebreaks against its further expansion also might be built by digging into some of the new, expanded sites for popular discussion afforded by such counter-systemic strategies.

INTELLECTUALS AND INFORMATIONALISM

In the final analysis, radical intellectuals have clearly played a vital role during most revolutions in industrializing agricultural and industrial societies. One must ask, however, if their role remains the same. To the extent that power works collaboratively rather than coercively, and given the code-intensive means whereby ideology and domination are coproduced by each individual at the particular screens he or she tunes in to daily, it would appear that the role played by intellectuals has changed significantly. In being mobilized to design and manage much of what constitutes informationalization, intellectuals seem to be losing some of their historic privileged isolation. Indeed, they now are increasingly a vital productive force in the everyday working world.

The real function of contemporary intellectuals, working on both the left and the right, arguably can be discerned more clearly now in the coded machine language of the cybernetic means of production defining American intellectual labor. That is, the intellectual's role today largely is that of word processor, image manager, value programmer, and symbol analyst. This position reveals many of the contradictions of personal and group collaboration under informational modes of production and power. Yet given this functional integration into the informational revolution, intellectuals now have much greater leverage as potential agents of resistance. The major task now facing critical intellectuals in these settings is assessing how to resist some of the trends toward total commodification, which their mental and manual labor in large part makes possible.

Ideology, it has been said, is the opiate of the intellectuals. Yet the remarkable resurgence of the New Right in American politics and society in the 1970s and 1980s demands that even the most hard-core junkies among today's leftist intelligentsia must immediately admit themselves into the rough detoxification program of ruthless self-criticism. For far too long, innumerable intellectuals have been mainlining megadoses of a potent ideological skag, namely, the New Class thesis, whose smooth high has entirely befogged the real role and function of most intellectuals under the administrative regime of corporate capitalism. During the 1970s, for example, Alvin Gouldner pushed a particularly powerful line of this stuff on the streets of many academic ghettos. Reaching into his boot, Gouldner pulled out "the best card that history has presently given us to play."[5] That is, the *intellectuals,* or "a new class composed of intellectuals and technical intelligentsia" that allegedly could seriously contest the "groups already in control of society's economy."[6] Ignoring the basic irrelevance and uselessness of most academic knowledge, Gouldner's designer drugs cast intellectuals as a vital new social group with immense potential power. As the creators and controllers of an apparently universal "speech community," whose boundaries are defined by an intersubjective, reflexive "culture of critical discourse," Gouldner's New Class allegedly would contest the old monied, propertied, privileged classes through its accumulation and circulation of "cultural capital." The gathering forces of the intellectuals as cultural capitalists, then, "are grounded in their *individual* control of special cultures, languages, techniques, and of the skills, resulting from these."[7] Because any further rationalization of advanced capitalism seems to require increasing submission to the intellectual and technical skills of the New Class, Gouldner claims that the intellectuals now have an unparalleled opportunity to revolutionize society through their collective command over cultural capital.

More recent events, however, have trumped Gouldner's historical card and are exposing the brittleness of the New Class scam to even the most wasted intellectual addicts. Many scientists, technicians, and bureaucrats have been pink-slipped by government agencies as the rollback of regulatory requirements and welfare deliveries sends their cultural capital crashing through the floor. Many thousands of intellectuals, in full individual control of their special skills, techniques, and cultures, are pounding the academic pavements as "gypsy scholars" seeking seasonal employment as migrant mental laborers. Even middle-level corporate managers, the celebrated indispensable elite of the professional/technical intelligentsia, have witnessed their personal fortunes collapse in the tumultuous global markets of the 1980s as corporate takeovers, foreign competition, and forced early retirement end their careers.

The intellectual members of the New Class, like all men and women, make their own history not as they please nor under circumstances chosen by them. As they seem to be at the threshold of revolutionizing themselves anew, they too conjure up spirits of the past to borrow their names, battle cries, and costumes. It perhaps is not surprising that Gouldner and other intellectuals have sought the austere traditions of the militant European bourgeoisie or the militant Russian intelligentsia to serve as their latest collective self-deception. These mystifications are needed by intellectuals in order to conceal from themselves the corporate limitations placed on their struggles to accumulate new forms of capital and power (like the bourgeois Jacobin entrepreneur) and then wield it as an avant-garde force to revolutionize society, like the radical Bolshevik intellectual. In the end, the smooth rush induced by this intellectual smack has only sustained a false enthusiasm among many contemporary intellectuals on the high plane of historical tragedy.

The real approach toward most intellectuals taken by supply-side, New Right entrepreneurs positioned at the key choke points of America's political economy in the 1980s illustrates the real value of mere cultural capital. In fact, critical intellectuals and the professional/technical intelligentsia tend to be powerless unless their work is strictly policy-relevant, corporate-connected, profit-oriented, and funded with its own hard money. Nonetheless, these synthetic ideological opiates do begin to clarify some of the contemporary intellectual's functions in the 1980s. The scientific intensification of production, which has attended the development of advanced corporate capitalism and the consumer society, in many respects has radically transformed the importance of words, symbols, skills, and images. Information is so precious that it is banked; knowledge has become a business; and culture itself is regarded as a capital asset. As Chapter 5 asserted, democratic politics have become an elaborate, continuously evolving videogame, while nuclear doomsdays, as Chapter 6 indicated, are simulated daily at military command, control, and comunications centers around the world in the mythic terms of

World War II. Yet the motivating forces behind these transformations are not the products of the intellectuals' "culture of critical discourse" as much as they are by-products of corporate capital's instrumental information-based technologies for purposive rational discourse. This discourse, in turn, is objectified in the newly emergent informational global networks of electronic devices communicating with each other, robotic machines constructing each other, and cybernetic systems designing, programming, and monitoring each other. To presume that the intellectuals and technical intelligentsia are the captains of industry in complete command of these new means of production remains a narcotic delusion of incredible proportions.

The intellectuals neither own nor control the physical capital or the cultural capital that anchors the corporate system. At best, the function of most intellectuals in the 1990s is that of the hired help. Intellectuals are the tellers at the information banks, the maintenance men at the great universities, the operators for the computer centers, the cameramen in the communications industry, the lifeguards at the data pools, and the counter clerks in the knowledge business. True executive command, however, rests elsewhere—with the corporate managerial strata or the state. And, quite benignly, the corporate managers and state administrators do not discourage such "secret" addictions to such synthetic symbolic substitutes for power, or the New Class thesis, in exchange for the intellectuals' continuing manufacture of those images and symbols that legitimize the real decision-makers behind the screens of power.

The function of intellectuals in the 1990s is largely the same as that shared by all other social strata: to produce through consumption. The special image of an intersubjective, reflexive speech community of the intellectuals as a nascent universal class, on a more important level merely mystifies the peculiar pre-programmed, stylized "consumption communities" assigned to the intellectuals in the growing world market. The role and needs of the intellectuals carefully have been grounded in distinctive bundles of material objects and professional services, which mediate the particular productive position of intellectuals as consumers. Just as the workers will control themselves voluntarily to gain access to Sears, the *Reader's Digest,* Levittown, secure jobs plus good benefits, "The Cosby Show," Pontiacs, and Disneyworld, so too do intellectuals accept their integration into the corporate system in pursuit of those objects and services that corporate product demography has assigned to them to dynamicize production: L. L. Bean, the *New Yorker,* high-tech Village lofts, tenured academic positions plus solid grant funding, "Masterpiece Theater," Volvos, and summers on Nantucket. Moreover, the intellectuals are doubly integrated inasmuch as they not only individually consume the particular objects assigned to them by the corporate sphere, but as a social strata, they also develop, manage, and program the symbols and signals that convert almost all material objects, as well as most human services, into the prepackaged needs and prescripted roles of all the other social strata. As individuals, intellectuals in America have the function of consuming those goods and services which they have coded as constitutive of their "speech community" and which they also produce as a strata of corporate capitalist society, as part and parcel of their unique "consumption community." As a strata, intellectuals find their real role emerging in these forms of labor as symbol encoders/decoders/recoders. In the machine language of the symbolic systems they work within, the intellectuals' roles are quite plain: they are word processors, literature scientists, symbol analysts, image managers, signal designers, cultural developers, public administrators, tradition retrievers, value programmers, and system coders.

Arguably, in the larger architecture of consumer society, the intellectuals are a minor modem for the master mainframe of corporate capitalism. Intellectuals have been charged with the task of retrieving and receiving the diverse analog data of traditional culture, images, symbols, values, and norms, and then transmitting and transforming these signs into more useful digital applications as commodities in the society of bureaucratically controlled consumption. In their work, for example, fragments of bourgeois, feudal, ancient, and non-Western culture are encoded, transmitted, and recoded by creative and critical minds to dynamicize corporate production. The examples are countless: plots from Shakespeare reprocessed as flashy space opera, African motifs recirculated as the summer rage for fashion boutiques, superficial ritualism of Anglo-Saxon tribal decision making reorganized as mediagenic democratic spectacle, bits of Old Masters reconstituted as packaging logos, strains of baroque music rescored as sitcom theme music, science fiction videogames reprogrammed as the life-size infrastructure of SDI planning, aspects of English family mores recycled as normal behavior for Haitian boat people, clips of Soviet Red Army films rerecorded as demonological images of the Free World's foes, parts of Indian peasant garb redefined as avant-garde chic for suburban teenagers, clichés in Greek building norms recast as necessary signs of municipal authority, pieces of Nazi insignia redefined as fetishes for adolescent imitators of the motorcycle lumpen, partial premises of historical materialism reconceptualized as the major integral of a multinational econometric forecasting model, glimmerings of the classical liberal arts retuned as babysitting games for public high schools, production values from television talk shows reformated as presidential debate scripts, minor courses in the Mexican diet repackaged as global fast food, and glimpses of Gothic icons reprojected as high-pressure salesmanship on televised drive-in rites for national televangelical audiences. Without the image management of contemporary intellectuals, advanced corporate capitalist life itself in today's transnational civil society would be impossible.

PROGRESSIVE POLITICS IN INFORMATIONAL SOCIETY

A critical task for radical intellectuals in the 1990s, then, must be the complete self-criticism of their own intellectual and practical activity under transnational corporate capitalism. As an engagé thinker, the critical intellectual should remain intransigently opposed to corporate capital's Sloanist developmental program of providing more material objects through increasingly rational productivity to more people. Yet, as radicals and as a major productive force, most intellectuals rarely question the means of development as much as they challenge its actual ends, that is, the continuing aggravation of inequality, deprivation, and alienation within a material culture capable of providing real equality, satisfaction, and community. At best, then, the engagé intellectual often only advances a program for some kind of socialist reconstruction against that of capitalist development, and this reconstruction would accept the material means of conventional capitalist development as it reordered distributive, structural, and moral ends to serve the program of progressive social movements rather than the managerial/state strata who currently benefit.

Unfortunately, there are no guarantees that the socialist reconstruction would be anything more than a mere reconstruction of capitalist development, remediating the ills of advanced technological society along old similar lines but through different "revolutionary" channels. Today, Gorbachev's perestroika and Deng's "to get rich is glorious" campaigns apparently are, to a significant extent, slightly different paths to getting Kentucky Fried Chicken, American Express Cards, Coke Classic, and Levis to socialist consumers, using Western capitalist know-how while maintaining the power of the party. The vanguardist sermons of the New Left in the 1960s about this or that evil in the Third World now justifying revolution in United States under socialist and reconstructive guidance typifies the basic uselessness of this strategy here. Without everyone engaged in seriously reconstituting present forms of community, personality, and politics along nonbureaucratic, nonadministrative, and nonhierarchial lines, the engagé intellectual will only reach the same ends as the corporate capitalist system. Each totally differs over the design of the vehicles for change, the rate of progress, the method of steering, and the scope of satisfactions; yet the final unsatisfying destination of total administration seems to be one and the same.

Radical intellectuals must also criticize and transcend the classical programs for progressive social reconstruction as bankrupt options in an informational age. Critical intellectuals now must recognize, first, that their codings never are received or accepted entirely as sent and, second, that they should work to deconstruct the entire means of symbolic management and administrative programming that prevent people from determining their own forms of everyday life, both under "developmental capitalism" and "reconstructive socialism." In helping to dismantle the repressive ensemble of administration, consumption, and production, critical intellectuals might help themselves and others guide the empowerment, reacculturation, and reskilling of individuals in their own households and communities through the thousands of local, limited, partial struggles that such a general cultural revitalization of commodified market culture implies.

Perhaps only on the local, immediate level of partial struggles can everyone resist the reduction of revolution to spectacle and of movements to single-issue pressure groups, which keeps the overall system rational through limited inputs of focused criticism. As image managers, the impulse among intellectuals to control and recast revolution in marketable packages, suitable for satisfying the need of mass audiences to visualize (but *not* realize) the possibility of historical choice, remains strong. Similarly, as symbol producers, many radical intellectuals find it difficult to resist the role of a taste-making avant-garde, appearing on Phil Donahue to mobilize the masses, smiling for *U.S. News and World Report* to spread the word in color glossies, cracking the college textbook market to raise consciousness, or substituting that "E.R.A. Now" bumpersticker on the Volvo for real ward-heeling for gender equality. Consequently, thousands of potential supporters then settle for mere passive participation in very limited social transformations as faithful customers of the new booming Marxist, feminist, libertarian, or environmentalist culture industries.

Radical change can proceed only if intellectuals refuse to aid and abet the recoding of their political acts as entertaining spectacle and the reprocessing of their critical thinking as system-affirming positive feedback in the existing modes of information. Regrettably, however, the master mainframes of corporate capital have proved all too effective at continually reassigning this role to intellectuals on the screens of power. In part, the radical student movement was manufactured and manipulated in order to pressure the state out of a pointless, destructive war; liberal feminism has been processed and programmed to assist in the restructuring of domestic labor markets to mobilize cheap, tractable labor and create new needs for goods and services no longer provided by women; and the ecological movement is being designed and developed to legitimate a new exurban, downsized, and "voluntarily" simplified consumerism as the corporate capitalist state recognizes that it cannot rebuild the cities, retain mass social services, and reinflate complex consumer expectations as it had prior to 1973.[8]

The continuing symbolic integration of all social strata will persist until critical intellectuals refuse to transmit and transform signs of human praxis into the matrices of mass management that advanced corporate society generates in the public and private sectors.[9] Gouldner is, in fact, basically wrong: the privileging of some particular intellectual elite with the job of "thinking" only indicates the extent of how far domination is institutionalized in informational societies. Actually, many people are thinking all the time—and much of the time critically. But, all have not had the same access or right voice as the intellectuals. Intellectuals, then, must not act as a separate caste, leading society on from above as a "correctly conscious" vanguard. They should, instead, rejoin their communities, working as coequals with their fellow citizens to revitalize local society and politics. Critical intellectuals could help revitalize many forms of resistance within the everyday vernacular dimensions of politics, language, society, and culture at the local, municipal, or regional level by creating new counterinstitutions. Their role, however, is not indispensable, because most people already know that many things are wrong and have ideas about what to do. Still, the intellectuals' contributions of critically grounded "good sense" might recombine with the popularly oriented "common sense" of other individuals in their local communities to resist the present administrative regime from within. Fortunately, a permanent resistance to these ideologies and their domination already exists among many diverse audiences, who are puzzled by—and question—many of the images they scan on the screens of power.

On the one hand, it could all fail. The alternative new media might simply become the latest means of containing the critical intelligentsia and resistance-minded citizens. The outcome of such experiments in the politics of image, as those outlined above, might simply devolve into eco-activist soap operas, feminist quiz shows, socialist sitcoms, or no-nukes talk shows. On the other hand, by questioning the production imperatives of mass marketing in the conventional media, the alternative media could move countercultural critiques beyond their state/corporate constraints, as weak channels of artifical negativity, into the realm of more authentic transformations. In the localist, popular discourses of the new media, some of the more real revolutionary forms and content in today's societies might be reclaimed from their spectacularization in the mass media as "the 1960s" or "student rebellion" or "new social movements" and given back as new ideas for local political struggles of communal transformation.

All of this, at the same time, would only be a beginning. By demystifying the processes of this spectacular corporate coding regime, and in elaborating local, popular, user-directed media networks, the users/consumers of new media have a chance to repossess their progressive past and reconstitute it in the present with new emancipatory discourses about a more democratic and ecological future beyond the confines of today's market culture.[10] The proof of this practice, however, definitely will be in its effective unraveling of the existing codes of commodification.

In the 1980s, and perhaps the 1990s, the peace movement, the anti-apartheid movement, the anti-nuclear movement, and the environmental movement will be organizing thousands who were infants or not yet born in the 1960s. Because these symbolic forms now are the conventional codes of popular political opposition, they often have had to borrow, in turn, from the disguises and languages of "the sixties" in their political campaigns. The answers to hard political questions rising from debates, such as those addressed in this book, about the role of the new electronic media in advanced corporate capitalism serve an important purpose. In recognizing the complex origins and ultimate conclusions of revolutionary activity in the 1960s as they oppose the current structures of power in the 1990s, activists might go beyond the allure of pure image and succeed in constructing resistance networks out of existing political opportunities, including those offered by alternative uses of the new media. By understanding the workings of the prevailing signs and symbols on the mediascape, however, they also might avoid repeating the tragedies of radicalism in the 1960s as farces in the progressive politics of the 1980s and 1990s.

NOTES

1. For an excellent discussion of this process, see Todd Gitlin, *The Whole World Is Watching: Mass Media in the Making and Unmaking of the New Left* (Berkeley: University of California Press, 1980). See also Adolph Reed, Jr., "The 'Black Revolution' and the Reconstitution of Domination," in *Race, Politics, and Culture: Critical Essays on the Radicalism of the 1960s*, ed. Adolph Reed, Jr. (Westport, Conn.: Greenwood Press, 1986), 61–95; and David Gross, "Culture, Politics and 'Lifestyle' in the 1960s," in *Race, Politics, and Culture*, 99–117.

2. See John Gaventa, *Power and Powerlessness: Quiescence and Rebellion in an Appalachian Valley* (Urbana: University of Illinois Press, 1980), 220–51, for a discussion, for example, of how grassroots political groups used home video technology to document the environmental problems they were fighting in Appalachia.

3. See John Downing, *Radical Media: The Political Experience of Alternative Communication* (Boston: South End Press, 1984).

4. For a critical consideration of alternative computer use, see Theodore Roszak, *The Cult of Information: The Folklore of Computers and the True Art of Thinking* (New York: Pantheon, 1986).

5. Alvin W. Gouldner, *The Future of Intellectuals and the Rise of the New Class* (New York: Seabury Press, 1979), 7.

6. Ibid., 1.

7. Ibid., 19.

8. See, for example, Gitlin, *The Whole World Is Watching*; James Miller, *"Democracy Is in the Streets": From Port Huron to the Siege of Chicago* (New York: Simon and Schuster, 1987); Alison M. Jagger and Paula S. Rothenberg, *Feminist Frameworks: Alternative Theoretical Accounts of the Relations between Women and Men*, 2d ed. (New York: McGraw-Hill, 1984); and Hazel Henderson, *Creating Alternative Futures: The End of Economics* (New York: Berkley Windhover, 1978).

9. For a more extended discussion, see Timothy W. Luke, "Informationalism and Ecology," *Telos* 56 (Summer 1983): 59–73.

10. For one very promising outline of these alternative forms of society, see Murray Bookchin, *Toward an Ecological Society* (Montreal: Black Rose Books, 1980), and *The Rise of Urbanization and the Decline of Citizenship* (San Francisco: Sierra Club Books, 1987).

Index

Adorno, Theodor W., 7, 20, 22, 23, 24, 27, 54, 55, 56, 57, 85, 128
Adversary culture, 65, 67, 80
Advertising, 8, 23–26, 36–39, 87, 105–10, 121, 122, 129–53, 171, 240–49, 252–54. *See also* Mass media; informationalism
Africa, 20, 23, 96, 102, 103, 113
Alternative media, 241–57. *See also* Mass media
Americanization, 118; and Fordism, 223–28
Amin, Samir, 14
Amott, Theresa, 239
Anderson, John, 135
Armstrong, Ben, 97
Arrighi, Giovanni, 238
Asia, 23, 74–76, 86, 95, 96, 102
Atherton, F. Christopher, 153
Avant-garde, 22, 29, 64–70, 80–81, 208–10, 250–57

Bakker, Jim, 88, 90, 96
Bakker, Tammy, 88, 90, 96
Balch, Stephen, 81, 82
Banfield, Edward, 63
Barnet, Richard, 14, 15, 237
Barthes, Roland, 6, 7, 12, 15, 16, 22, 23–26, 46, 51, 55, 58, 161–62, 171–72, 179, 201
Bates, Stephen, 135, 155–56, 157
Baudrillard, Jean, 7, 12, 16, 22, 27, 30–46, 56–58, 111–13, 117, 119, 126–28, 154, 161–62, 179–80, 237
Beecher, Catherine, 105

Bell, Daniel, 14, 62–63, 65–70, 71, 74, 76, 82–83, 127, 236
Bendix, Reinhard, 155
Beninger, James R., 14
Bennett, William J., 61, 81, 83
Bentham, Jeremy, 47
Biskind, Peter, 54
Black, Gregory, 179
Bluestone, Barry, 14
Blumberg, Paul, 126
Boggs, Carl, 220, 236–37
Bolling, Richard, 84
Bolshevism, 65–68, 251
Bookchin, Murray, 258
Boorstin, Daniel, 128
Bourgeoisie, 19–22, 65–81, 103–5, 216, 251. *See also* Capitalism
Bowles, John, 84
Braverman, Harry, 57, 127, 238–39
Brick, Howard, 69, 84
Brzezinski, Zbigniew, 14, 84
Burawoy, Michael, 58
Burch, Noel, 54
Burgess, Ernest, 119
Burnham, James, 127
Burnham, Walter Dean, 153
Bush, George, 78, 124, 136, 143

Caddell, Pat, 141, 156
Calleo, David, 237
Campaigning, 13, 129–53, 154, 155–58
Canada, 155, 230, 234
Capitalism, 4, 20–21, 22–46; corporate capital, 4, 20–21, 31–39, 45–46, 47–54, 64–100, 126, 207–14; 240–57; entrepre-

neurial capital, 102–3, 105–7, 113–14; monopoly capitalism, 32, 35–39, 45; transnational capitalism, 19–23, 51–53, 74–77, 95, 100–101, 119, 159–68, 177–78, 207–14, 220–21, 223–24
Carnoy, Martin, 238
Carter, Jimmy, 76, 135, 137–38, 140
Charisma, 13, 129–53
Chernobyl, 13, 44, 181–201
Christianity, 88–97, 207
China, 113, 127, 149
Clark, Rodney, 84
CMEA (Council for Mutual Economic Assistance), 165, 220, 230, 232
Cohen, Jean, 209–10, 220, 236–37
Collins, Robert, 126
Commentary, 61, 63
Commodification, 10, 19–46, 51–52, 88–93, 98–122, 240, 249
Commodity fetishism, 19–21, 31–33, 86–97, 98–126, 228–29, 240–49
Computers, 3, 4, 8, 10–11, 20–23, 30–54, 210–23, 249–54. *See also* Informationalism; Mass media
Connally, John, 135
Consumerism, 21–22, 26–30, 32–46, 73, 75, 86, 87, 90, 93–97, 98–126, 132–53, 159–78, 197–201, 208–36, 240–57
Consummativity, 100, 101, 107, 110–26, 145–53, 187–201, 240–57
Consumption communities, 4, 14, 88–93, 111–16, 145–53, 159–78, 181–201, 214–23, 240–57
Corporatism, 75, 98–122, 208–23
Critical theory, 3, 5, 7–10
Crespi, Irving, 153, 154
Crozier, Michael, 82, 236
Culler, Jonathan, 55
Cultural contradictions of capitalism, 61–81
Culture of narcissism, 76

Dadaism, 26, 27
Dahrendorf, Ralf, 14, 58, 126, 238
Dallmayr, Fred, 16
D-Day, 13, 160–78
Debord, Guy, 7, 12, 16, 22, 26–30, 46, 55, 56, 130–31, 154, 156, 159, 178, 181, 201
Decter, Midge, 63

Democracy, 22, 129–53, 208–23, 240–57
Deng Xiaoping, 29, 77, 254
de Saussure, Ferdinand, 15, 42
Diamond, Edwin, 135, 155–56, 157
Diamond, Martin, 63
Domination, 7–13, 46–54, 107–26, 145–51, 159–78, 181–201, 207–23, 245–54. *See also* Ideology; Power; Resistance
Downing, John, 258
Drucker, Peter F., 14
Dukakis, Michael, 124, 136

Eagleton, Terry, 7, 16
Eagleton, Thomas, 140
Eco, Umberto, 5, 6, 15, 16
Eder, Klaus, 208, 216, 219–20, 236–39
EEC, 160, 177, 229
Eisenstein, Elizabeth, 58
Elections, 13, 129–53, 212–14, 219, 230. *See also* Democracy
End of ideology, 67, 86
Environmentalism, 63, 207–8, 210, 217, 227–34, 245, 255, 257
Epstein, Joseph, 82
Europe: Eastern, 86, 181; Western, 4, 23, 75, 77, 78, 102, 126, 134, 155, 159–78, 181, 182, 193, 198, 208, 210, 227, 232, 235, 240, 242, 245, 247
Evans, Christopher, 14
Ewen, Stuart, 126
Exchange value, 31–46

Falwell, Jerry, 88, 93, 96
Family, 12, 13, 87, 98–126
Feminism, 61, 63, 106, 124, 125, 207, 245, 255, 256
Ferguson, Kathy, 15
Ferguson, Thomas, 83, 153, 151
Ferraro, Geraldine, 143
Firestone, Shulamith, 127
Fiske, John, 138, 155
Fonda, Jane, 118, 245
Fondaism, 116–22, 125, 245, 249
Ford, Daniel, 204
Ford, Gerald, 140
Ford, Henry, 118
Fordism, 116–18, 217, 223–28, 231, 234, 235, 245
Forty, Adrian, 54
Foster, Hal, 58, 180, 236

Foucault, Michel, 34, 40
Fox, Richard Wrightman, 54
France, 23, 25, 160, 164, 196–97, 212, 213
Frank, Andre Gunder, 15
French, Marilyn, 128
Fuller, Tony, 156
Fundamentalism, 86–93, 207, 210, 248
Furniss, Norman, 127

Galbraith, John Kenneth, 14, 126
Gartner, Alan, 14
Gaventa, John, 258
Geertz, Clifford, 70, 84
Gerbner, George, 97
Germany, 20, 103, 127, 159–78; West Germany, 166, 167, 178, 192, 193, 198–99, 200, 219, 230, 232
Germond, Jack, 85, 155–56
Gideon, Siegfried, 127
Gitlin, Todd, 257–58
Glasnost, 188–90, 233
Glazer, Nathan, 63
Glenn, John, 136, 143, 146
Goldhar, J. D., 238
Goldman, Peter, 156
Goldwater, Barry, 137
Gorbachev, Mikhail, 29, 77, 182, 188–92, 233, 254
Gouldner, Alvin, 250–51, 256, 258
Graham, Billy, 23
Graham, Hugh, 83
Gramsci, Antonio, 12, 118, 120, 128, 207, 236, 238
Great Britain, 20, 154, 164, 165, 187, 212, 213, 230, 232
Great Society, 76, 149, 168
Greens, 181, 212, 219
Gross, David, 257
Guattari, Felix, 236
Gurr, Ted, 83

Habermas, Jürgen, 83, 215, 219, 236–38
Hadden, Jeffrey, 9
Harrison, Bennett, 14
Hart, Gary, 135, 137, 141, 143, 146, 149
Hartley, John, 138, 155
Hartman, Geoffrey, 179
Hartz, Louis, 83
Hawkes, Nigel, 202–4
Hayden, Delores, 55

Hebdige, Dick, 55
Hedonism, 65–70, 71, 80–81, 93
Held, David, 16
Henderson, Hazel, 258
Hillenbrand, Martin, 237
Hiller, Bevis, 55
Hine, Thomas, 55
Hirsch, Joachim, 216–18, 224, 237–38
Hjelmslev, Louis, 15
Hopkins, Raymond, 239
Hopkins, Terence R., 238
Horkheimer, Max, 7, 20, 22, 23, 24, 27, 54, 55, 56, 57, 85, 128
Howe, Irving, 82
Hudson, Hugh, 154
Hudson, Michael, 14, 237
Humphrey, Hubert, 135
Huntington, Samuel P., 63, 82, 236
Hutcheson, Richard, Jr., 97
Hyperreality, 35, 37, 39–46, 48–49

Ideal type, 10–12
Ideology, 4, 7, 8–9, 12–14, 22, 26–29, 46–54, 61–64, 86–97, 110–22, 130–51, 159–78, 181–83, 197–201, 240–57. *See also* Domination; Power; Resistance
IMF, 229
India, 113
Industrialism, 3–5, 46–47, 65, 207–8, 217–18, 223–34
Informationalism, 3, 6, 7, 8, 10–14, 21–23, 40–46, 47–54, 62, 71, 76, 86, 93, 116–22, 130–36, 145–53, 159, 207–8, 210–20, 221–23, 232–36, 240–57. *See also* Ideology; Mass media
Inglehart, Ronald, 236
Innis, Harold A., 4, 46, 58
Intellectuals, 9, 13–14, 22, 52, 61–81, 82, 240–51
Italy, 103, 127, 166, 230

Jackson, Jesse, 137, 143, 146, 148
Jagger, Alison M., 258
Jakobson, Roman, 6, 15
Jamieson, Kathleen Hall, 153, 155, 157–58
Janowitz, Morris, 127
Japan, 4, 74–76, 77, 78, 81, 85, 103, 125, 127, 134, 149, 166, 167, 193, 198, 208, 227, 230, 231, 232, 235, 240, 242, 245, 247

Japanization, 74–76, 81, 84
Jay, Martin, 16
Jelinek, Mariann, 238
Jencks, Charles, 55
Jervis, Robert, 239
Jessop, Bob, 58
Johnson, Chalmers, 84
Jong, Erica, 121, 128
Joyce, James, 49

Kahn, Herman, 63, 84
Kennedy, John F., 134, 151
Kennedy, Robert F., 134, 137
Keohane, Robert O., 237
Kern, Stephen, 58
Knabb, Ken, 55
Konrad, George, 236
Koppes, Clayton, 179
Krieger, Joel, 239
Kristol, Irving, 61–63, 82, 83
Kyshtym, 187, 190

Lamberton, Donald M., 14
Landes, David, 58
Lasch, Christopher, 76, 85, 109, 126–28
Latin America, 20, 23
Lavers, Annette, 55
Lears, T. J. Jackson, 54
Lefebvre, Henri, 37, 55, 57
Leiss, William, 56
Leninism, 65
Liebs, Chester, 55
Lipset, Symour M., 63, 212–13, 237
London, Herbert, 81, 82
Lukács, Georg, 19–22, 28, 30, 32, 54, 55, 56

Machlup, Fritz, 14
Mandel, Ernest, 14
Marc, David, 55
Marchand, Roland, 55
Marcuse, Herbert, 3, 7, 14, 16, 22, 53, 58, 114, 127–28, 222
Marples, David, 202, 204
Marx, Karl, 7, 10, 19, 21, 30–33, 39, 40, 42, 54, 80, 85, 88, 210
Marxism, 10, 26, 29, 30–33, 39, 61, 63, 80, 209–10, 214–15, 255

Mass media, 3, 4, 5–8, 10–14, 20–23, 23–29, 34–35, 44–54, 68–81, 72, 86–97, 101–2, 110–26, 129–52, 155–58, 159–78, 210–20, 240–57. *See also* Alternative media; Informationalization
Masuda, Yoneji, 14
McCarthy, Eugene, 134, 137
McGovern, George, 61, 140
McLuhan, Marshall, 4, 14, 35, 46, 47, 49, 58, 237
Mediascapes, 4, 12, 21, 22, 43, 48, 70, 72, 74, 97, 240
Medvedev, Roy, 188
Mendelsohn, Harold, 153, 154
Miliband, Ralph, 58
Miller, Henry, 121
Miller, James, 258
Millet, Kate, 127
Minc, Alain, 14
Mitchell, Juliet, 127
Modernism, 62, 64–81, 84, 207–20, 234–36
Modernity, 22, 35–39, 61–81
Mondale, Walter, 140–41, 143, 146, 148, 150, 156
Morris, Charles, 5, 15
Moynihan, Daniel P., 62, 63
Mueller, Ronald, 14, 15, 237
Mumford, Lewis, 58

Naisbitt, John, 14, 50
NATO, 23, 160, 163, 165, 166, 177, 211, 229, 230, 232–34
Neo-authority, 64, 70
Neo-Confucianism, 74, 81, 95, 125
Neoconservatism, 12, 61–81, 82, 229–36
Neo-religion, 64, 70
Neo-tradition, 64, 70, 74–76
New Class, 66, 68, 250–52
New Deal, 61, 62, 63, 70, 71, 76, 149
New Frontier, 62, 70, 168
New Left, 61, 63, 240–57
Newman, Charles, 58
New Right, 71, 250
New social movements, 63, 207–36
News media, 129–53, 142–45, 160–78, 181–201, 240–54. *See also* Alternative media; Mass media; Informationalism

1980s, 72, 74, 95, 97, 100, 120–26, 150, 151, 152, 240, 252, 257
1950s, 4, 49, 62, 63, 67, 68, 71, 72, 86, 93, 95, 114, 151, 154, 240, 243
1940s, 62, 64, 65, 86, 95
1970s, 49, 62, 76, 95, 100, 124, 240, 243
1960s, 4, 12, 49, 61–64, 68, 72, 73, 76, 82, 87, 93, 95, 96, 99, 114, 124, 240–45, 257
Nisbet, Robert, 63
Nixon, Richard, 139
Noble, David, 127
Noelle-Neumann, Elisabeth, 143, 153, 156
Nora, Simon, 15
North, Oliver, 93
Nuclear arms, 44, 167–68, 174–77, 184, 200–201, 232–34
Nuclear deterrence, 44
Nuclear energy, 181–201, 222–23, 225–28
Nye, Joseph S., 237

O'Connor, James, 15, 236
OECD, 23, 160, 165, 177, 181, 182, 187, 190, 198, 209, 211, 213, 221, 229, 230, 232–36
Offe, Claus, 237
Ohmann, Richard, 16
O'Neill, John, 16
Ong, Walter, 15, 58
Ouchi, William, 84

PACS (political action committees), 129, 134, 151–53
Paris Match, 25
Patterson, Thomas, 153
Pax Americana, 62, 86
Peele, Gillian, 83, 126
Peirce, Charles, 15
Pentagon, 79, 229
Permissive individualism, 52, 98, 100, 110–26
Phillips, Kevin, 84
Piccone, Paul, 58, 236
Podhoretz, Norman, 63, 83
Polling, 139–42, 145–53. *See also* Elections
Porat, Marc Uri, 14
Possessive individualism, 47, 110
Poster, Mark, 49, 56, 58

Postindustrial society, 3, 4, 21, 207–20, 235. *See also* Informationalism
Power, 4, 8–10, 12–14, 22, 26–29, 31–46, 46–54, 61–81, 93–97, 110–26, 130–53, 160–78, 197–201, 208–36, 240–54. *See also* Domination; Ideology; Resistance
Private sphere, 101–10
Protestant Ethic, 65–69, 71
Public, 33–39, 44–46, 101–10, 130–53, 160–78, 187–99, 208–23, 240–57
The Public Interest, 63, 65
Public opinion, 130, 131, 132, 133, 134, 135, 136, 137, 138, 139–42, 145–53, 190–99. *See also* Polling
Puchala, Donald, 239

Ranney, Austin, 154
Reagan, Nancy, 143, 150
Reagan, Ronald, 61, 76–80, 124, 134–38, 140–41, 143, 146–52, 155–57, 163, 165–68, 170, 175, 177, 189, 192, 194, 229, 231
Reaganism, 75, 76–80, 81, 95, 123, 229–34, 235
Reed, Adolph, Jr., 126, 257
Reformation, 66, 102
Reich, Robert, 14
Religion, 64, 68–70, 73–74, 86–97
Resistance, 5, 12–14, 22, 46–54, 123, 207–36, 240–57. *See also* Domination; Ideology; Power
Reissman, Frank, 14
Roberts, Oral, 88, 96
Robertson, Pat, 68, 88, 93, 96, 136, 143, 248
Rogers, Joel, 83, 153, 157
Rokkan, Stein, 212–13, 237–38
Roszak, Theodore, 258
Roth, Guenther, 155
Rothenberg, Paula S., 258
Rothman, Sheila, 127–28
Rothschild, Emma, 239
Rothstein, Robert L., 237
Russudello, John, 154

Sabato, Larry, 153–54
Sabel, Charles, 238
Schiller, Herbert, 237
Schuller, Robert, 88

Semiotics, 3, 5–8
Sexuality, 98–126
Shannon, Claude, 15
Shupe, Anson, 97
Sign value, 32–33
Simon, William, 83
Simulation, 30, 35–46
Situationism, 26–29
Sloan, Alfred P., 228
Sloanism, 228–29, 231, 234, 235, 254
Society of the spectacle, 26–30, 89, 130–
    32, 145–53, 164–68, 181–83, 197–201,
    240–54
South Korea, 74, 75, 85, 148, 149, 161
Soviet Union, 4, 5, 79, 81, 143, 165, 166,
    181–201, 233
Starr, Martin, 85
State, 11–14, 46–54, 71, 75, 78–81, 98–
    102, 108, 124, 125, 207–14, 215–21,
    229–36
Steinfels, Peter, 64, 83
Surrealism, 26
Swaggart, Jimmy, 68, 96
Swann, Charles, 97
Sweden, 192, 193, 200

Taiwan, 74, 75, 85
Taylorism, 121, 223, 228, 231, 234
Teletraditions, 71–81, 84, 86–97
Televangelism, 12, 73–74, 86–97
Television, 3, 4, 10–11, 13, 21, 43, 45, 48,
    71–76, 87–93, 129–53, 241–45. *See also*
    Mass media
Thatcherism, 75
Thody, Philip, 55
Three Mile Island, 187, 196, 197, 200–201
Tilton, Timothy, 127
Toffler, Alvin, 14, 50
Touraine, Alain, 14, 214–16, 219–20, 236–
    37
Tradition, 62, 64, 65–70, 71–73
Trilling, Lionel, 63

United States, 4, 5, 12–13, 20, 61–81, 86–
    97, 98–126, 129–53, 160–78, 187, 191–
    201, 210, 223–35, 240–57
Use value, 31–46

Van der Pijl, Kees, 237
Vaneigem, Raoul, 55, 162, 179, 201
Vietnam, 71, 161, 168–71, 174, 233, 245
Vogel, Ezra, 84

Wagner, David, 82, 83
Wallace, George, 137
Wallerstein, Immanuel, 15, 126, 238–39
WTO (Warsaw Treaty Organization), 165,
    220, 230, 232
Wasserman, George R., 55
Watanuki, Joji, 82, 236
Weaver, Warren, 15
Weber, Max, 10, 16, 21, 58, 64, 65, 83, 130,
    133–34, 155
Welland, Colin, 154
White, Stephen K., 16
Wildavsky, Aaron, 63
Williams, Frederick, 14
Williams, Raymond, 16
Williamson, Judith, 55
Wills, Garry, 79, 85
Wilson, James Q., 63
Windscale, 187
Witcover, Jules, 85, 155–56
World Bank, 40
World War I, 65, 174, 175
World War II, 20, 26, 77, 125, 126, 159–78

Yergin, Daniel, 237
Young, Ed, 88
Young, Oran, 239

Zaretsky, Eli, 103, 126–27
Zimmerman, James, 85
Zone-regime, 4, 160–68, 174–78, 190–
    201, 209–14, 220, 229–36

Note on the Author

Timothy W. Luke is an associate professor of political science at the Virginia Polytechnic Institute and State University. He received his Ph.D. in political science from Washington University in St. Louis in 1981. Luke is a prolific author, with a wide array of scholarly publications to his credit, including articles in *Social Research, Philosophy of the Social Sciences, Sociological Forum, History of Political Thought, The American Political Science Review, The Journal of Politics, Studies in Comparative Communism,* and *International Studies Quarterly.* He has also been the frequent recipient of academic teaching awards in the midst of writing reviews and presenting scholarly papers. He also is the author of *Departures from Marx: Constructing an Ecological Critique of the Informational Revolution* (University of Illinois Press, forthcoming).